How to Conduct a Practice-based Study

How to Conduct a Practice-based Study

Problems and Methods

Silvia Gherardi

University of Trento, Italy

Edward Elgar

Cheltenham, UK • Northampton, MA, USA

Published by
Edward Elgar Publishing Limited
The Lypiatts
15 Lansdown Road
Cheltenham
Glos GL50 2JA
UK

Edward Elgar Publishing, Inc.
William Pratt House
9 Dewey Court
Northampton
Massachusetts 01060
USA

A catalogue record for this book
is available from the British Library

Library of Congress Control Number: 2012939098

ISBN 978 0 85793 337 9 (cased)

Typeset by Servis Filmsetting Ltd, Stockport, Cheshire
Printed and bound by MPG Books Group, UK

Contents

Acknowledgements

I am entirely responsible for this methodological reflection on the practice turn in organization studies. However, it would not have been possible without the collaboration and the fertile cultural environment provided by the Research Unit on Communication, Organizational Learning and Aesthetics, at the University of Trento (www.unitn.it/rucola), which began work on these topics in 1993. I therefore extend particular thanks to my colleagues, and especially to Attila Bruni, with whom I shared the experience of teaching and preparing a first version of this book (Bruni and Gherardi, 2007), which we tested with students at the University of Trento.

I am also indebted to all my colleagues and friends who have worked on these topics and allowed me to describe their works and help make them better known. I hope that I have been respectful of their thoughts, and I apologize for any errors or omissions.

Every book is a collective undertaking, and numerous people have contributed to this one, among them Adrian Belton, its patient translator, the reviewers and the staff at Edward Elgar Publishing who attended to its publication.

Introduction

This book springs from my experience during the past twelve years of teaching undergraduates and doctoral students at the University of Trento and other universities, and from the innumerable international doctoral seminars which I have organized in Trento, together with my colleagues of the Research Unit on Communication, Organizational Learning and Aesthetics. The purpose of the book is to present the methodology developed by scholars using the practice-based approach in organizational studies. Nevertheless, this is not a book on research methodology in the conventional sense. It is not intended to be a handbook of the 'how to do it' type, because I believe that it is not through a prescriptive and routinized methodology that one can learn how to conduct research. Instead, the book intends to solicit a methodological sensibility that the reader may possess and/or have developed from contact with research by others, gaining understanding of the types of questions that other authors have posed, how they have sought answers to those questions, what further questions remain and how to set up future search. The book's aim is therefore to engage in dialogue with those who share common interests in the study of working practices and to construct an ideal community of intellectual inquiry.

In setting and pursuing this objective, I have made a specific methodological choice. It consists in introducing the reader to research which may be considered in a certain sense 'classic' within practice-based studies, the purpose being to provide contact with authors and topics that, to my mind, are significant in developing a methodological sensibility. The reader will therefore find numerous examples drawn from empirical research intended to present or to illustrate a concept, a perspective or an experience in the field. In this way, the reader will be introduced to diverse authors who have conducted field research, and he/she may enter in contact with the methodological apparatus evinced by the examples. I have accordingly constructed brief case studies consisting of extracts from field research that I have previously tested in teaching situations. My intent is therefore to familiarize the reader with the topics, methods and issues that can be included under the heading 'practice-based studies' so as to elicit methodological reflection which reasons inductively.

I shall anticipate in this introduction some of the basic assumptions of the approach, although these will only be discussed expressly in the book's conclusions. I shall therefore start by framing the practice-based approach within organizational studies and the conception of organization that they adopt.

To assume a practice point of view is therefore to develop a conception of the organization as a texture or web of practices which extend internally and externally to the organization. We may therefore say that practices constitute a mode of ordering the flow of organizational relations. They furnish an ordering principle as the institutionalization of activities and ways of doing which are sustained by both material and social relations. Simultaneously, however, this ordering principle is also temporary and unstable, and is therefore a disordering principle as well. By means of practices, organizations solve the problem of their everyday reproduction, so that practices are an answer to the problem of how to reduce uncertainty. It can also be said that they introduce indeterminacy because they always express a rationality that is contingent and in a 'becoming'.

Why assume practices as the units of analysis of organizations? The simplest answer is that practices are loci – spatial and temporal – in which working, organizing, innovating or reproducing occurs. At a disciplinary level, this makes it possible to bring the study of work closer to the study of organizing, and to view both of them not only in their interrelations but as processes which take place in time and therefore in a 'becoming'. The categories of performance, practical accomplishment and becoming will be those that illustrate the temporality and processuality inscribed in practices.

If practices are used as the lenses through which to look at organizations, one sees the fine details of how people use the resources available to them to accomplish intelligent actions, and how they give those actions sense and meaning. The study of practices can be associated with the simply descriptive purpose of depicting the activities that make up a practice, so that the term 'practice' denotes a set of activities which form a pattern. Vice versa, if the purpose is what Rouse (2002) has called 'normative', then the interest in their study becomes more complex. The term 'normative' may be misleading if it is associated with a prescriptive stance (how practices should be), whereas giving normativity to practices is a dynamic internal to the devisers of practices, who define them as such on the basis of judgements as to what constitutes a good practice or a beautiful practice. In other words, practices are sustained by normative conceptions. Hence, when studying practices, the researcher is interested in understanding how they are seen 'from inside', how conceptions and discussions form around the mode of practising a set of activities, and therefore how society is produced and reproduced through practices.

There is consequently an empirical interest in assuming practices as the units of analysis of organizing; but there is an epistemological reason as well. The renewed interest in the study of practices has arisen within the so-called 'post-epistemologies'. The aim of a renewed interest in practice is to go beyond problematic dualisms (action/structure, human/non-human, mind/body), to see reason not as an innate mental faculty, but as a practice phenomenon, and to question individual actions and their status as building blocks of the social (Schatzki, 2001). Hence a practice should not be viewed as a unit circumscribed by given boundaries and constituted by defined elements, but rather as a connection-in-action: that is, as an interweaving of elements which are shaped by being interconnected. Humans do not occupy a privileged position in this field of dynamic interconnections. To use Law's (1994) expression, it is relational materialism which provides the basis on which to construe the interconnections between humans and non-humans and sociomaterial relations.

The book is organized so that the reader can gradually acquire partial notions about practices and develop a sense of how to set about identifying the salient aspects of a practice-based approach and the elements that are of theoretical importance for empirical analysis.

The first chapter invites the reader to consider practices as working practices. Its purpose is therefore to emphasize that working and organizing are situated processes. From the theoretical point of view, this chapter introduces the topics of situatedness, and of knowledge-in-practice as a situated knowing which connects one activity to the next. The second chapter introduces a circumscribed scenario in which coordination centres are the prototypical workplaces where issues to do with knowing-in-practice were first studied, and where the interaction between humans and artefacts is the main unit of analysis. This set of studies has generated one of the most useful concepts with which to understand practice as a collective knowledgeable doing. Putting a set of activities into practice requires both individual and collective work; and competent participation in a practice is achieved by maintaining a common orientation. From the theoretical point of view, this chapter demonstrates the continuity between learning and knowing, and between knowing and doing.

The third chapter introduces the topic of materiality through the presence of the body and sensible knowledge. The body can be regarded as an awkward presence, so much so that it was removed from organization studies. I have consequently considered it important to mention the body at the outset of an analysis intended to destabilize taken-for-granted dichotomies. This interpretative lens reveals numerous features of practice, primarily the facts that people work through bodies, that bodies are differently sexed and that organizational practices are gendered. But the main theoretical contribution originates from showing that the body knows, that it is the seat of embodied knowledge, and therefore that the notion of sensible knowledge entails detachment from the cognitivist view of knowing and organizing. The concept of practice gives visibility and thematizability to the tacit, sensory and aesthetic knowledge comprised in knowing as a collective and situated activity.

The fourth chapter introduces the world of non-humans and what they do and get done. From the theoretical point of view, this chapter concerns sociomaterial relations with artefacts within a framework of relations that Knorr Cetina (1997) has called 'post-social'. When analysing a practice, the objects of that practice, the technologies and the material setting itself can be considered the relational infrastructure (Star, 1999) which supports performance of the practice while at the same time being invisible.

The fifth chapter focuses on discursive practices. It stresses that the concept of practice, qualified in the previous chapter as sociomaterial, can also be defined as materialsemiotic. Discursive practices are of particular importance for showing that people work not only by doing, but also by saying. Saying in a situation is also a 'doing', and discursiveness is both an end of a practice, as for instance in institutional discourses, and a means by which researchers (and not only practitioners) gain access to how individuals in situations construct those situations themselves and the objects/ subjects of discourses.

The sixth chapter deals with what we may call another relational infrastructure: namely the support which rules – given and emergent – provide for situated practices. From a theoretical point of view, practices enable us to see how normativity (of sense, consensus, as well as prescription) emerges from situated action; whilst from the methodological point of view, the practice-based approach enables us to analyse a practice as the locus of ordinary prescription. We may say that the analysis of practices comprises the methodological recommendation that researchers should investigate prescription using a 'bottom-up' or emergent approach. It is curious to note that one of the inducements to study situated practices and one of the meanings implicit in the term 'in practice' are constructed by the opposition between what is prescribed – for example, how the work should be done – and how 'it is really done'. The antithesis between formal and real, between prescribed work and real work, has for a long time been an interpretative key used by the sociology of work, even before the 'practice turn' resumed similar topics with a different vocabulary.

The seventh and eighth chapters slightly change the expository logic hitherto followed. In fact, whilst Chapters 1 to 6 showed the principal supports for the performance of a practice, and which therefore constitute its resources – like maintaining a common orientation, sensible knowledge, the technological infrastructure, discursive practices and the normative infrastructure – the next two chapters address the problem of how to represent practices and why. They start from the assumption that practices are as opaque to practitioners as they are to researchers, but precisely for this reason their description and reflection on practice are potential means to empower practitioners. Chapter 7 seeks to answer the question of why use should be made of a practice-based approach which is not solely descriptive but can be included in the action-research tradition in the general sense – or which anyway is of applicative interest. The eighth chapter illustrates how a second tradition of research – which seeks to construct or describe technologies for the support of situated work – has engaged in the study of practices and with what methodological tools. The methodological discussion becomes more explicit in these two chapters. Chapter 7 examines what research design is able to consider the constant interconnection of practices, and therefore how to explore a 'texture of practices', while Chapter 8 illustrates the relation between the study of practices and rediscovery of ethnographic studies within the analysis of organizations and information systems.

It will have been noted that the book is structured around methodological concerns, but while space is given to the themes of research design, the choice of topics, and the aims of an anti-rationalist and anti-cognitivist approach, little space is devoted to research techniques. This is not to imply that the latter are of little importance; but rather that, like all the tools of a good craftsperson, they must be adapted, invented and made the object of bricolage, not of worship. It will also have been noticed that qualitative research is better able to answer questions as to the 'how' of a process, its temporality and the meaning attributed to it. It will be seen that many of those who adopt a qualitative research strategy resort to participant observation, the ethnography of objects, shadowing, conversation analysis and the interview with the double, but the range of possible tools is not restricted to these techniques, and the development of a new approach should also stimulate the invention of new research techniques.

The book finishes with a concluding chapter which has two purposes: on the one hand, to review the theoretical background that has generated the interest and field of studies that have formed under the umbrella concept of practice-based studies; on the other hand, to systematize the conceptual and analytical framework on which this book is based.

1. How ordinary work is practically accomplished

What do people do when they work? When they work is that all they do? How does work differ from non-work? The more traditional sociologists of work have preferred to consider it a 'macro' social phenomenon – as employment – leaving 'micro' analysis to other disciplines or to other sociological traditions. This is the so-called 'missing what' (Garfinkel and Wieder, 1992, p. 203) which escapes traditional studies on work. It is this perspective that has been resumed by the practice-based studies that continues the phenomenological and ethnomethodological tradition, and takes up Barley and Kunda's (2001) invitation to 'bring work back in' organization studies. The study of situated working practices also responds to a need for better understanding of the difference between prescribed work and real work (Licoppe, 2008) – a problem long present in the European sociology of work.

To understand this latter perspective, consider the phenomenological definition provided by Alfred Schütz (1962, p. 212), which treats work from another point of view 'Working, then, is action in the outer world, based upon a project and characterized by the intension to bring about the projected state of affairs by bodily movements'. This definition places particular emphasis on work as an activity directed towards the world, that is intended to accomplish a project, and above all one that involves the human body. Too often, in fact, it is forgotten that work activities are performed by a body, by its psycho-physical capacities, and that bodies are differently sexed. Workers are not abstract labour but sociomaterial and symbolic bodies. Gender relations are therefore part of working practices. Jobs are connoted along gender lines, and interactions in workplaces are not so much work interactions as gender constructs.

For symbolic interactionism, Everett Hughes's (1958; 1971) studies on work are of particular interest within practice-based studies, 'work as interaction is the central theme of sociological and social psychological study of work' (1971, p. 304). To give an idea of their position within a non-traditional perspective, we cite just one example, that of the division of labour. Traditionally the division of labour is considered as the condition which determines job roles and the set of individual and collective responsibilities, with the consequent assumption that individuals work on the basis of job roles. For Hughes (1958, p. 380), the division of labour does not consist of the simple difference between the work of one person and that of another, but in the fact that different tasks and different results are parts of a whole to whose production all to some extent contribute. Therefore the division of labour derives from interaction among people; interaction which unfolds step by step, and as it does so, constitutes the work as a collective and emergent product.

From this perspective, working is a being-in-the-world tied to the accomplishment of a project through physical activities that are situated in time and space. Defining work as a situated activity means focusing the sociological analysis of work on working practices as modes of action and knowledge, emerging *in situ* from the dynamics of interactions (Gherardi, 2006). This definition is rooted theoretically in social phenomenology, ethnomethodology and symbolic interactionism. Since the 1990s (together with other studies on distributed knowledge, cultural cognitive psychology, activity theory and situated learning), it has given rise to a new strand of social studies on working and organizing which fall under the heading of 'practice-based studies' or 'studies of knowing-in-practice'.

At the basis of this renewed interest in work as a situated activity there are two phenomena that have contributed to redefining the nature of work, and that have consequently challenged the analytical categories with which it is analysed:

1. The increased 'knowledge' content that characterizes work in 'technologically dense' environments (Bruni, 2005; Suchman, 1996).
2. The spread of information and communication technologies (computer, Internet, cellphones, to mention only the most common of them), which have redesigned workplaces, as well as the meaning itself of 'workplace' as a spatial and temporal locus marked by the co-presence of different human actors in interaction (Heath and Button, 2002; Llewellyn and Hindmarsh, 2010).

Emerging today is a perspective of study founded on working practices as an analytical and interpretative alternative to the traditional one, because study of work as a knowledge-based activity is necessary to gain better understanding of technological practices where interaction takes place both in co-presence and at a distance, where the reliability of technological systems is vital, and where communication and responsibility are crucial for the support in real time of the capacity to think and act collectively and cooperatively.

This perspective is also of applicative interest for those who design technological systems to support working activities, and who have come to realize that many failures in the introduction of new technologies are due to simplistic representations of the working activities that they are intended to support. As we shall see (Chapter 7), the resumption of ethnographic studies[1] on work is in fact also due to the interest of information system designers in 'thick' descriptions of working practices able to unveil the aspects of collectively performed working practices.

1.1   WHAT DO PEOPLE DO WHEN THEY WORK?

Work is much more than an activity undertaken in order to achieve a predetermined purpose. To familiarize the reader with this idea, Box 1.1 presents a brief description of the workday of Marco, an express delivery courier (Tiddi, 2002). Marco's is an apparently banal job, but for precisely this reason it illustrates the plurality of reciprocally interacting elements implicated in a working practice.

The example shows how achieving a simple goal (delivery of a package) requires complex abilities and involves the entire person.

First, Marco is involved with his body: travelling from one side of the city to the other forces him to breathe car exhaust fumes, weave through the traffic on his scooter and take comfort from the fact that at least it is not raining and not too cold. His five senses are therefore 'at work' and his body receives diverse aesthetic perceptions that contribute to increasing (or decreasing) 'pleasure' gained from performing the activity. Marco's communicative and relational abilities are also part of his body, so that he knows that politeness is one of the modes of interaction required by his job, and that the absence of a gesture by the girl who took delivery of the package meant that he would not receive a tip. This prompts

---

BOX 1.1   THE PONY EXPRESS WORKING PRACTICE

Marco is sitting on his scooter, his radio transmitter at his ear, waiting for a call from the express delivery depot. He has asked for details about an address given to him. He wrote it down as he always does, but now he cannot find it. 'This happens when you're in a hurry,' he thinks. Marco has worked as an express delivery courier since he was made redundant by his previous employers. He waits, but he knows that he will not have to wait long: with Christmas approaching, there is a lot of business, and the office is under pressure. The answer soon arrives, and he is given the details he needs. Addressee: Service & Co. Marco looks at what he has just written down. He realizes he cannot remember where the street is. He fishes the Rome city map out of his scooter trunk. He looks for the street and finds it: it is on the other side of the city. He thinks, 'I've got to get across the whole of Rome, and at this time of the year the streets are murder even when you're on a scooter. When you get long-distance deliveries like this one, you feel like leaving them at the depot . . . but then you get on with it . . . It's obvious that the easiest deliveries go to the older guys. You can't cause problems, because if you do, they won't give you work. The only solution is to be ready to deal with hassles as quickly as possible. At least, let's hope I get a tip. But if I take the ring road, it's gridlocked at this time of day. And then I might be fined, because you can't ride a scooter on the ring road. I'd better go through the city centre, enter the restricted traffic zone, where the traffic wardens can't be bothered with scooters even if they're not supposed to enter.' Marco starts up his scooter and sets off. He dodges the traffic wardens, crosses the city centre, and heads for Nomentana. He reaches his destination. Macro thinks 'I've inhaled so many exhaust fumes it's like I've smoked a packet of fags, but the weather's been good. It isn't raining and it isn't cold. It doesn't even seem like winter. Here we are, street number 32.' Marco parks his scooter and approaches the intercom. He looks for the name of the firm, finds it, and rings. A girl answers. 'I have a package for Service & Co.' he says. The girl buzzes him in. 'Third floor' she says. The lift is out of order. Marco walks up three floors, finds the door and rings the bell. The door opens automatically. Marco enters. He goes to the girl seated in the lobby, gives her the envelope, and gets her to sign the receipt. He lingers for a moment, hoping for a gesture from the girl, but she does nothing. 'So there's no chance of a tip. I'd better be polite otherwise the management will be on my neck. That's all I need,' he reasons. He bids the girl goodbye. Marco looks at his watch: 'I told Lella that I'd get off at five, I can still do another one.' He goes back to the depot to pick up another delivery.

Source: Tiddi (2002, pp. 37–9).

reflection on how such modes of interaction (what Hochschild, 1983, called 'emotional labour') are not specific to the work of an express delivery courier but relate to broader social practices which impact on (and are reproduced by) everyday work relations.

Second, Marco is also at work with his mind, given the cognitive labour required to deliver the package. What is the exact location of the company? What route should he take to get there? We see from how Marco answers these two questions that cognitive labour does not follow an abstract logic but draws on situated knowledge. Marco uses the street map to find the exact location of the company, but he decides which route to take by relying on his personal knowledge (and experience) of traffic and road conditions. Hence, the knowledge which Marco applies is knowledge that he has acquired from his everyday experience, and which he must activate because it comprises the practical solution to his problem.

However, it would be over-hasty to conclude that the success of Marco's work depends solely on his personal abilities and that it is entirely individual. He is in fact in contact (by radio) with an operations centre which gives him the delivery coordinates, and to which he can refer when some unforeseen event occurs (such as losing the recipient's address). Thus one understands that Marco's work also depends on (and impacts on) that of others, and that in general it requires the coordination of multiple activities in different times and places (the depot which receives the delivery order, communication of the address to the courier and delivery by the latter).

Moreover, Marco's world is populated not only by human actors but also by technologies and objects. The radio transmitter (which connects him to the operations centre), the scooter (which gives him mobility), the lift (which is out of order), the receipt (which certifies delivery), are all elements of differing technical complexity intrinsic to Marco's work and which can help or hinder its performance. For that matter, the automatism of the gesture with which Marco extracts the street map from the trunk on his scooter is enough to evoke the pervasive role of objects in any practical activity.

The working practice of an express delivery courier therefore takes place within an ecology of intimately connected elements: the body, language, prior knowledge, and the human and non-human actors that everyday activities bring together. Moreover, it is supported by background knowledge, by the tacit rules of the community of practice to which Marco belongs (the reason why 'the easiest deliveries go to the older guys'), as well as by the historical, institutional and cultural context in which the work takes shape. In fact, like many other jobs in the so-called 'new economy', Marco's job is marked by precariousness and an unstable position in the labour market, but it is important to note that this does not diminish the value of such jobs evidently rich with knowledge.

We may conclude that while people work, they perform activities of different kinds; they produce and reproduce society in its work relations, and they affirm an individual and collective work identity. We may also say that there is work that is necessary for a person to be able to work. This has been variously defined and studied, and it is the subject of the next section.

1.2   RELATIONAL WORK AND ARTICULATION WORK

The above account has demonstrated that work involves numerous other activities. The set of these activities can be called 'relational work' (Gherardi, 1990), the purpose of which is to maintain and reproduce everyday sociality, both within the workplace and externally to it (with other social relations). One should always bear in mind, in fact, that working and spending a part of the day engaged in work is only one aspect of life; for life is also made up of other activities which usually interweave with the routine of work. Recall, for instance, that Marco the express delivery courier, thought about his date with his girlfriend, and took decisions about his practical activities considering other activities not related to work.

Relational work, moreover, is not the only work performed alongside work as a change-directed activity. Together with the latter, a large amount of work is undertaken so that activities may proceed smoothly. This is 'articulation work', a term used by Corbin and Strauss (1993) to denote the work necessary to establish, maintain and change the arrangements necessary to work both within one's own organizational unit and among different units.

Hospitals, for instance, are workplaces in which a very extensive set of people interact to perform a large number of different tasks whose accomplishment requires supplementary articulation work. If the nursing staff are to do their work, they must agree with the doctors in the ward and with other departments (the pharmacy, the kitchen, the operating theatres, the analysis laboratories and so on). Without these agreements, the nursing staff cannot be sure that medical schedules are updated and available to each shift so that the requisite medicines are present in the correct department, the patients are fed and treated, the wards are clean and the technologies are working. The set of these interactions are customarily established within the units and among them through a series of collaborative and competitive strategies that require negotiation and persuasion; but once established they do not last forever and are often interrupted (or disrupted) by unexpected events, breakdowns or contingencies requiring further articulation work.

When unexpected events occur, the work is delayed, it is of poor quality or it is simply not done. This produces conflicts, anxieties, frustrations and further repair work on the social relationships that have been unintentionally severed. The normal and quotidian breakdowns in normality therefore require work which repairs and renegotiates previous arrangements.

An example of articulation work in response to a contingent event is provided by Corbin and Strauss (1993) and is described in Box 1.2.

BOX 1.2   THE HOSPITAL WARD CASE

During an afternoon shift, a hospital pharmacy found itself short-staffed because two pharmacists had taken sick leave. Moreover, during that shift, several medical emergencies had occurred to which the pharmacy had to give priority to. As a consequence, a medication which should have been sent to a unit arrived too late for it to be administered during the afternoon shift. Because the doctor was anxious that the patient should receive the treatment, the nurses on the afternoon shift made arrangements with those on the night shift for the latter to administer the medicine. However, the treatment required that the patient be kept under constant observation while the medicine was being administered (intravenously). Because there were fewer nurses on the night shift than in the afternoon, the night-shift nurses assumed an attitude of resentment and frustration. They did not have the power to request more personnel; nor could they choose whether or not to administer the medicine ordered by the doctor. They discussed the tardiness of the afternoon-shift nurses in starting the treatment: why had they waited? Why had one of them not gone personally to the pharmacy to fetch the medicine? The afternoon-shift nurses tried to explain that the delay had not been their fault. In the end, the nurses on the night shift had to include this task on their schedule. But the next morning, when reporting to the head nurse, they complained vociferously about what had happened. The head nurse had to investigate the causes of what had happened, make peace between the two shifts, and reply to the doctor's protests that the treatment had not been administered in due time.

Source: Corbin and Strauss (1993, pp. 74–5).

What does this example tell us about practice? It shows that the execution of work is a collective and coordinated action. It is not enough that the work has been divided among specialized and coordinated tasks; that division must be constantly and cooperatively reproduced.

Because there are so many different types of work, it is necessary to agree on what must be done, to what standards, in what places, with what resources, with what counterparts and so on: all this constitutes articulation work. But these agreements must be reached, maintained and revised through a constant process comprising diverse interaction strategies, like negotiation, discussion, education, persuasion, threat or coercion.

Corbin and Strauss (1993) propose three concepts with which to analyse articulation work:

1. The *arrangements* made among people in the same operational unit or among different units. These are agreements reached on the actions necessary for the work to be performed. For instance, within a particular unit, agreement is reached on what is to be done, by whom, with what resources, for how long, for what purpose, to what standard; among different units, agreement is reached on resources, technologies, execution times, spaces, competences and so on. The same applies to agreements within organizations and between these and other institutions. The arrangements are always temporary and subject to re-negotiation, and it is for this reason that articulation work is routine work.
2. *Working things out.* That is, the strategies of interaction by which arrangements are made, maintained and revised. These are interaction strategies in response to what has been said or done by others, before the work starts and during the arrangement-making process.
3. *Stance.* That is, the position assumed by each participant towards both the work and the process of working things out. It therefore concerns each participant's perception of his/her capacity to control and influence the situation and context in which the arrangements are made. Individual stances also depend on (and change) the stances of others.

The concept of 'articulation work' well expresses the set of activities necessary to accomplish a working practice. But besides this concept, there are several others which are variants of it. To be stressed in particular is the importance (especially in service jobs) of *arbitrages* (Grosjean and Lacoste, 1999) when agreement must be reached on values, orders of magnitude and the action appropriate to the situation; in short, cases in which the deontological dimension of the profession is called into question (as often happens in hospital settings or in relation to care and service jobs). The collective production of values-based rules of behaviour is therefore a dimension of work, in that social groups produce, legitimate, observe, negotiate, comply with or disregard the rules while people work and deal with practical problems.

Another concept which can be associated with the previous ones is that of *knotworking* developed by Engeström (1999b, p. 31) to recall (and oppose) the idea of *networking*. The expression suggests that it is not sufficient to create relations; these must then be fixed – knotted together – and made relatively long-lasting, also by means of objects or *ad hoc* solutions. This therefore requires collaboration which constructs temporary organizational relations and which involves (for instance) customers, producers and reciprocal learning among the parties engaged in the solution of a problem, and so on. Knotworking is a self-organized activity based on the practical knowledge of those who discern and resolve a problem.

What people do when they work, therefore, is much more complex than the simple execution of a planned activity. We thus intuitively realize that work contexts are much more than simple containers of work activity, and that the latter can be studied as a (more or less 'competent') performance. The concept of 'performance', in fact, makes it possible to regard work as an activity which follows a script, but whose interpretation is situated. It is an individual and collective activity that may consequently vary according to the participants involved in it, or those who are prepared to be involved. Finally, it is an activity which constructs itself through knowing how to move in space and among different materials, and which therefore requires choreographic ability.

We can consequently explore what is meant by work as a situated activity in light of the intellectual history of what has been called the 'paradigm of situated action'.

1.3   THE PARADIGM OF SITUATED ACTION

In 1994 the French journal *Sociologie du Travail* devoted a special issue, edited by Anni Borzeix, to the theme 'Work and Knowledge'. The monograph had the merit of bringing together the North American, English and French schools, and of anticipating the developments thereafter which gave rise to the body of inquiry known as 'practice-based studies'. In 2000 and in 2002 two other special issues appeared (see Gherardi, 2000; Heath and Button, 2002) and when we compare their list of articles, shown in Table 1.1, we can easily see an ongoing conversation at distance among authors who share similar concerns.

Table 1.1   *Comparison between special issues related to practice-based studies*

SOCIOLOGIE DU TRAVAIL, 1994	ORGANIZATION, 2000	THE BRITISH JOURNAL OF SOCIOLOGY, 2002
Editor: Anni Borzeix	Editor: Silvia Gherardi	Editors: Christian Heath and Graham Button
Aaron Cicourel	Etienne Wenger	Lucy Suchman, Randall Trigg and Jeanette Blomberg
Edwin Hutchins	Dvora Yanow	Christian Heath, Paul Luff and Marcus Sanchez Svensson
Barnard Conein and Eric Jacopin	Alessia Contu and Hugh Willmott	Michael Lynch
Dominique Vellard	Frank Blackler, Norman Crump and Seonaidh McDonald	John Hughes, Mark Rouncefield and Peter Tolmie
Christian Heath and Paul Luff	Yrjo Engeström	Jack Whalen, Marilyn Whalen and Kathryn Henderson
Jacques Theureau and Geneviève Filippi	Lucy Suchman	Daniel Neyland and Steve Woolgar
Isaac Joseph	Silvia Gherardi and Davide Nicolini	Graham Button and Wes Sharrock
Bruno Latour	John Law	Randy Hodson

The special issue of *Sociologie du Travail* contained an illuminating article by Barnard Conein and Eric Jacopin (1994) which reconstructed the intellectual roots of the concept of situated action and connected it with subsequent developments. We shall refer to this article to show that the interpretative framework of situated action draws on the thought of Alfred Schütz (1962) and George Herbert Mead (1934) – that is, on interactionist approaches.

We owe to these two authors the idea that situated action is anchored in space. Both of them emphasized that all work presupposes a self-referred space made up of objects. They also stressed that contact with (and manipulation of) objects, is the support for the execution of work. Schütz (1962, p. 187) described work as 'the world within my reach', as an activity which both depends on the context and constitutes it. Mead (1934) drew a distinction between the object within range of manipulation (what can be seen and touched) and the object at a distance, out of reach but present in the visual field. He thus showed that the space of work is progressively created through manipulation with tools and objects. Manipulatory activity presupposes the reciprocal construction of space and action, because action (bringing objects 'within reach') marks out the boundaries of the same space that it thus constructs.

This idea was taken up by cognitive ethnography (Lave, 1988), which acknowledged that cognitive activities are not solely mental but also rely on the material elements in the context which anchor the necessary information supports. When Jean Lave and colleagues (1984) studied arithmetic calculations in supermarkets, and how the arrangement of purchases in trolleys reproduced the order of the aisles in which the goods were displayed, they showed how the spatial environment gives shape to situations, and how our 'practical arithmetic' follows rules different from those learned at school.

An anecdote widely cited to exemplify practical arithmetic (and, by extension, many of the characteristics of practical knowledge) is called 'the case of the cottage cheese' (see Box 1.3).

Calculation by adults in work situations follows a situated logic which uses visual supports and aids devised in relation to the context. Objects help us remember, measure and compare. A pile of files on the desk is an indicator of the amount of paperwork still to be done and the amount of time that it will take (Bruni, 2005). In a similar manner, Beach (1988) has shown how barmen use the shapes and places of glasses, as well as the

---

BOX 1.3   THE COTTAGE CHEESE CASE

A person on a *Weight Watchers* diet programme must measure out three-quarters of a half portion of cottage cheese. After a first perplexed glance at the cheese and the instructions, the person has no doubts: he/she tips the contents of the tub onto a plate, uses a knife to shape the cheese into a round pancake, draws a cross on the surface, removes half of it, then reshapes the remaining cheese into a round pancake draws again a cross on the surface, and then removes a quarter. Measuring out three-eighths of a tub of cottage cheese would not only have been more complicated but probably would not even have come to that person's mind – also because fractions pertain to school practices, whilst in everyday life the practical reasoning used to measure, compare, weigh and so on, employs other resources found in the environment.

Source: Lave (1988, p. 88).

colours and quantities of liquids, as reminders – anchored in the environment – of how to prepare cocktails. The workplace is an active context and not a mere container of activities: it helps us remember; it allows us to do some things and not others (for example, ones that might put our safety at risk); it solicits our action with visual or auditory signals; it furnishes programmes that help us diagnose possible breakdowns and suggests how we should intervene.

The situated action approach extends the original idea of work as interaction to encompass action with objects in relation to the physical environment and situations. The aim of the approach and its research methodology is to understand how work environments, equipped with artefacts and objects, may significantly facilitate the performance of tasks by those who work in those settings.

The first lesson taught by the paradigm of situated action is that the context is not a mere container but rather a resource for action; the second lesson is that the term 'situated action' has a privileged relationship with the idea of the 'Other' (first introduced by Mead) and with Goffman's theory that ties it to communication. In fact Erving Goffman (1956; 1959) developed a theory of situation using the terms 'situated activity system' or 'encounter'. When two people communicate, they reciprocally make an attention space manifest, and therefore accessible, and their action is situated because it is oriented by and dependent on the action of the recipient of the communication. The situation is the result of the interaction between those two people.

'Situated action'[2] became a well-recognized concept through the work of Lucy Suchman (1987) who resumed Goffman's theory in one of her books (significantly entitled, *Plans and Situated Action*) and asked whether the concept of interaction may be extended to machines, or whether interaction presupposes communication among humans. Are social interaction and interaction with machines the same thing? Whilst a non-sociological current of thought – Human–Computer Interaction (HCI) – answers in the affirmative, Suchman drew a distinction between the two types of interaction. To exemplify it, she used the relationship between people and an 'interactive' photocopier.

Suchman studied the communication and cooperation between two novice users trying to understand how to operate the expert help system incorporated in the photocopier. Not only were the two humans recipients of a communication system, but so too was the help system in the photocopier, in that it asked questions and gave answers to the users. In the case of an interactive machine 'in dialogue' with its user, the face-to-face interaction furnishes a model for understanding the action, and the presence of the two novices made it possible to analyse interaction with the patterns of oral communication. Nevertheless, the interaction between those persons differed from their interaction with the photocopier. Access to the situation, in fact, was not symmetrical for the persons and for the machine. The situation of the 'expert help system' comprised a plan for the use of the machine written by the designer and implemented as the program that determined the machine's behaviour; while for the humans the situation was open, and it was modified in the interaction and through it. The machine did not have access to the situation because it did not produce any spontaneous understanding; nor could it improvise *in situ* the circumstances of the situation. Therefore, Lucy Suchman (1987) concluded, analysis of the social interaction furnished a model for analysis of the interaction with the machine, but only the social interaction was situated.

In other words, plans (or programs) for machines, are not plans for people. During the 1980s, plans attracted a great deal of research, especially in robotics, but the criticism brought by Suchman (1987, p. 3, original emphasis) was that:

> The model treats a plan as something located in the actor's head, which directs his or her behaviour. In contrast I argue that artefacts built on the planning model confuse *plans* with *situated actions*, and recommend instead a plan as formulations of precedents conditions and consequences of action that account for action in a plausible way.

Before action, plans have only a predictive or organizational purpose; after action, plans serve to justify the actions undertaken. An example provided by Suchman is canoeing down a river. Before setting off, the canoeist may plan a course for descending the river, but when he/she reaches the rapids, he/she sets the plan aside and resorts to all his/her skills. Hence a plan is an ingredient of practical action, in the sense that it is an artefact that helps one to reason on the action, but it is not a mechanism generative of the action.

Generally, therefore, describing an action as 'situated' means considering the organization of the action as emerging *in situ* from the dynamic of the interactions. This dynamic results from two processes:

- Each participant's understanding of the action of the other or others;
- The perception and interpretation of the signals emitted by the surrounding environment.

Central to the paradigm of situated action is a revised conception of context as no longer a container of action but a situation in which the interests of the actors and the opportunities in the environment meet and are reciprocally defined. Of central importance in work, therefore, are interactions with others, situated communication, the construction of situations, the relationship with the physical environment and the objects in it, but especially the idea that these elements are 'held together' and express a contingent logic embedded in the situation.

We shall see later how the term 'situated' has different meanings for other strands of analysis. For the time being, however, we shall consider the theoretical link leading from the notion of work as situated action (which characterized the 1990s) to the notion of work as knowing-in-practice.

1.4 WORKING PRACTICES AND KNOWING-IN-PRACTICE

What does the concept of practice bring to the study of work as situated activity? Why is knowledge in this case qualified as 'practice'? Around these concepts there has developed the paradigm of situated action which subtends the study of knowledge comprised in practices and on which practice-based studies are grounded.

The concept of 'community of practices' first arose within analyses of organizational learning as the precursor to studies on practical knowledge and how it is created, disseminated, and conserved in working practices and in the community that forms around a practice. Numerous authors (Brown and Duguid, 1991; Lave and Wenger, 1991; Zucchermaglio, 1996) have identified the community of practice as an informal aggregation defined not only by its participants but also, and especially, by the way in which these act and interpret events. A community of practice is a network of relations among people, activities and the surrounding environment, in constant communication and interaction with other communities. The relations are constructed around activities, and activities take shape through social interactions, so that specific competences and experiences become part of the individual and are stabilized within the community. In this regard,[3] of interest are the ways in which knowledge is transmitted from one community to another: how new conversations develop between them and how the interdependence among activities creates opportunities for innovation through the hybridization of conversations. This theoretical background – developed mainly by Brown and Duguid (1991) – has given rise to the idea of practices as loci of learning, organizing and innovating. More recently, practices have been termed 'sites of knowing' (Nicolini, 2010) in order to underline the non-distinction between knowing and practising.

To convey a preliminary idea of the theoretical and methodological framework in which working practices are analysed as knowing-in-practice, we may say that knowledge can be seen and analysed as an activity, rather than as an object (a body of knowledge), and that it can therefore also be studied as a situated activity. In other words, knowledge emerges from the context of its production and is anchored by (and in) material supports in that context. We may also say that knowing is an activity both individual and collective; that it is an activity situated in working practices; and that, therefore, practical knowledge is contextual as opposed to being decontextualized and theoretical.

A metaphor which aptly illustrates how a practice emerges and is socially and materially sustained is that of climbing, as described by Hennion (2007, pp. 100–101):

> What climbing shows is not that the geological rock is a social construction, but that it is a reservoir of differences that can be brought into being. The climber makes the rock as the rock makes the climber. The differences are indeed in the rock, and not in the 'gaze' that is brought to it. But these are not brought to bear without the activity of the climb which makes them present. There is co-formation. Differences emerge, multiply and are projected. The 'object' is not an immobile mass against which our goals are thrown. It is in itself a deployment, a response, an infinite reservoir of differences that can be apprehended and brought into being.

Hennion thus illustrates the relationship of co-formation between sociomateriality and identity, but he only alludes to the fact that the same relationship exists between the doing – climbing – and the knowing: that is, knowing how to read the rock, seeing the handholds that become such only at the moment when the climber sees them and makes them handholds for his/her next move. This knowing how to read the context as a 'reservoir of differences', knowing how to identify the handholds for the next action, knowing what the next action will be (Garfinkel's, 1996, 'what next'), and possessing the vocabulary to talk competently about climbing, are things that are collectively learned, transmitted and transformed during practice, and as an effect of it.

To work is therefore to use a set of knowledges as resources for action, and working produces further knowledges. Working is knowing, therefore, and not simply applying acquired knowledge. And, as we shall see, knowing is a collective knowledgeable doing, and by focusing on knowing rather than knowledge, the distinction between knowledge and learning is avoided.

The shift from knowledge to knowing allows its analysis in terms of a phenomenon that according to Blackler (1995, p. 1039) is: (a) manifest in systems of language, technology, collaboration and control (that is, it is mediated); (b) located in time and space and specific to particular contexts (that is, it is situated); (c) constructed and constantly developing (that is, it is provisional); and (d) purposive and object-oriented (that is, it is pragmatic).

Consider, for example, the practice of cardiological teleconsultancy in order to see knowing as a practical achievement. The general practitioner records the patient's ECG with a portable apparatus. The recordings may be made at the doctor's surgery or in the patient's home, because the apparatus can store around ten traces that can be transmitted at a later time. The call centre coordinates the referral procedure, establishing contacts between GPs and cardiologists, and handling transmission of the ECGs. The traces are sent by the doctor, downloaded using special software at the call centre, and distributed among the cardiologists, who can read them on their PC screens. The traces are discussed by telephone with the GPs and then sent back to the GPs by fax with the report attached. The GP usually sends the trace immediately after recording it and uses the remote consultation service while examining the patient.

The service takes almost the form of a 'cardiological examination at a distance',[4] and the activity which emerges from this new workplace distributed in space is substantially different from already existing medical practices: it is neither a cardiological examination nor a general one; it is not a simple consultation between experts nor a training exercise within a course. Teleconsultancy, therefore, is a new kind of medical practice, a sort of hybridization of already existing practices which obliges the two experts to learn new modes of work and action in the social, but also material, system in which they are embedded. The distributed setting made possible by the new technologies requires the two experts to learn how to act in a sociomaterial system characterized by different types of knowing distributed among different actors, objects and relations. To practise telemedicine is therefore to activate a knowing-in-practice that indeed involves the medical knowledge acquired at university and refined through working experience but does not consist merely of the application in situation of already existing knowledge.

Box 1.4 presents what can be considered a typical telephone call. The telephone call reported shows that, when the ECG and the patient do not align (the ECG is normal but the patient feels ill), various elements are discursively mobilized, and the trace moves into the background, losing its status as a privileged object. To paraphrase Latour (2002, p. 251), it is as if the trace has become a 'labyrinth' through which the two doctors must find their way. Thus, previous ECGs, reports on other examinations, medications, family histories, become elements that must be discursively activated

BOX 1.4   THE TELECONSULTANCY CASE

[Greetings.]

GP: I've had this ECG done on a patient already affected with chronic ischemic cardiopathy, because he felt ill while he was eating, he felt faint and a weight on his stomach.

C: The trace doesn't seem . . . how is he now?

GP: He's lying down now . . . he feels weak . . . he hasn't got dyspnoea, absolutely not . . . he still feels this weight . . . I think it's indigestion, I mean, he needs to vomit . . . but, you know . . . I preferred to do the ECG . . .

C: I'd say . . . there aren't any evident alterations . . . of course, then you have to look at the clinical [assessment] . . . because these things, sometimes . . . these things are a bit tricky . . . For the moment I'd keep an eye on him . . . there's a left axial deviation . . . there's . . . some ventricular extra-systole . . . Is he taking Cardioaspirin?

GP: No, in fact I wanted to give it to him . . .

C: But he has a history of ischemic cardiopathy but he hasn't had acute episodes?

GP: No, no. Perhaps . . . five years ago, there was something . . . when the chronic ischemia diagnosis was made . . .

C: I'd wait a bit longer . . . how old is he?

GP: 85.

C: The risks are clearly there, if the thing doesn't sort itself out, I'd have him looked at, just to be on the safe side . . . but, at the moment the trace doesn't show anything . . .

GP: . . . out of the ordinary . . .

C: . . . although traces can sometimes be negative . . .

GP: . . . right . . . in fact . . . that's true, you can't always rely on the trace . . .

C: . . . no, no there's a good percentage of heart attacks with normal traces . . . except that this . . . well . . . I mean . . . at 85 years old, of course, some problem always comes out!

GP: Yes, I'll give him an antacid and then we'll see.

[Salutations.]

Source: Bruni et al. (2007, p. 93).

and aligned in order to restore meaning to the situation. The cardiologist and the GP seem almost to be suggesting interpretations to each other, as in a dance where two actors must lean on each other to find a point of balance which permits their movement. The action of the cardiologist and the GP, in fact, does not take place in an empty space, but internally to a broader medical practice. It is consequently to the broader medical practice that they turn in the absence of points of contact between patient and ECG.

From a methodological point of view, a sociologist who studies work as knowing-in-practice wonders what network anchors the distributed and fragmented knowledge that gives form to the teleconsultancy. He/she establishes that it consists of:

1. *The patient.* The patient possesses, and contributes to the teleconsultancy, knowledge about his body and sensations. In this case, knowing consists in the ability to perceive an 'anomaly', translate it into an account through language, and narrate the symptoms to the doctor. This preliminary description and bodily knowledge is supported by the general practitioner, who translates the patient's subjective knowledge (which medicine assumes to be strongly influenced by individual factors and therefore unreliable) into elements of 'scientific' knowledge through its 'translation' into medical terminology.

2. *The medical community.* The doctor's expert knowledge is expressed in the transformation of the patient's idiomatic and colourful expressions into an 'objective' knowledge through the systematic use of medical terminology and the application of medical expertise to common sense (Cicourel, 1986). In the above telephone call (for example) it is noticeable that the two doctors exchange their opinions on the reliability of the trace representing the patient. Doing so is not only functional to the medical decision, it also helps maintain the sense of belonging to the medical community and the sharing of knowledge within it.

3. *The organizational rules.* When hospitals hire specialists, they internalize bodies of already codified knowledge and simultaneously codify other types of knowledge by institutionalizing models of behaviour and knowledge in norms and/or operational routines. Medical protocols, in particular, are based on the segmentation of therapy and surgery into one 'correct sequence' of micro-actions, and they result from a process of rationalization of medical knowledge (Berg, 1997). When performing the teleconsultancy, the cardiologist follows a protocol inscribed in the computer's software which requires him to complete all the fields on a form. Thus the protocol structures the conversation between the two doctors.

4.   *Artefacts.* Knowledge resides not only in humans and rules but also in artefacts such as the instruments, technologies and objects that participate in and constitute the setting of the activity. In the case considered here, the patient-file which the cardiologist must compile not only defines the sequence and the content of the questions put by the cardiologist to the general practitioner; it is also an instrument of organizational accountability.[5] That is to say, the set of questions is not only predetermined by the form of interaction between the cardiologist and the general practitioner; it also mirrors the forms of knowledge deemed legitimate and relevant in that medical practice. Besides the patient-file, there is another artefact which shapes medical knowledge through the constraints and rules that it imposes. This is the software used in the service to regulate how the teleconsultancy report must be written. It makes accountable not so much the activity or interaction with the general practitioner as the rationality that reconstructs (a posteriori) the medical action in terms of legal liability. Moreover, use of a further artefact – the electrocardiograph (for recording the ECG) – incorporates the knowledge that has been necessary for its design and implementation. It is this technical object that transforms the impulses emitted by the human body into elements representing its activity. But, at the same time, the image of the patient furnished by the ECG artefact assumes value according to the narrative in which it is embedded – that is, as and when it is situated within a field of practices.

5.   *The technological infrastructure.* The teleconsultancy is made possible by a technological infrastructure consisting of computer, telephones, cables and electrocardiographs, but also of the languages and codes necessary to render them compatible, as well as a call centre responsible for interconnecting general practitioners, ECG traces, cardiologists and the transmission of reports. The practical knowledge mobilized by the teleconsultancy is therefore anchored in a technological infrastructure, that when it is in operation, is not visible/hearable in the telephone call, but on which the possibility of the teleconsultancy depends.

Knowledge, therefore, does not reside in the heads of people; on the contrary, it is anchored in the material world, and working requires activation of a fragmented system of knowledge (Bruni et al., 2007). We use this expression to emphasize that all those who interact within a specific working practice possess different 'pieces' of knowledge which, as in a jigsaw puzzle, must be fitted together to acquire intelligibility.

I have used the example of the teleconsultancy in order to show that what we call 'knowledge' is a cooperative activity, a practical accomplishment. My purpose is also to underline that the way in which new technologies 'enter' medical practice is very close to what happens in many other computer-mediated types of work, where working at distance entails the dematerialization of work and the loss of sensible knowledge. Observing, touching and listening to the patient, is an activity typical of medical examinations which disappears in the teleconsultancy process, with the consequent loss of the sensory (aesthetic) abilities. Moreover, there is an impoverishment of the 'material-objective' basis of knowledge which is offset by an increase in communicative competence. Because the patient's body is absent, it is reintroduced and mainly represented by the ECG trace and the account given by the general practitioner. Compiling the clinical report becomes a cooperative activity mediated by information and communication technologies within a rarefied interactive space.

We may therefore start with the example of the teleconsultancy to illustrate some of the characteristics of work in the knowledge society, but also to propose an interpretative and methodological frame for analysis of situated practices as knowing-in-practice. Accordingly, the characteristics of practical knowledge are the following:

- *A pragmatic stance.* Practical knowledge is directed to doing, to taking decisions in situations, to solving problems, to maintaining and reproducing a community of practices;
- *A specific temporality.* Practical knowledge emerges from the situation and from situated action;
- *An anchoring in materiality.* Practical knowledge uses fragments of knowledge embedded in objects and technology, and in the material world that interacts with humans and interrogates them;
- *An anchoring in discursive practices.* Practical knowledge uses the discursive mobilization of cues for action and their positions within a narrative scheme that gives sense to what occurs phenomenologically;
- *A historical-cultural anchoring.* Practical knowledge is also mediated by what has happened in the past and has been learned from experience and in experience. If we consider the setting in which practices are developed, we must include within it both the institutional context and the social system of the division of labour and the rules that regulate social roles.

1.5   TO SUM UP

Generally, the adjective 'practical' related to knowledge implies a devaluing meaning: practical knowledge is acquired through doing, which does not have to be taught formally, which needs only to 'work' to be valid, and which is therefore a commodity of little value with respect to 'theoretical' knowledge. The common sense that has sustained this (widely held) vision is today radically contested by the definition of contemporary society as a knowledge society (Castells, 1996) or of cognitive capitalism (Boutang, 2002). The knowledge content of contemporary work is in constant growth: the more work dematerializes, the more knowledge becomes one of its main products and, therefore, one commodity like many others.

The vision of practical knowledge that derives from research on organizational learning and from the consolidated tradition of philosophical and sociological inquiries today merge into what have been called 'practice-based studies'.[6] These studies are part of the critique of rationality and the use of rational models to interpret social action. In this sense, the purpose of studying work as practical knowledge and situated activity is to replace objective rationality (as a regime of 'optimizing' or 'satisficing' logic) with the logic of situation (and therefore a regime of 'contextual rationality'). On this view, the context in which work is undertaken is not preconstituted. On the contrary, it is actively constructed in 'situational frames' which interpret situations by isolating them from the environment. Work is thus 'knowing how' – knowing how to contribute constantly to the working practices.

Although there is no unified theory of practical knowledge, the concept of practice has a long tradition in both philosophy and sociology.[7]

To briefly summarize the sociological study of practices, the sociologists who have made the greatest contribution to it (Garfinkel, Bourdieu and Giddens) are indebted to Schütz (1962) and his definition of the 'social world' as a reality constituted by innumerable and finite provinces of meaning. Following his phenomenological tradition the world of everyday life is seen as province of meaning dominated and structured by the so-called 'natural attitude'. The world therefore is not the private world of the single individual but an intersubjective world shared by all of us and in which we have, not a theoretical, but an eminently practical interest. However, individuals are usually aware that they have different perceptions of reality, and they are also simultaneously aware that there is a degree of accessibility to the perceptions of others which may be minimal but suffices to perform the normal activities of everyday life. The meanings of experiences undergone in the external world are therefore considered 'empirically identical' – in particular as regards practical goals. The result is a sharing of sense which becomes essential for communication and for that particular aspect of reality conferred on the world of everyday life. Hence, work represents the highest degree of interest in life and attention to it, and, simultaneously, the way in which women and men can alter the external world.

Studying work in its everyday settings requires that working practices and their day-by-day reproduction be assumed as the units of analysis. The attention therefore shifts from analysis of work as production to work as the reproduction of society and social relationships. The production of social life thus becomes a 'skilled performance' (Giddens, 1990, p. 4), in that social practices are constructed (as ethnomethodology demonstrates) as procedures, methods or techniques opportunely performed by social actors. Practice can thus be viewed in light of the idea of society put forward by Garfinkel (1967), that is, not as an already existing structure in which animals and human can enter, but as a performance that must be constantly refined.

Whilst action is an individual act performed by a social actor and is considered in its unfolding, a practice is something more (although is composed of activities and courses of action). What makes it recognizable and recognized is its being socially sustained and constantly reproduced. A working practice is such if it is recognized by a community, and if it is sustained by a normative basis both ethical and aesthetic. Communities of practitioners sustain their practices by negotiating and discussing what is a good practice, which of them is better or more beautiful, when a practice should be changed and how, or whether it should be discarded.

We shall also see in the following chapters that the coordination of work and the discursive practices of coordination rely on the 'accountability' of situations, and of the people who interact in those situations. This term, generally used to denote a 'motive', 'reason' or 'explanation' was used by Garfinkel (1967) to emphasize that people make their actions explainable (accountable) at the moment when they name (and enact) them. Hence, accounts contribute to the environment of which they themselves are part, and they are interpreted and understood procedurally. This is because large parts of our actions and interactions are not based on shared arrangements but instead on a set of tacit presuppositions, neither made explicit nor entirely explicable, and which are taken for granted. Knowing how to see (and therefore to develop a professional vision), knowing how to speak (to use technical vocabulary with competence) and knowing how to do: these, therefore, are the 'observable and reportable' competences that the sociologist of work considers when describing and interpreting working practices.

Therefore, in our analysis of working practices as processes by which people perform the practical knowledge necessary to accomplish their everyday work, we shall start from the following assumptions:

- Human activity in situations does not comply with absolute rationality. The reciprocal intelligibility of the actions of those involved in a practice derives from recognition of reciprocal intentions according to a plan considered a resource for action;
- Cooperation in practice is the result of the constant adjustment of the unforeseen events which arise from the context;
- Technology is an artefact that transforms and distributes representations: it incorporates knowledge and ensures that, in the work environment, knowledge is distributed between human and non-human actors;
- Work is a practical activity constructed by actors in situations and interactions which may occur face-to-face or be mediated by information and communication technologies, but which in all cases must be studied *in situ*.

In this chapter I have referred to four classic studies in order to illustrate the single points of interest and application of practice-based studies and, in so doing, offer insights into their methodology:

1. The pony express case illustrated how a practice is an ecology of interacting elements (such as the body and bodily knowledge; artefacts and the knowledge materialized in them; organizational and societal rules).
2. The hospital ward case was an example of articulation work, and therefore of how arrangements of elements should be negotiated and renegotiated while practices unfold in time.
3. The cottage cheese case showed how the context of a practice is not a simple container of it, but rather is a resource for practical reasoning and acting.
4. The teleconsultancy case represented an instance of a practice that, in its being practised, connects all the 'pieces' of fragmented knowledge together into a coherent whole. It shows how knowing-in-practice is achieved as a practical accomplishment.

NOTES

1. Ethnographic studies of work are based on the systematic observation of the routine activities of people in their specific work environments. They furnish minute descriptions

of those activities and environments. The focus is on both constants and variants, and the aim is to reconstruct and interpret the everyday processes and practices of organization and work performance (Bruni, 2003).

2. The term 'situated action' is used in the field of artificial intelligence and the study of man/machine interaction in opposition to the abstract representation of knowledge. Its best-known proponents, Winograd and Flores (1986) and Suchman (1987), argue that when designing interfaces, it is better to study the concrete use that people make of computers, rather than focusing on how people think or on what computers can do. Besides these authors, Lave (1988), who worked in the area of educational studies, contributed to the debate by showing that abstract knowledge (acquired in educational contexts, for example) is not transferable to the real world, and that there is a substantial difference between knowing in everyday situations and decontextualized knowing. Various disciplinary fields, therefore, have attacked the representational and cognitive conception of knowledge as produced in people's heads by mental processes. For a good example of this debate see the special issue of *Cognitive Science* (1993), edited by Donald Norman, which sets out the two positions together with a defence of representationalism by Alonso Vera and Herbert Simon.

3. The concept of community of practice has given rise to lively debate, which is omitted here for reasons of space. Nevertheless, one should bear in mind that the concept has been reversed, so that the study of communities of practices has given way to the study of the practices of a community. For details see Gherardi (2009a).

4. I have chosen here to illustrate this working practice because it can be followed from its beginning to its end, whereas practices usually last much longer in time and involve a larger number of people and places.

5. The term 'accountability', in Garfinkel's words (1967, p. 1): 'When I speak of accountable . . . I mean observable-and-reportable, i.e. available to members as situated practices of looking-and-telling'. Literally, the term derives from the *account* used to explain what is happening to ourselves and to others. Accountability therefore comprises moral responsibility (of the person who explains) and reasonableness (of what is being explained). Also deriving from the same root is the word *accounting*, so that the adjective *accountable* means justifiable according to explicit and demonstrable procedures.

6. For an overview of research in practice-based studies see the 2000 special issue of the journal *Organization*, whose introduction presents practical knowledge as the third way between a mentalist conception of knowledge as a product of the mind and a conception of it as an object or new type of commodity (Gherardi, 2000). A reconstruction of the development of practice-based studies can be found in Corradi et al. (2010).

7. For an overview of the philosophical and sociological roots of the concept of 'practice' see Gherardi (2006; 2011).

2. Working in coordination centres

Just as the factory represented the ideal-typical workplace for the study of work in the industrial age, and just as the laboratory has been the locus in which science has been studied as the outcome of the working practices of scientists in flesh and blood (Latour and Woolgar, 1979), so coordination centres have become the main places of reference for studies on knowing-in-practice.

Coordination centres are airport control towers, the control rooms for railway or subway traffic, the call centres which handle emergency calls and deploy ambulances, as well as all those work situations characterized by information and communication technologies used to support cooperation at a distance.

Coordination centres are representative of a set of situations which have to do with 'working together', where 'together' refers to the world of humans interacting with the world of non-humans and, mainly, with the information and communication technologies which support distance work. These places are interesting for the study of working and organizational practices because they make it possible to revise standard categories of analysis like cooperation and individual/collective work, as well as 'organizing' understood as an activity situated in practices (Czarniawska, 2008; Weick, 1979). They are also interesting because they allow analysis of the invisible work (Star and Strauss, 1999) required of communities of practice so that technological systems can operate. For the same reason, also those who concern themselves with the design and development of technological systems to support distance work are interested in understanding how 'working together' takes place on an everyday basis and in situations of crisis. Paradoxically, in fact, the success of this strand of ethnographic and naturalistic inquiry into work has also been due to failures of the technologies that support human work.

The episode presented in Box 2.1 is recounted by Christian Heath and Paul Luff (2000, pp. 1–2) at the beginning of their book *Technology in Action*, and their subsequent comment is that this disaster was nothing compared with the costs caused by the introduction of a computerized system at the London Stock Exchange. It will be objected that technology has made giant steps forward, and that the social costs of innovations

BOX 2.1   THE LONDON AMBULANCE SERVICE CASE

In 1992 the London Ambulance Service installed a computerized system in its control room. The purpose was to replace the manual practice of noting down emergency calls on slips of paper. The information about emergency calls entered into the computer was to be matched with the locations of ambulances dispatched by the same computer system, so that crews and ambulances could be automatically allocated. The system was intended to change the routine working practices of both control room staff and the ambulance drivers.

Problems began to emerge on the day when the system came into operation, although it was not an 'extraordinary' day: response times were longer, fewer than 20 per cent of the ambulances arrived within the target time or with a delay of less than 15 minutes; and the time taken to answer calls increased alarmingly with the average time that a call remained unanswered rising to 10 minutes. Together with the greater delays, there was also an increase in the number of calls, because patients rang to know whether an ambulance was arriving. The ambulance crews felt frustrated; for the system required perfect information about the location of ambulances which could not always be provided in sufficient detail. Without this perfect information, the system began to allocate crews incorrectly. More than one ambulance would arrive at the scene of an accident, or the closest ambulance would not be despatched, so that the crews sent requests to the control centre to check the correctness of what they were doing. As a consequence, the control centre was overwhelmed with messages and problems. Particular emergencies (marked in red and appearing above all other messages on the computer screen) formed such a long list that they were soon forgotten, and the dispatchers lost track of how calls, ambulances and crews had been allocated and whether they had dealt with the cases assigned to them. After the second day of problems, the service returned to a mixed system – manual and computerized. And when at the end of the week the system crashed completely, the paper-based system was resumed.

Source: Heath and Luff (2000, pp. 1–2).

are among the risks of contemporary society. However, the concern here is not with anecdotal aspects of technological failures; the intention instead is to emphasize that the many difficulties surrounding computer-mediated work, and the numerous dissatisfactions expressed in regard to 'knowledge management' (McDermott, 1999) are based on inadequate knowledge of how groups actually work in situation. Consequently, those who set out to develop systems to support human work do so on the basis of a deficient, decontextualized and schematic representation of how cooperation and practical knowledge develops within the community that generates working practices. This conclusion was reached by the numerous authors whose studies in the 1990s (Galegher and Kraut, 1990) centred on Computer-supported Cooperative Work (CSCW – a topic to which we shall return later) and others who, from the organizational learning perspective, emphasized the need for closer study of how practical knowledge is produced and transmitted in the communities producing it.

There are some studies on coordination centres which have marked an epoch with their contributions to both theory and methodology, and which, besides ethnographic observation and conversational analysis, have made large use of video (Hindmarsh and Heath, 2007). Perhaps most notable among these pioneering studies are those by Christian Heath and Paul Luff (1992) on the Bakerloo Line control room in the London Underground; by Isaac Joseph (1994) on Line A of the Paris Réseau Express Régional (RER); by Lucy Suchman (1997) on air traffic control at an airport on the west coast of the United States; another by Christian Heath and Paul Luff (2000) on the London Underground; and by Michèle Grosjean (2004) on the Paris emergency call centre.

Before describing how people work – and how working practices are studied – in coordination centres, we define the features of the latter and what, by extension, likens them to so many other workplaces which do not necessarily have to do with traffic: 'Centres of coordination are characterizable in terms of participants' ongoing orientation to problems of space and time, involving the deployment of people and equipment across distances, according to a canonical timetable or the emergent requirements of rapid response to a time-critical situation' (Suchman, 1997, p. 42).

These, therefore, are physical places in which work groups coordinate the activities of other people at a distance, and where the crucial components of their articulation work are the management of time and of the consequences triggered by unforeseen events. The study of workplaces of this kind thus provides a model for understanding coordinated and cooperative work understood as knowing-in-practice and as situated action aimed at maintaining and reproducing a space-time order.

2.1 MAINTAINING A COMMON ORIENTATION: THE BAKERLOO LINE CONTROL ROOM

The control room of the Bakerloo Line in the London Underground (like the control room of any other line) hosts the Line Controller (LC), who coordinates the day-to-day running of the railway, and the Divisional Information Assistant (DIA), whose responsibility is to give information to passengers through a public address system and communicate with station managers.[1] Both of them sit at a semicircular console which includes touch screens, a radio system to contact drivers, the keys for the public address system and closed circuit television monitors for viewing platforms. The console faces a line diagram which occupies almost the entire room and displays traffic movements along the Bakerloo Line (from Elephant and Castle to Queens Park). Figure 2.1 depicts the control room.

The service is coordinated by a paper timetable which states the numbers, transit times and routes of trains, the crews with their shifts, and all other relevant information. The timetable is not simply an abstract representation of the service's operation; it is an instrument used by various staff to coordinate the traffic flow and passenger movement, as well as by the LC and the DIA to determine the adequacy of the service and to initiate remedial action if necessary. The LC, in fact, is regarded as 'the guardian of the timetable', although his work is informed by the simple principle of ensuring that trains transit at regular and brief intervals. The timetable

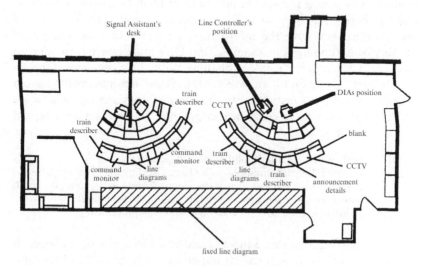

Figure 2.1   Technology in the Bakerloo Line control room

serves not only to identify potential difficulties but also to manage them. The LC, for example, makes small adjustments to the running times of trains to ensure that the necessary intervals elapse among them. In the case of more serious difficulties, such as staff absences, train breakdowns, suspicious packages in stations or on trains, the LC uses a pen to mark adjustments on the timetable. But it is also important that other people, like the drivers, the DIA, the shift crew manager and so on, are informed. Otherwise they will be unable to understand the current operation of the service and may act incorrectly. This is the crucial juncture for coopera- tion in the control room.

There is clearly a division and specification of the respective tasks and responsibilities of the LC and the DIA, but they are sustained in prac- tice by a close-knit system of collaboration. In fact, the control room personnel have developed a body of complex practices for monitoring each other's behaviour and for coordinating activities and tasks accord- ing to a flexible and emergent division of labour which allows them both to support the activities of others and to deal jointly with difficulties or crises. These practices seem to be independent of the people who enact them, and in effect, one observes personnel who have never previously worked together implicitly and informally coordinating their behaviour. The LC and DIA rarely inform each other explicitly about what they have done or are about to do – especially because the pace of work when handling difficulties or emergencies is such that they would not have time enough to leave what they are doing to inform the other about their actions. However, it is essential that both of them be aware of what the other is doing, not only so that they can coordinate their actions but also so that they have the information necessary to understand how the service is running. For example, the DIA must give information to passengers when some incident disrupts normal service, and if neces- sary to give advice on alternative routes. These announcements have a number of recurrent features. We can see how they emerge in practice and through knowledge embodied in practices by considering a typical announcement:

DIA: Hello and good afternoon Ladies and Gentlemen.
          Bakerloo Line information . . . we have a slight gap in our south bound
          Bakerloo Line service towards the Elephant and Castle, your next south
          bound train should depart from this station in about three minutes . . .
          [A little later the DIA produces a second announcement.]

Even though this announcement is addressed to a generic audience, it acquires its performative force, its importance, because it has been con- ceived for a specific category of passenger: in fact, it is transmitted only to the stations concerned, and therefore only to those passengers waiting at a particular station and who will suffer a delay in their journey.

In order to produce timely information of importance to passengers, the DIA constantly monitors the service and the action of his colleague and transforms these bits and pieces of information into announcements tailored to particular categories of passengers using the service at that time. To show how this happens in practice we return to the scene of the previous fragment but just before the announcement, when the LC calls a Driver (D):

> LC: Control to the train at Charing Cross south bound, do you receive?
> [LC switches CCTV monitor to platform.]
> D: Two Four O Charing Cross south bound.
> LC: Yeah Two Four O, we got a little bit of an interval behind you, could you take a couple of minutes at the platform for me please?
> D: Over.
> LC: Thank you very much Two Four O.

The video recordings made by Heath and Luff (2000) show that the announcement to the public by the DIA begins before the LC has finished his conversation with the driver. This is because the DIA overheard what was being said and has translated it into the consequences for the passengers waiting at Charing Cross. It is in fact crucial for provision of the service that information emerges while the LC is making adjustments. Technology is important for mutual cooperation: it is through the fixed line diagram that the DIA is able to see what the LC is doing and is able to infer what the consequences of his actions will be. In fact, at the beginning of the call he looks at the diagram for an explanation of why the LC is calling the Driver. By the LCs second attempt to call the Driver, the DIA has already moved to the console and has his finger on the announcement button. When he hears the word 'couple', he can estimate how long the delay will be and makes the announcement before the Controller/Driver conversation has concluded.

The DIAs glance at the diagram in the room and his gathering of a fragment of information suffice for him to perform his task. As he does so, he maintains with the LC the 'social distance' which Hughes (1958) calls 'elbow contact': a closeness/distance that leaves each with his responsibilities while they keep in contact. As the DIA prepares to make his announcement, he does not look at the LC, nor observes what the LC does. The DIA is absorbed in doing something else. Apparently, the only thing that he does do is turn a distracted ear to what is happening in the room, and take action when he hears certain key words.

This small fragment of activity enables Heath and Luff (1992; 2000) to make interesting considerations in regard to the meaning of individual or collective work. They show how individual tasks, based on a precise division of labour and responsibilities, rest on collective work; that is, on the ability to maintain a common orientation to the activity, a distributed attention – and therefore how, at the coordination centre the intelligibility of the scene, the possibility of coordinating tasks and activities, rests on socially organized communicative practices.

Also the division of labour, as a prerequisite for action, proves to be a property emergent from interaction. The individual tasks of both the DIA and the LC are made reciprocally visible so that the articulation work can proceed. Both of them independently monitors the flow of information by means of the diagram and the monitor; but at the same time each of them keeps an eye or an ear open to what his colleague is doing.

Finally, technology not only supports collaboration in the coordination centre; it is also the medium through which some activities become collectively visible and accessible. There is in fact an aspect of study on coordination centres that we only mention here (but to which we shall return later; see Chapter 7). This is the translation of the knowledge acquired through ethnographic analysis into the design of work systems and technologies to support them. When it is realized that tasks traditionally conceived as individual (reading, writing, speaking on the telephone) have a collective importance because they support the cooperative orientation of work, then the way in which their enabling technology is designed becomes crucial. Not by chance, an approach to design (called 'user-centred design') has been developed in order to study day-to-day work (and coordination) practices so that the introduction of new technologies does not obstruct, but instead facilitates, articulation work. As we shall see more clearly later (Chapter 7), therefore, the study of situated work is a prerequisite for the development itself of technological systems.

The case of the Bakerloo Line illustrates how at coordination centres, the maintenance of activities within a practice is made possible by this common orientation to the object of the work, and by this alternation between individual and collective work.

2.2 ACTS OF PRESENCE: THE A LINE OF THE PARIS RER

We now turn to the coordination centre of the A Line of the Paris RER, and we consider the issue raised by Isaac Joseph (1994): coordination centres perform a centralization function, but their centrality does not come about on its own; rather, it is the effect of a set of acts of presence in which the participants in the practice of 'traffic regulation' engage individually, in pairs, or collectively. Participation in a practice is therefore an activity deployed through several and distinct 'acts of presence'.

This theoretical issue concerns the conditions for reciprocal understanding in situations characterized by multiple perspectives among people who share the same workspace. It is for this reason that the study of control rooms has been of path-breaking importance: (a) for understanding the professional competence of those exposed to traffic and its disruptions; and (b) because of the intrinsic dangerousness of situations and, therefore, for the study of technologies to support work, and also safety. Coordination centres can be studied both from a Goffmanian theoretical perspective as ecologies of behaviours in a public place, and from the perspective of distributed knowledge as the shared space of action and communication (Hutchins, 1990).

These studies have highlighted the shortcomings of another key concept concerning work: that of 'task'. This is not appropriate in contexts where activity is inscribed in complex and irregular processes, and where the worker's attention resembles that of someone walking along a road: it oscillates between focused attention and distributed attention (Joseph, 1994, p. 566). The personnel of control rooms alternate between the two. They are attentive to understanding 'the state of the system', having a data set accessible to them either by telephone, or in graphic form, or on a computer screen. This information – which makes it possible to know 'what is happening' – is highly sensitive to the subjectivity of the reader, and it is perceived from various points of view. Those people working in situations like this work 'in public' in the sense that they are always in co-presence and, in the case of perturbations and ambiguities in 'what is happening', they are careful to maintain co-presence in the workplace. The most important aspect is that this work indeed mobilizes resources at a distance, but it is distance work performed with close 'elbow contact'. Consider, for instance, how responses to an accident entail mobilization of dispersed people and resources.

Dealing with a problem in a shared workspace therefore means:

- Perceiving it, formulating it and *bringing it to the attention* of those whom it may concern;
- *Mobilizing* the technological and human resources that may contribute to its solution;
- *Controlling the consequences* of the mobilization work, so that a provisional time limit can be set on the sequence in which the activities are coordinated, thus signalling that the problem has been taken care of. The set of these activities (sedentary or in motion, discursive or gestural) establish the 'participation frame' (Goffman, 1981, p. 3),

which changes (and alters the role of the actors) according to the situation;

- *Differentiating participation* and therefore (as with people who work together on a stage set) by distinguishing between those engaged in a specific task and those instead contributing to group work.

This work, which consists in maintaining decorum, giving a 'tone' to the situation, preventing mishaps, and ensuring that all goes well, is sometimes manifest in that particular interactional form that Goffman (1959) described as 'familiarity' or 'intimacy without warmth', and Hughes (1958) characterized as 'the elbow room with which to fulfil his colleague's particular duties'.

Friendliness or teasing, greetings rituals, games-playing and joking not only reveal the spirit of the group but they construct it at the same time, because in circumscribing a space of co-presence, they activate it. The abilities that the participants develop are therefore based on a capacity for reciprocal understanding and on an ability to maintain co-presence. These abilities are activated in different ways in different frames of presence according to the attention that the situation requires.

The dynamics of attention, presence and distributed knowledge unfold through four situations: 'being informed', 'putting oneself forward', 'standing aside' and 'regaining control of the situation'. I will examine each of these situations, but first I introduce the concepts of distributed knowledge and distributed attention, and show how acts of presence relate to them.

Hutchins (1990), in his study on how knowledge is distributed within a community that works together (in this specific case, the team steering a ship into harbour and supervising the docking operations), distinguishes three situations which structure the distribution of attention and knowledge:

1. *No awareness* (everything is fine): each member of the team attends to his/her own task;
2. *Local awareness:* the members of the team look at the results of their tasks or at interactions with the tasks of others;
3. *Global awareness:* the members keep an eye on what is happening externally to their tasks and have an overview of the situation.

Also attention – as already said in regard to the false opposition between individual and collective work – is not a dichotomous category (attention/disattention), but rather a process in which 'the gear is changed' and more or less attention is paid according to the social dynamics that signal when it is necessary to change that gear.

Following Hutchins's classification of modes of awareness Joseph (1994), in his study on the RER coordination centre, identifies four modes of participation – called 'acts of presence' – common to many other work practices in which a group collectively mobilizes attention and a shared orientation:

1. *Being informed.* Attention and distraction are both forms of presence and of participation by simple presence. Being aware has the function of soothing anxieties (of both station managers and passengers) and of allowing an informed presence on the coherence of the work process and the objectives of distributed work. Being aware of the general progress of a team and being informed about the progress of collective work constitute a minimal form of active participation.

2. *Putting oneself forward.* Abnormal situations are those in which the cooperative ties within the team change and modify the structure and frame of participation. It is now that someone comes forward to take charge of the situation and to manage the emergency, assuming responsibility and speaking on behalf of the group – although to do so he/she requires the cooperation of everybody and is not a solitary hero. In fact, contrary to the rhetoric of emergencies, whoever acts as the leader (if not the 'saviour') is already late with respect to the accident. In fact, he (the rhetoric almost always identifies this person as a male) resumes the course of an incident that has occurred before his arrival. He supports the person or persons who have been vigilant (and who have alerted him), and who he needs in order to disentangle what is happening. Putting oneself forward is therefore a process which establishes an 'anticipated certainty' while subverting procedures and calling the tasks assigned into question.

3. *Standing aside.* Though maintaining a structure of distributed and changing attention during activities is the prevailing model of cooperation in teams, also to be considered are the activities complementary to it. Standing aside is to abstain from intervening and to rely on what the others do. It consists in not claiming to understand something that has begun previously and waiting for its clarification; it is to look at the autonomy of others and support it with vigilance. Backing and being backed are the verbs and the dynamics of interaction that unfold in a constantly changing environment where, independently of hierarchical positions, people are active or passive in a dance of mutual control and collaboration. Standing aside is not to withdraw; rather, it is to reassure, to assist, to inquire, make a gesture or utter a word in the workspace of the other, but without interfering

or taking the other's place. It is therefore to make one's presence felt and be willing to collaborate, but without necessarily taking an active part.

4. *Regaining control of the situation.* Understanding and anticipating the other may take the form of skilful turn-taking and overlapping between complementary initiatives whose purpose is to achieve a shared goal emerging from the action. However, one should bear in mind that this process may produce misunderstandings, create gaps in the presence and engender situations in which one of the members of the team momentarily does not follow (or is 'out of step' with) the others. These are the cases in which conciliation work is important. Reconciling means finding a solution to a problem which is always and simultaneously technical and human; it is an activity undertaken to repair normality which is shaped with the means available on site. Unlike authority actions, which interfere in the action and seek to redirect it, reconciling is to activate and orient existing connections without disturbing the attention of the individual actor and/or work group.

We may conclude from this analysis that maintaining a common orientation and a distributed collaboration structure is part of the articulation work performed through acts of presence. In a situation, 'being there' is the fruit of individual and collective practical knowledge, not a simple datum but a learnt competence. In fact, the core feature of enactment of a cooperative activity is co-vigilance, as a working practice that unfolds through acts of presence in an environment in which attention and knowledge are distributed, that is, co-shared. Co-vigilance, co-visibility and co-audibility are therefore the conditions (and the strategies) whereby an 'individual' becomes accessible to an entire team, constructing (and maintaining) a shared horizon for the activity in progress.

2.3 CO-PILOTING, SCAFFOLDING AND EMERGENCY CALL CENTRES

Constructing a common horizon and orientation makes it possible both to handle several cases in parallel (as in the emergency call centres discussed shortly) and to transmit knowledge within the community.

Consider the following exchange given in Box 2.2 (Grosjean, 2004) between a novice operator (NO) and an expert operator (EO), in an emergency treatment centre (*centre de traitement des alertes*). The telephone call concerns a knife wound.

BOX 2.2   THE EMERGENCY CALL CENTRE CASE

EO: What is it, a haemorrhage? Did he tell you?
NO: It's a butcher who's stuck a knife in his arm.
EO: So inform the ambulance.
NO: No, the system hasn't been working. Now it is. Shall I tell the ambulance to call back?
EO: Of course, tell it to. But did he tell you it was a haemorrhage?
NO: He told me he'd stuck a knife in his arm.
EO: But was it [the blood] spurting? Did you ask him?
NO: No, no. I didn't ask him.
EO: Listen! Tell them that a butcher has stabbed himself. That he's haemorrhaging. They should call there. Then they'll tell you whether or not they're going.
NO: We won't call the police, then? And, if there's a problem?
EO: You can't always call them!

Source: Grosjean (2004, p. 35).

The expert operator is sitting next to the novice. He notices his uncertainty and realizes that the call to the ambulance would create an ambiguous situation (is it a haemorrhage or is it not? Is it an emergency or is it not? Should the police be told?), and intervenes. Michèle Grosjean (2004) interprets this action as an example of the parallel treatment of cases between operators and the law, and therefore treats it in terms of 'co-piloting'. She identifies in it a situation similar to the complementarity that arises between two equally expert operators (and/or whose experiences are complementary). The image of the second pilot who supports, checks or takes his/her colleague's place at the controls is useful in interpreting how novices acquire competence and how experts transmit codes of behaviour and encoded knowledge about the usual way of doing things.

As exemplified by the above exchange, knowing-in-practice is transmitted in imperative form (do it like this; do not do it like that), without much time being spent on explicit explanations of why something must or must not be done in that way. In the course of an action, the novice is requested to trust the expert and follow his/her advice, that is, to learn pragmatically, while explanations – both requested and given – are provided as and when necessary in the interstices of the activity or in negotiative situations. This co-piloting recalls the situation of driving schools and of cars fitted with dual commands. The same concept is expressed by the term 'scaffolding', which denotes the support in a situation that the expert gives to the novice during his/her apprenticeship. The metaphor of 'scaffolding' has been widely used in the literature, both by psychologists and educationists, to describe how experts support novices' learning-on-the-job, especially in the case of apprenticeships in traditional trades.

In the search for vocabulary to describe the emergence, complexity, multiplicity and interdependence between work and communication, the metaphor of scaffolding (Orlikowski, 2006) has been proposed to convey the organizational elements of what we may call the support and co-piloting work that enables transmission of the knowledge and culture of a practice. The properties of a scaffold are the following (Woener et al., 2005, pp. 4–5):

- It is a *temporary* structure that typically exists for the duration of a project and is dismantled when the building is completed and is self-supporting.
- It is a flexible *structure* erected on the building site and adapted to local requirements, but which can be used in many different situations.
- It is a *portable* structure which is easily moved, assembled and reassembled.
- It exists in *numerous forms*: there are structures that allow workers to walk on the outside of a building, others that allow workers to lower themselves from above, others that serve to support poured cement, others that provide reinforcement and are incorporated into the building's structure.
- It is *heterogeneous*, in that it consists of different components according to what must be supported and the materials available.
- It is *emergent* because it is erected over time according to the needs, dimensions and purposes of what is being built.
- It is *generative* in that it serves as the basis for further creative work and to support certain human activities that would not be possible without a material support.
- It gives a certain *stability* to the set of people, materials and spaces loosely coupled together.
- It is *constitutive* both of human activity and its results. For example, scaffolding shapes the building to be erected and the results when it has been built.

This metaphor introduces the idea that working practices require a support structure which is sufficiently malleable to be removed when it is no longer useful but which is absolutely necessary for the construction work. Coordination centres demonstrate how work activity is situated in a physical environment which supports (or otherwise) material-discursive practices.

2.4 THE THEMES OF IMPORTANCE FOR UNDERSTANDING SITUATED WORK

Coordination centres have become paradigmatic for the analysis of working practices in all places characterized by the shared orientation of participants to problems of space and time, and which deploy people and instruments in space both according a schedule and in response to unexpected contingencies. This, therefore, is a type of work in situation not restricted to coordination centres alone. More generally, every working practice functions as a collective and recursive action, on the basis of the common orientation which the various participants enact as they coordinate activities distributed in space and time through the reconfiguration of diverse human, material and discursive elements.

On studying the operations of an air traffic control tower at an airport in the United States, Suchman (1997, pp. 45–57) lists the principal themes suggested by her research, and which, more generally, are relevant to our purposes here in regard to working practices and knowing-in-practice.

The first theme concerns *technology as material practice*. A work environment consists of its architecture, furniture, telephone lines and radio links, computers, video monitors, documents and other similar objects, which assume multiple identities according to their importance for the working practice in which they are embedded. For example, an airplane may be for one person at a particular moment *that* specific airplane; for another an example of a flight; for another a container to be loaded or a machine to be repaired. According to the circumstances and the activities, people seek to make the environment functional to what they must do. In doing so, they leave the mark of their activities on that environment, thereby conditioning future actions. During these activities, the elements of the environment (the objects and the technologies) are experienced as more or less central to what is being done, more or less negotiable or resistant, more or less focal, facilitating or constraining for the activity. Coordination centres must maintain their centrality while providing connections to other places and keeping track of their activities over time. This is made possible by a set of technologies. Suchman describes the monitors which show what is happening at the gates from television cameras located at them, and the technologies which connect the image with the number of the gate and the flight. To obtain a map of the status of arrivals and departures, the operators in the control tower rely on a process that Latour (1990) has called *alignment*: the use of a two-dimensional board makes it possible to manipulate a large number of spatial and temporal relations among objects distributed in space. A clock is then used to associate the images on the monitors with the order represented on the board. Access to the database (via computer) enables manipulation of the spatial and temporal relations with other sites during the course of events.

There is then *the reading of a scene*. The principal task of the operators is to assemble knowledge about past, present and future events by juxtaposing and relating technologies and artefacts. Access to information and its distribution to all those concerned comes about through interactions with multiple technologies related to each other, and which must be read in ways structured by the task being performed. The competence of the operator resides in knowing how to read a scene (for example checking a departing flight) through the juxtaposition and interpretation of verbal reports, visual images, other forms of text, in real time and in the emerging situation. This is a competence similar to the one that Bourdieu (1972) describes in players when they anticipate the move of the opponent because they know the game and are therefore oriented to what is about to happen. Bourdieu calls this 'practical sense', emphasizing the sensory nature of this kind of knowledge. As we shall see (Chapter 3), the theme of reading the situation has a marked aesthetic component, and it is a competence that pertains to learning a professional vision.

The ability to read a scene is essential for *(re)producing the normal order*. As the operators envisage a solution to a problem, they refer to a sequence of expected events (for instance, removal of the ramp suggests that the airplane is ready for departure). They thus rely on the reproduction of a certain order and they contribute to recreating it. At the same time, the operator who makes his/her activity visible to the other participants does so within other normative orders. So-called 'normality' is dependent on its faithful reproduction through competent practices. For instance, Jordan (1992, cited in Suchman, 1997, p. 44), in a study on how problematic situations are resolved, highlights the relation between routine and improvisation, and proposes the concept of 'typified action sequence' to interpret how the members of a work group orient themselves to a normal course of events, and this is the horizon in which unforeseen events can be absorbed. The reproduction of routines is not guaranteed from the outside, but accomplished by those who put them into practice.

Attention should be paid to *structures of participation*. What characterizes coordination centres, in fact, is the way in which a common orientation and a shared responsibility for the results of the work are maintained.

Coordination requires reciprocal orientation among the workers and a simultaneous shared orientation to the development of multiple situations. The order of interaction is therefore emergent from the communications that the workers hear or do not hear, and from a continuous state of 'incipient talk'

Another theme is the *constitution of the workspace*. The use of new technologies means that work groups are no longer held together by simple physical space. For example, at certain moments during their work two operators sitting next to each other may be more closely connected with people located kilometres away than they are with each other. This means that a workplace is not simply constituted by its physical location; rather, it is constituted by a shared field of perceptions and interactions maintained throughout the duration of the working day. Goffman (1971) calls this field 'situational territory',[2] and as we shall see, the concept has been reprised by Suchman (1997) to show how work positions within a radar room are *physically* defined by workspaces which in their turn are connected to other places outside the room and *socially* by a network of relations which, all together, define the visible and invisible boundaries of a particular workspace. The division of labour in the room is reflected by the usual workspaces, each oriented towards the equipment that connects the individual worker with colleagues in other places. The stability of these situational territories derives from the collective ability of the participants to project the location both of their colleagues and of specific equipment. Moreover, the mutual visibility and accessibility of the workers in the room enable reciprocal substitution or a variety of associations between people and 'materials' like airplanes, flights or other instruments, without there being specific ownership of an activity. The operations in the room – a situational territory shared by numerous people physically or socially co-present – can be analysed as processes of convergence, alignment, disalignment or realignment of activities, and whose resources are talk, gaze, gesture, body position, space, furnishings and equipment.

In this scenario, the *development of competence* is a further aspect to investigate. The analysis of work in situation consists of observation of the order that emerges from the interactions among workers. It is not analysis of decontextualized work expressed as a set of elementary tasks (task analysis) or as a job description. For this reason it is essential to consider the processes of learning and transmitting knowledge within the community and as a historical-cultural process. To exemplify this we may refer to a routine task in ground operations which consists in calculating an airplane's weight and balance. The weight/balance of an airplane is the relation between the total load of passengers, baggage, fuel and other materials, and the settings necessary for the stability of the aircraft. In the case of newer airplanes this calculation is directly readable on the computer screen in the cockpit. But in older aircraft, such data appear in the radar room and are communicated to the pilot in an oral exchange called 'radio call-out'. In this regard, Suchman (1997) gives an example drawn from Charles and Marjorie Goodwin (1996) (who have studied the coordination of air traffic) which illustrates the coordination between a young apprentice and an expert operator during a radio call-out. The expert, on noticing the difficulty of his/her inexperienced colleague in finding the data, intervenes on the computer screen and momentarily modifies it while at the same time using his/her finger to direct his/her colleague's attention to the necessary data. Competent participation in operations involves learning to see the work environment in an informed way. A similar example was cited by Polanyi (1958) when he described how an expert doctor teaches a junior doctor to read an X-ray. Through verbal explanation and gestures, he/she helps the junior doctor to give sense and order to what are apparently only patches of different colours. Both in formal situations of training on the job, and informally in the sharing of knowledge between peers, the possibility of sharing and creating knowledge is tied to mutual access to activities, to interaction in situation, and to the features of the surrounding environment.

Another theme is the *authoritativeness of knowledge*. The expression 'authoritative knowledge' is intended to highlight the relation between access to, and control over, technologies and the forms of knowledge considered to be authoritative – that is, legitimate grounds for drawing inferences and acting. In this case, Suchman (1997) refers to Jordan's (1992) study, and to her example of a situation in which airplanes had to be moved between gates so that one of them could be repaired. This involved towing an airplane (which had arrived at one gate) to a different gate for departure, as well as reassignment of the crews, passengers and baggage. Jordan describes the 'horizontal' distribution of knowledge necessary to reassign the aircraft and passengers to the new gate and to manage the requisite technologies. This distribution of knowledge was made possible by the frequency with which the operators spoke out loud without addressing anyone in particular, made comments on the situation, or addressed generic questions to the room as a whole. The group's members were therefore aware that information could be relevant for another participant, and that some other colleague might have information important for what they were doing.

The study of work in situation is not only descriptive in its purpose; it is also intended to yield practical outcomes. This introduces the theme of *design for change*. Indeed, it is precisely this applicative intent which has induced rediscovery of the ethnography of work, and other qualitative methodologies, which have led to revaluation of the sociologist's role in analysis of the relation between work and new technologies. The methodological assumption is that, in order to design any aspect of a work setting, it is necessary to understand the relationship between this aspect and the set of activities and technologies of which it is only one part. It is also necessary to bear in mind that the products of any professional design (objects, technologies, environments and so on) have been conceived and produced on the basis of a partial and situated projection of the circumstances in which they will be used. Consequently, such products must not be taken as definitive, but rather as starting points for the development of artefacts-in-use which will be inevitably adapted or changed so that they can be introduced into the work environment. This applies to technologies and their problematic introduction into work groups and spaces, as well as to every object of day-to-day use which is transformed in its use. Therefore, in general terms, when the theme of working practices is related to the design of technologies and collaborative work settings, it is assumed that the requirements for their design/production are discovered and/or created through the contingencies of their everyday use, and through the solutions that the participants invent to deal with problems and ambiguities. Moreover, bearing in mind that changes in one component of a work system usually have repercussions on other components (both within the same workplace and in others connected to it), one deduces that new requirements and new interpretations will constantly emerge. It is consequently important that those people who do the work are involved in its design. Design-in-use can be conceived as resembling musical improvisation, which exploits knowledge of a motif to elaborate changes and phrasings suited to the circumstances in which the piece is being performed.

2.5   TO SUM UP

We have shown that coordination centres are places paradigmatic for the study of work as a knowledge-based practical activity undertaken in technologically dense environments. Such environments demonstrate that new categories are needed for the analysis of work, and that certain dichotomic concepts (for instance, individual or collective work) should be replaced with complementary pairs of concepts (individual and collective work). Cooperation at work, therefore, does not derive from the division of labour and formal coordination mechanisms, but instead from emergent and situated forms of cooperation based on maintaining a common orientation, on practices of co-piloting and scaffolding, and on the acts of presence that mobilize knowledge and distribute attention.

In regard to coordination centres, Suchman (1997) has proposed eight themes for research and analysis: technology as material practice, reading a scene, reproducing the normal order, structures of participation, construction of the workspace, the development of competence, authoritative knowledge and design for change. We believe that these themes of relevance to understanding work in coordination centres are also of central importance for the study of practices. Consequently, they will be partly resumed in the following chapters, beginning with close examination of what is meant by 'practice' and 'knowing-in-practice' as a situated activity.

In this chapter I have referred to four classic studies in order to illustrate and introduce the reader to the main themes in practice-based studies:

- The London Ambulance case was paradigmatic of what may happen when a new technology designed to support work disrupts routine working practice.
- The Bakerloo Line case illustrated how a practice involves common orientation, and how common orientation rests on co-audibility, co-visibility and co-presence.
- The Paris RER case summed up the theme of learning as participation and of awareness in maintaining a common orientation. It helped conceptualize participation in a practice in terms of four acts of presence: 'being informed', 'putting oneself forward', 'standing aside' and 'regaining control of the situation'.
- The emergency call centre case posed the theme of the transmission of knowledge between an expert and a novice in terms of co-piloting. This theme was developed further through the concept of scaffolding, that is, providing a temporary structure for the development of competence.

NOTES

1. This section is based on an article by Heath and Luff (2000). We have omitted the page references so as not to encumber the text. We hope that our summary of a much more composite and detailed text is respectful of the authors' intentions.
2. Goffman (1971, pp. 29–35) employs the concept of situational territory to specify the space in use, that is, that territory immediately before or around a person who claims it as his/her own and which others respect for instrumental reasons. Workspaces are good examples of territory that does not belong by right to the person who uses it, but is appropriated as workspace and, consequently, personalized and made private in its use. In very open workplaces or ones with multi-person transits (for instance lobbies or corridors), the idea of the workspace is recreated by specific situations.

3. Sensible knowledge and knowledgeable bodies

In the two previous chapters I have sought to illustrate, through the description of research experiences, the interpretative opportunities brought by the 'practice turn'. But I have not made a theoretical presentation of what is meant by the term 'practice'. I shall further postpone this issue, being content that I have shown at least one opportunity furnished by the practice-based approach. When working practices are studied, description of the activities comprised in a practice is less important than the pattern of connectedness which holds it together. This pattern ties the actions occurring within the practice to the actors of that practice, whether human or non-human, so that they actively construct its situational context.

As Lave (1991) notes, one should bear in mind that 'situation' is not simply another term for the immediate, physical context. A situation has to be explored in social and historical terms. As we have seen in the case of the coordination centre, people in a room are not inevitably and identically situated, and the situated constraints on practice do not simply arise in and through such isolated interactions. The people and the constraints have social and historical trajectories that should be understood within the texture of connections linking one practice to another and the texture of practices[1] in cultural and historical terms (Gherardi, 2006). A context is not a container of practices; rather, practices create their own context (Fox, 1997).

Study of the practical organization of knowledge, in the form of methods of reasoning and acting and the association of human and non-human elements, is one of the most important directions taken by practice-based studies. Nevertheless, inspection of the literature shows that a unified field of practice studies does not exist; rather, that there are three types of relations established between practices and knowledge (Gherardi, 2006, p. 38):

- A relation of *containment*, in the sense that knowing and learning are processes that take place within situated practices. On this view, practices are constituted as objective entities (in that they have been objectified) about which practitioners already have knowledge (that is, they recognize them as practices) and which comprise bits

and pieces of knowledge anchored in the material world and in the normative and aesthetic system that has elaborated them culturally.
- A relation of *mutual constitution*, in the sense that the activities of knowing and practising are not two distinct and separate phenomena; instead, they interact and produce each other.
- A relation of *equivalence*, in the sense that practising is knowing-in-practice, whether the subject is aware of it or not. Acting as a competent practitioner is synonymous with knowing how to connect successfully with the field of practices thus activated. The equivalence between knowing and practising arises when priority is denied to the knowledge that exists before the moment of its application, so that when it is applied, something already existent is not performed but the action instead creates the knowledge formed in the action itself and by means of it.

However, the three relations do not exclude each other, and emphasizing one of them does not prejudice the others. In this chapter I shall focus more on the first type of relationship because I wish to introduce the theme of sensible knowledge in order to stress how a practice-based approach contributes to a non-cognitivist and non-rationalistic view of organizing. In other words, I want to show how knowledge embedded in practices is an embodied knowledge, and how people use their bodies to relate with the world and shape a knowledgeable body.

3.1   SENSIBLE KNOWLEDGE AND A KNOWLEDGEABLE BODY

Within organization studies during the 1970s and 1980s, a controversy arose on forms of knowledge, and it culminated in the critique waged against the rationalist paradigm. Many authors in those years stressed the importance of the emotions, symbolic constructs, and the institutionalization and aesthetic approaches to organization (Carr and Hancock, 2003; Dean et al., 1997; Gagliardi, 1996; Guillet de Monthoux, 2004; Linstead and Höpfl, 2000; Ottensmeyer, 1996). Within aesthetic approaches, there is a strand of inquiry which has a common root with practice-based studies because it focuses on sensible knowledge and on how people use their sensibility in workplaces and employ their bodies in working practices (Hancock and Tyler, 2000; Strati, 2003). In fact:

Sensible knowledge concerns what is perceived through the senses, judged through the senses, and produced and reproduced through the senses. It resides in the visual, the auditory, the olfactory, the gustatory, the touchable and in the sensitive–aesthetic judgement. It generates dialectical relations with action and close relations with the emotions of organizational actors. (Strati, 2007, p. 62)

I will now present some empirical studies in order to show the connection between sensible knowledge and practice-based learning, focusing on the knowledge and learning that derive from the sensory faculties of touch, hearing, sight and smell. I shall examine the problematic nature of sensible knowledge and the relations among aesthetics, emotion and affectivity in practice-based studies.

3.1.1   With the Hands

The first sense considered is touch and the intelligence of hands. Strati (2007, p. 68) refers to an ergonomic study that he conducted in sawmills in the north-eastern Alps which is presented in Box 3.1.

What is described in Box 3.1 is an act of measurement learned through practising under the guidance of a more expert worker. For some sawmill workers this action had become a habit, endowed with social legitimacy and based on individual dexterity – that is, on an ability that not all individuals possess in equal measure and the learning of which cannot be prescribed. In other words, it was a skill that had to be learned and transmitted in practice by drawing on the sensible knowledge possessed by the individual worker. And not all workers may be skilled in the same way!

3.1.2   With the Feet

The perceptive-sensory faculty of touch is not restricted to the hands. Moreover, it is not only an individual skill but may be deployed as a collective skill when there is a sharing of instrumental tools. Research in a dental

---

BOX 3.1   THE CASE OF THE WORKERS IN THE SAWMILL

During my research, I observed that the workers in the plank-stacking yards of some sawmills did not use the gloves prescribed by the regulations to protect their hands. Working in pairs, the men – all the yard workers were men – would grab planks of the same length but different thicknesses and call out a number: 'two-and-a-half', 'three', 'four-and-a-half', 'three', 'two-and-a-half' and so on.

Working in rapid rhythm, according to the number called, the men would lay the plank in their hands on the stack of others of the same thickness. The number indicated the thickness in centimetres of the plank, which the stackers measured 'by hand' without using a gauge or some other instrument. Gloves would have interfered with this touch-based operation. The fear of injuring themselves with splinters, or of freezing their bare hands in the bitter winter air of the stacking yard, was not part of the men's workplace safety culture. The workers in the plank-stacking yard drew on a form of knowledge and action that was based, not on intellective–analytical understanding, but on aesthetic understanding, and it was on this dimension that they performed their work. Knowledge in this particular work practice was based on 'interpretation by touch', after which the workers: (1) verbally formulated the number indicating the thickness of the plank – and therefore the discursive practice; (2) agreed or otherwise on the number; (3) moved towards the correct stack; and (4) placed and arranged the plank, again using their hands because it was by means of the perceptive-sensory faculty of touch that the two workers adjusted the plank's position so that the stack was stable and ready to receive further planks.

Work and organizational practice in the yard was therefore a complex matter. It depended on the ability of the senses to know and act simultaneously; it was made possible by the capacity for action furnished by speech acts; it interwove with the capacity for ratiocination. It was performed in the interaction between the two workers, who coordinated themselves in sensory interpretation and then enacted their corporeality by bending over and grasping the plank. It followed the rhythm with which they formulated the number and decided whether it was the correct one, moved towards one of the stacks in the yard, synchronizing the few steps taken and assuming the correct bodily posture to lift the plank the short distance necessary to place it on the stack, and then checked the stability of the stack, which they shook and rearranged if necessary. 'Feeling' with the hands was knowledge and action at the same time; so was moving around the yard 'touching' the organizational space with the feet; so too was assuming the correct posture to perform this particular work practice at the sawmill.

Source: Strati (2007, p. 68).

clinic (Hindmarsh and Heath, 2000; Hindmarsh et al., 2011) illustrates how students learn 'to look with the demonstrator' and to sense through sharing of the dental mirror. In fact novices learn first by watching, looking, sensing and listening to others while carrying out meaningful activities; by learning how to talk with competence; and how to claim and exhibit their understanding with bodily conduct. Hindmarsh et al. (2011, p. 501) notes that 'the assessment and the display of competence in the clinic is underpinned by more mundane orientations and displayed understandings of the structure of talk and the body in interaction'. I shall return to this point in Chapter 5. For the time being, I want to stress that knowing by touching involves not only the hands but the rest of the body as well, and therefore movements around the work setting in order to explore and gain familiarity with the organizational space. The example that follows is intended further to illustrate the complexity of the knowing and learning furnished by the sense of touch with the feet.

The example is again provided by Strati (2007, p. 69), and is presented in Box 3.2, who observed a group of workmen as they stripped the roof from a building.

The roof-strippers' sensible knowledge is of vital importance for their choice of work, for confidence in their workmates, and for selection of new team members. Strati (2007) observes that knowledge which has not been formalized in scientific terms is difficult to teach even when an explicit desire to learn is manifested. This is because – as Polanyi (1958) has pointed out – in everyday practice we are often aware of being able to do something but unable to describe analytically how we do it, to explain it scientifically, and thereby turn it into explicit rather than implicit and entirely personal knowledge. Sensible knowledge has precisely this characteristic: it evades logical–analytical description and scientific formalization and is better expressed evocatively and metaphorically.

Knowing-in-practice is dwelling in and making sense of practice. Brown and Duguid (1996) noted that even though instruction is minimal, quite complex practices can be learned effectively and easily where the social context is evident and supportive; by contrast, it is almost impossible to make enduring, coherent sense if the individual is cut off from the practice in which his/her particular activity makes sense.

3.1.3 With the Ears

The next example illustrates sensible knowing with hearing. One of the best-known examples in this regard is provided by Cook and Yanow (1993). It concerns flutemakers and how apprentices are trained to learn when a

BOX 3.2   THE CASE OF THE WORKERS ON THE ROOF

From a second-floor window in a building opposite the roof-strippers I had a good view of them as they worked. There were three of them, and judging from his movements one of them was the foreman. In fact, he moved around the roof, helping one workmate and then the other, and he took over work from the others when they seemed unable to cope. He gave orders which I could not hear but which were apparent from his posture and gesticulations. Although very overweight, he moved with surprising agility across the steeply sloping roof, which became increasingly perilous as the work proceeded. The other two roof-strippers worked, sometimes alone, sometimes together, on removing the section of the roof beneath their feet. As they did so, they threw the debris down into the courtyard below, with loud crashes. They worked quickly, only slowing down to deal with particular difficulties. How – I asked myself – can they avoid overbalancing and falling if they have to use their hands to work? I put this question to the workmen during their lunch break. Their immediate response was to say generally that 'the important thing is not to be afraid', but then they began arguing among themselves because, they said, that reply was wrong. I went back to talk to them on several occasions, and also asked how I could learn to perform the work they were doing. They told me that the most important thing was 'to feel the roof with your feet', indeed 'feel that your feet are fastened to the roof', and that this feeling had to come by itself, because it could not be taught. Other important aspects to their work were 'almost leaning on the air' between the body and the roof, or 'listening' to noises and paying attention to suspicious ones, or again 'appreciating the beauty' of working up there. In short, aesthetics emerged as a form of knowledge: the roof-strippers knew by 'feeling with the feet' or by 'leaning with the body' or by 'listening to noises' and also by 'enjoying a sentiment of beauty'.

Source: Strati (2007, p. 69).

BOX 3.3   THE CASE OF THE FLUTEMAKERS

A flutemaker would typically make only cryptic remarks, such as 'It does not feel right' or 'This bit doesn't look quite right'. The first flutemaker would then rework the piece until both were in agreement that it had 'the right feel' or 'the right look'.

When the apprentice became a judge of his/her own work, this marked of the end of the apprenticeship, and in this way, at one and at the same time, an apprentice would both acquire a set of skills in flutemaking and become a member of the informal quality control system that has unfalteringly maintained the style and quality of these instruments.

Source: Cook and Yanow (1993, p. 380).

---

flute 'sounds right'. In this production process each flute is worked on by several flutemakers in succession and each craftsman is skilled in only a few aspects of the process. A flute goes down the line but also up it, until it is finished. Box 3.3 describes how this takes place.

In this example, we may note a collective activity that I name 'taste-making' (Gherardi, 2009b) and it is further illustrated in Section 3.3 of this chapter. This refers to the aesthetic judgement on the practice and it is performed through (few) words, gestures and the tacit negotiation surrounding the development of sensible knowledge. The material and discursive practices that allow the negotiation of sensible knowledge simultaneously construct the normative accountability of the practice and the taste for 'the right sound'. In what follows I shall examine the relationship among sensible knowledge, aesthetic judgement and taste-making as an activity that sustains or changes practices. The reason for anticipating the concept of taste-making is to underline the role of language and collective appreciation of the object of the practice in the examples of sensible knowledge.

3.1.4   With the Nose

The next sense that I examine is smell. To provide an example of how language and discursive practices constitute 'handholds' for practice, I refer to an article by Geneviève Teil (1998) which describes how she learned to develop taste during a course to train the sense of smell. This sense and the professional skills associated with it constitute a field of expertise in demand by both the food and perfume industries. This ability can be

---

BOX 3.4   LEARNING TO BECOME AN EXPERT AROMATHICIAN

How, therefore, does one become a taster? Teil (1998) describes how learning produced changes in tastes and in olfactory practices during the training course, and how this brought about a change in the relationship between the novice and the object through:

- Learning how to manage one's body and brain, so that the 'olfactory tool' is circumscribed within the body;
- Learning how to use it in accordance with collective norms; and above all
- Learning how to check its operation in a suitable way.

The trajectory of learning therefore proceeds through: (a) feeling (perception of sensory impressions which delimit a context and an olfactory measure, and control over the brain's interpretations); (b) describing (development of a classificatory language with which to categorize sensations and to communicate, abandonment of the hedonism of feeling oneself naive, acquisition of an expert aesthetic to judge sensations); and (c) using (to stabilize the link between the odour and its olfactory descriptor, gaining control over application of the metrological criteria that enable measurement of the relationship between describer and odour, and relying on the network of practitioners in order to heighten the performance of the olfactory tool).

Source: Teil (1998, pp. 507–19).

---

learned in the surprisingly short period of five days, but its maintenance requires constant practice. In order to study the transmission of this knowledge, Teil attended the course and conducted self-ethnography, as well as participant observation (see Box 3.4).

From Teil's (1998) theoretical analysis we learn not only that the learning of sensory knowledge develops through stages extending from the mundane knowledge of the novice to the mastery of expert knowledge within a professional community, but also how participation in the community is contextual to the learning of an expert language with which to express aesthetic judgements.

From Teil's experience we draw direct communication through reflection:

> I acquired [during the course] confidence and control over my sensations that enabled me to assert and to defend my description of a wine, for example, even if it was disputed by other experts, and also to continue the dialogue with them, without beating a retreat before the idiosyncrasy of tastes. . . . I know who I can trust, even if we do not share the same tastes, I know how to re-translate the preferences of others into my system of descriptors, and thanks to this I can understand their admiration for some or other product. I gain great pleasure from discussing the possibilities offered by aromas in gastronomy, from searching for restaurants that use them. . . . To my great surprise, this capacity for dialogue has made my tastes very versatile. (Teil, 1998, p. 519)

This subjective account of the experience of learning highlights both individual and collective dimensions: acquiring confidence in one's judgement and having the means with which to argue for one's judgement; knowing how to set value on other people's opinions, incorporating them into a system of evaluations; knowing how to share pleasure. As this process unfolds, the novice changes into an expert, and the expert into a critic of taste; and each of these figures has a different relationship with the object, because it engages in practices specific to each community: simple amateurs, experts or critics.

I have illustrated how taste starts from sensible experience to become an aesthetic judgement, and finally a professional competence. My purpose has been to show that 'with taste the faculty to judge is freed from every logical function . . . taste is a reflexive or evaluative judgement that enables the discovery of the subjective conditions of knowledge' (Brugère, 2000, p. 5).

3.1.5 With the Mouth

Taste is the most intimate of all the senses. But how is taste routinized, stabilized, but also innovated within a community so that it becomes an organizational element, as in a restaurant? The example that follows in Box 3.5 concerns Chef Passard, who radically innovated French cuisine.

If practice is stripped of pathos (Gagliardi, 2007), involvement, passion and the profound meaning of doing as a relation with the world (praxis as defined by Marx), the subjectivity of practitioners cannot be understood, nor can the cultural system in which that practice is embedded (Gherardi et al., 2007). On the other hand, all this makes practice difficult to express verbally, both for practitioners and for researchers, who have difficult access to this knowledge resource and a paucity of vocabulary with which

---

BOX 3.5   THE CASE OF CHEF PASSARD

Sensitivity is one of Passard's distinctive dispositions. His grandmother taught him to be particularly attentive to gestures and sounds: 'you need to listen to the food products, you need to master the flame so that it never damages, but rather caresses' (interview). This sensorial dimension is also visible in the kitchen and in his cooking gestures: we observed that Passard, more than other chefs, likes to bend over the pan to keep a closer eye on the preparation; he stirs the air about with his hands to breathe in the air of his cooking, he pricks up his ears to listen and requires silence in the kitchen (observation). He has even removed clocks from the walls so that his chefs would be aware of their senses rather than focusing on timing (observation and interviews).

Source: Gomez and Bouty (2011, p. 930).

---

to describe it. I wish to emphasize that practitioners are in no better position than researchers as regards their capacity to know in terms of objectified knowledge and to express in words a savoir-faire, an embodied knowledge, and an ability that resides in the fingers, the eyes, the nose or the ears. These abilities, which are apparently an individual 'endowment', and seemingly reveal a particular talent, are in reality the effect of a social practice and a collective process of learning and knowledge transmission. The term 'feeling' well expresses the act of knowing with the body.

3.1.6   With Feeling

The following example is taken from a study on safety as a social practice. Although safety is an organizational outcome deriving from the nature of the extant work practices, and as such cannot be reduced to the sum of the competencies of the individual members, experts acquire or, better, develop a 'sense of what is safe'. Gherardi and Nicolini (2002b) observed the following presented in Box 3.6.

Feeling, having a sense of what should or should not be done, and similar expressions may be subsumed under Bourdieu's (1990, p. 66) 'feel for the game'. The best image with which to sum up Bourdieu's theory is that evoked by the expression '*sens pratique*' as the immediate and anticipatory perception of the sense of the social game. An expert's practical knowledge

---

BOX 3.6   A SENSE OF WHAT IS SAFE

A heavy load of bricks needs to be taken off a lorry and positioned at the far side of the site. Although a special crane-sling for this kind of job is available, it is complicated and too time-consuming to fit. The senior operator decides to use the sling already mounted on the crane. The sling is possibly under-sized for this job. After positioning and securing the load, he asks for the crane to lift it a few centimetres from the ground. Then he glances at it, looks at the crane and 'feels' the tension of the sling. He then gives clearance for the operation to be concluded. Having watched the scene, I ask him 'How could you be sure it wouldn't fall?' His unequivocal answer is: 'I can't say . . .'.

Source: Gherardi and Nicolini (2002b, p. 214).

---

resides in the ability to understand immediately – for example, to recognize a tune from its first two notes – to know, recognize and reproduce a practice after seeing it done a number of times.

This special sense is described by Bourdieu (1990, pp. 81–2) thus:

> A player who is involved and caught up in the game adjusts not to what he sees but to what he fore-sees, sees in advance in the directly perceived present; he passes the ball not to the spot where his team-mate is but to the spot he will reach a moment later, anticipating the anticipations of the others. He decides in terms of objective probabilities, that is, in response to an overall, instantaneous assessment of the whole set of his opponents and the whole set of his team-mates, seen not as they are but in their impending positions. And he does so 'on the spot,' 'in the twinkling of an eye,' 'in the heat of the moment,' that is, in conditions which exclude distance, perspective, detachment, and reflexion.

As noted, insofar as these skills can be practised but not fully described, they depend on social processes of interaction and participation in joint activities to be 'transferred' to the body and kept alive.

3.1.7   With Tools

Like a partially sighted man with his stick, tools, whether they are simple artefacts or complex technological equipment, become prostheses which sustain activities during a practice and whose use is learned and taught by developing the ability to use the body, sensible knowing, and the

BOX 3.7   THE CASE OF THE BIOPSY

P: The first thing to do is locate the posterior iliac crest [demon-strates by moving her hands on the patient's lower back: her fingers rest on the skin where the iliac crest is anatomically situated], by touching, you can feel a kind of bow-shaped ridge. This is what you have to follow with your finger. [She lets the trainee try and feel with her thumb.]

JD: Must I push hard?

P: No, not too much pressure . . . also because if the patient is well positioned, you can feel it easily! When you've found the correct point, use your fingernail to make a small mark. When you've found the point, you have to prepare the sterile field, disinfected . . . before putting the sterile gloves on, touch the place again and try to 'take a snapshot' of the exact point. Then you put the gloves on. Without touching any-thing, find the point again with your finger . . . but you mostly find it again by trying to visualize where you were previously, because the gloves decrease sensitivity.

       Now proceed with the anaesthesia.

       [P asks the patient if all is well. On receiving an affirmative reply, P addresses the JD.]

       You make a small superficial incision with the scalpel, you know how to do it. Grasp the needle firmly, push it in, and remember that you have to find the marrow, not the blood . . . Hold it firmly because you have to use your body to increase the pressure . . . it's a bone!

       If you have absolute silence and you concentrate, you can 'hear' the bone breaking . . .

JD: Do you hear the noise?

P: It's difficult to explain. . . how can I put it? The rupture of the trabecula makes a 'scratching' noise. Like a needle scratch-ing a surface . . . you immediately feel a loss of resistance, like a vacuum, and then you feel softness. When I was a student, my tutor used to say: 'When you're in, let go of the hilt and do like this [touches the part of the needle outside the patient's body with her finger], if it tends to bend, you're only just inside'.

       Now remove the stylet and attach the syringe . . . you'll feel that you're aspirating something different . . . air and something thicker. Remember that you're not collecting a blood sample.

You know, when you reach the bone you have the sensation of a needle scratching a shell . . . a clam, see what I mean? It's just like scratching the crest of a clam.

Source: observations by Nurse Laura Linetti in 2010.

appropriate discursive practices. The example shown in Box 3.7, drawn from clinical practice, illustrates these three components. It concerns bone marrow biopsy, or haematopoietic marrow biopsy, which consists in the aspiration, using a specially designed needle, of a small quantity of marrow which is then examined under the microscope. Although the marrow can be collected from various bones, most frequently used in adults is the posterior or anterior iliac crest (a bone in the pelvis). After disinfection of the cutis, a local anaesthetic is administered to the skin and to the most external part of the bone selected. A small incision of a few millimetres is usually made on the skin with a scalpel, the purpose being to facilitate the needle's penetration into the bone and, especially, to prevent the loss of the small specimen of marrow when the needle is withdrawn. The needle is then inserted to a depth of two centimetres and a small cylinder of marrow is aspirated. The case presented in Box 3.7 shows how Dr Paola (P) teaches a junior doctor (JD) to perform this operation.[2]

This passage illustrates the intelligence of the hands, the interference of gloves which reduce sensitivity, and testing the needle's resistance so as to know whether it can support the operation, but it also illustrates the element of 'visualization' and the language used to transmit a sensation analogically and metaphorically. The trainee is told to 'take a mental snapshot', 'to feel a vacuum and a softness'. Finally explained to the junior doctor is what kind of noise she will probably hear – or will probably imagine that she can hear. In other words, the experienced doctor is teaching her to see with the eyes of her mind.

A working practice therefore comprises sensory knowledge which is individual and collective, and which develops through learning how to use all five of the senses professionally, as well as the body in its entirety and its interaction with other bodies in movement within a shared space. In their turn, these bodies become professionally trained, that is, disciplined by the practices in which they are embedded. Practices are inscribed in bodies, and bodies are therefore the artefacts through which people know and work. Becoming a competent member of a community of practice requires incorporating bodily abilities and developing what Goodwin (1994) has called 'professional vision'.

3.2   PROFESSIONAL VISION

Goodwin's discussion of professional vision is based on research conducted on a field course for young archaeologists and in a courtroom. He defines professional vision as 'socially organized ways of seeing and understanding events that are answerable to the distinctive interests of a particular social group' (Goodwin, 1994, p. 606). Goodwin uses videotapes as his primary source of data to illustrate how the two professions learn and teach how to see. An archaeologist, a farmer or a builder will see different things in the same patch of dirt, because they look at it with different professional 'visions'. In fact Goodwin (1994, p. 606) states that: 'all vision is perspectival and lodged within endogenous communities of practice'.

Goodwin (1994) has investigated three practices that shape a domain of occupational knowledge:

- Coding, which transform phenomena observed in a specific setting into the objects of knowledge that animate the discourse of an occupation;
- Highlighting, which gives salience to specific phenomena in a complex perceptual field by marking them in some manner;
- Producing and articulating material representations, which embed and structure the knowledge produced and transfers it through space and time.

On introducing the concept of professional vision, I would stress that it does not refer solely to the dimension of the transmission of knowledge and the fact that practitioners have a professional vision whereby their way of seeing is apprehended as 'participatory appropriation' (Rogoff, 1995). Participatory appropriation is the process by which individuals transform their understanding of, and responsibility for, activities through their own participation. The notion is thus used in contrast to the term 'internalization' employed by the cognitive approach to learning and cognition, which suggests some form of transfer of knowledge. Novices play an active part in their learning process and differ in their ability to see and in their willingness to seize learning opportunities.

The work of Goodwin (1994; 1997; Goodwin and Goodwin, 1996) is relevant to practice-based studies because it enables the empirical study of how knowing-in-practice is a collective activity accomplished through the three micro-practices of coding, highlighting and producing material representations. We have already seen in Teil's (1998) research how coding allows articulation of the linguistic categories that classify odours; and we can refer to Bowker and Star (1999) to explore the role of classifications not only in materializing knowledge but also in constraining actions and furnishing an infrastructure for the practices based on them. The activities that produce material representations will be discussed in the next chapter. Here the concern is instead with the activity of highlighting. It is suggested that the professional vision is centred on the sensible knowledge which, on the one hand, anchors knowing how to look to be able to see in the practitioner's body and, on the other hand uses a performative language – in the form of knowledge pointers – to transmit and consolidate this knowledge within a community's practices.

I have called 'knowledge pointers' (Gherardi, 2006, pp. 76–81) those linguistic devices used mainly when giving instructions and shaping how a novice learns to see when following those instructions (see Box 3.8 for an example).

In becoming a practitioner, Gianni developed the ability to grasp the knowledge pointers contained in the instructions he received and which gave him access to socially organized ways of seeing and understanding. It was through the social relations that tied Gianni to his workmates that the opportunity arose for him to learn and tacitly to coordinate himself with them, both to understand the implied meanings of the language which they used and to develop the capacity to view the work with the eyes of an expert. Becoming an insider requires the ability to participate with competence in the discourses of a community and to look at a shared reality with a gaze situated within that community's culture of practice.

The skill of seeing (and looking) is structured through constant and situated use of directions and micro-explanations: the novice is *taught how to see*. The ability to see a meaningful event is not an individual and psychological process; rather, it is a social situated activity accomplished through discursive practices which employ specific knowledge pointers.

BOX 3.8   LEARNING TO SEE IN A BUILDING SITE

A building site is a context in which the members of several occupations shape events subject to their professional scrutiny. Our novice Gianni learned what elements were important within the domain of building construction through a mechanism of instruction/imitation/emulation: 'you learn the job by watching: all right, you do it, but first you watch how it's done.' Moreover, imitation involved complex micro-social interactions in which language, observation and workmanship mixed and merged. Looking and seeing, and listening and understanding are the main components of a professional vision. The use of the performative utterance 'Look!' can be considered a knowledge pointer because it signals the importance of what is happening. More specifically, 'look' implies 'look carefully because what is happening is important and should be understood and remembered for the same occasion or similar ones in the future'. Looking carefully – 'stealing the job with the eyes', as an expression collected in the field aptly put it – means understanding the prescription by making the effort to watch and memorize.

However, knowledge and competence are also acquired through simple perceptive exposure, that is, through automatic non-reflexive 'seeing'. The habits of a community do not need to be explicated or explicitly talked about; they are probably are 'picked-up' through 'constant seeing'. Looking, with its 'intentional' dimension, is utilized only in situations of micro-difficulty when it is necessary to redirect the action ('look, this is how you do it', or simply 'this is how you do it' – the 'look' and what to look at being implicit in the latter utterance).

Language is used in other learning situations as well, often in concomitance with ostensive reference to examples and with suggestions ('you do it like this . . . no, not like that'), in judgements ('well done', 'good work', 'that's the way to do it'). The combination of language, observation and ostensive reference thus reduces the need for extensive linguistic explanation without losing comprehension and coordination.

'Watch out!' is also a sort of reproof which serves the purpose of learning. If something unexpected or dangerous happens, a near-accident or a minor one, the statement is used as criticism which indicates what should have been done – for example, 'You should have been careful, and you weren't, and this is what might have happened' – and as a generalization, as shown by the following fragment in which after a near-collision one of the two workmen involved generalized the need to give proper warnings: 'Beware of moving loads . . . *always call out* [emphatically] . . . you should . . . be careful lads . . . when you're walking around the site, be careful.'

Source: Gherardi (2006, pp. 76–81).

The importance in professional work of practices of seeing, always accompanied by verbal or written accounts of what is observed, has been analysed in relation to the 'architect's gaze', that is, as the embodiment of a range of skills and competencies that architects tend to regard as their domain of jurisdiction. This capacity of 'seeing as an architect' (Styhre, 2011, p. 266) 'is acquired through a combination of formal training and education, practical work, and ongoing discussions with peers'.

3.3 TASTE-MAKING

Sensible knowledge helps us to understand that practices are performed through a 'sapient' body that knows through the senses, and that there accumulates in the body a capacity to act in the world, and to do so both individually because it possesses a professional vision, and collectively because professional seeing is a practical activity that has been anchored in materiality and discursiveness. To this should be added two further, closely interrelated elements. On the one hand, we must consider how aesthetic knowledge is based on aesthetic judgements (for instance concerning beauty or ugliness) and, on the other, how attachment to practices (or better to the objects of practices) is a subjective phenomenon ('I like it' or 'I detest it') but is simultaneously an evaluative and normative element which sustains practices.

The attachment that ties the practitioner to his/her practice and its object, as well as to his/her identity as a practitioner and to other practitioners, is a passionate and pleasurable or painful relation both shared and collectively elaborated (Gherardi et al., 2007). Belonging to a choir and gaining pleasure from music, and belonging to a scientific community and gaining pleasure from a particularly brilliant article, are forms of attachment socially supported by the respective communities, which have developed vocabularies and specific criteria of taste in order to communicate, share and refine the ways in which such practices are enacted. Attachment is not only the relation with the object of practice and the associated feelings; it is also the effect of the collective formation of the taste at the moment when the aesthetic judgements supporting the practice are formed. Taste may therefore be conceived in terms of taste-making (Gherardi, 2009b), that is, a situated activity that rests on learning and knowing how to appraise specific performances of a practice.

Polanyi (1958, p. 195) uses the expression 'dwelling in a practice' in order to emphasize that it is both intimate acquaintance with, and mastery of, a practice that generates the pleasure of practising it: 'astronomic observations are made by dwelling in astronomic theory, and it is this internal enjoyment of astronomy which make the astronomer interested in the stars. This is how scientific value is contemplated "from within"'.

When work practices are viewed 'from within', what is of interest to the researcher is the intellectual, passionate, ethical and aesthetic attachment that ties subjects to objects, technologies, the places of practices and other practitioners. In particular, I shall pay attention to the elaboration of taste 'from within' a community of practitioners and to the deployment of discursive practices for expressing aesthetic judgements, since taste is learned and taught as part of becoming a practitioner and it is performed as a collective, situated activity – taste-making – within a practice.

The sociology of attachment furnishes a theoretical framework (and a methodology) particularly suited to the study of practices as collectively supported by the constant refinement of taste within a community of practitioners, because it is based on a set of 'shifts' which propose a different conception of action (Gomart and Hennion, 1999):

- From *action* to *passion*. Instead of focusing on the subjects the researcher asks: through what mechanisms is this kind of 'active passion' performed?
- From '*who acts*' to '*what occurs*'. Instead of focusing on action, the researcher turns to events and asks: what occurs, how is the effect produced, which mediators are present?
- From *making* to *feeling*. The researcher asks: how can certain people tentatively help events to occur? How is feeling actively accomplished?

With these questions in mind we can regard taste-making as a collective achievement realized through three processes that I shall analyse in this section:

1. The collective development of a lexicon of taste;
2. The formation of a sense of belonging to an epistemic community; and
3. The refining of performances through the negotiation of aesthetic judgements.

Gaining pleasure from the object of a practice and sharing this pleasure with other practitioners is something that is learned and taught to newcomers through the collective elaboration of a shared lexicon for communicating about sensible feelings. We have already seen in the example of the flutemakers taken from Cook and Yanow (1993). Another example, is provided by Patricia Martin (2002, p. 867) in an ethnography on old people's homes where she describes how: 'I saw OPH [old people's home] staff socially constructing residents' bodies through talk and practice. They enacted a conception of bodies – as strong or weak, able or disabled, touchable or untouchable, clean or dirty, fair or foul smelling – in ways that shaped residents' perceptions, experiences, and feelings'. Martin introduces the term 'spirit of a place' in order to focus on a form of organizational knowledge that reflects a facility's culture and *emotional climate* relative to social relations, practices, routines and tacit understandings. The spirit of the place is an efficacious expression with which to convey the type of emotional attachment, sensible knowledge and the aesthetic judgement that a collectivity expresses through the situated activity of taste-making.

Other researchers, for instance Kathy Mack (2007), who studied sailors' attachment to the sea, suggest that workplaces are sensed through multi-sensory experiences (sight, sound, taste, smell and touch) that bring forth the 'senses of place' and make them more accessible. For example, sea-scapes are *sensed* through the stories accumulated in the nooks and crannies of sailors' steel mobile homes that form a structure upon which they may build a sense of seascapes. For seafarers, these stories carry the tacit knowledge of seafaring and at the same time construct and express it.

The elaboration of an appraisal vocabulary (be it cryptic expressions, indexical accounts or full narratives) allows practitioners to communicate aesthetic judgements, express their passion for the object of practice and their sense of place.

The attachment to the object of the practice sustains identity; but the object may be contested, and within larger communities of practice different ways of relating to it may give rise to different identities and different tastes. For example, we can see how epistemic communities elaborate their objects and their subjectivities in the academic field.

Scientific disciplines consist of bodies of knowledge that are situationally practised within competing 'schools of thought'. Mathematics, for example, can be 'done' in many different ways. What is it that sustains the practice of a particular school, and the identity of its practitioners?

A historical study by Paolo Landri (2007) on the 'school of Naples' which formed around the charismatic figure of Caccioppoli at the end of the Second World War shows how passion for an innovative development in functional analysis mobilized an epistemic community around its founder. In those years, doing mathematics in the school of Naples was a practice clearly identifiable by the international academic community; and for the mathematicians belonging to the school it meant producing a distinctive 'epistemic community'.

Landri (2007, p. 410) writes that 'the fabric of mathematics develops within an epistemic community; it unfolds through the differentiation of schools of mathematics implying differences in terms of practice, and reflects diversities in aesthetic judgments on the objects of knowledge'. Objects of knowledge are the focus of ongoing collective aesthetic judgements that put an end to controversies within the epistemic community and mobilize passion for knowledge.

The mobilization of passion for the object of one's own practice contributes to the emergence of a distinctive epistemic community. Strati (2008, pp. 232–3), in a study on a department of mathematics, reports how a mathematician defined the object of knowledge in ethical/aesthetic terms:

> The most beautiful result is one where the author has been able to identify fundamental ideas, after which he works out his theory following a line of reasoning and a generally geometric intuition, and the thing acquires a particular significance, it becomes clearer, it's easier to understand . . . A beautiful result is often one in which the author demonstrates more than he says.

The author comments how here, as often happens in organizations, aesthetics and ethics interweave so that it is often very difficult to determine whether or not 'beautiful' is being used as a synonym for 'good' or vice versa. Ethics and aesthetics are often intertwined in language, and judgements on correct or incorrect practices take into account not only criteria of instrumental rationality, but also of style, elegance, skill, innovativeness and so on.

The attachment of practitioners to the object of practice is constructed in the moment and in the space of the practising, in intuitive knowledge, and judgements on the correctness or otherwise of the practice are not external to its practising, but are formed within the action and are not only *sustained* by practice but *constitute* it.

Internal appraisal of performances, done from 'within' the community, elaborates the vocabulary of taste necessary to refine practices while skilfully repeating them. And, within repetition, the sharing of pleasure of doing is also the sharing of the pleasure of being. Taste shapes work practices and refines them through negotiation and reflectivity which suspend the flow of the action in order to intervene and savour the practice and express an aesthetic judgement upon it. We may say that practices are constantly refined through the taste-making process which works both on a sentiment of the perfectible and on repetition as tension toward a never-achieved perfection. Artistic practices easily illustrate this dynamic. The following excerpt (see Box 3.9) recounts an episode concerning the Duke Ellington orchestra (Crow, 1990, cited in Weick, 1999, p. 550) and aptly describes the discursive modes in which this ability to grasp the taste of a practice is transmitted.

BOX 3.9   PLAYING LIKE BUDDY BOLDEN

'Duke came to me and said: "Clark [Terry] I want you to play Buddy Bolden for me on this album."

I said: "Maestro, I don't know who the hell Buddy Bolden is!"

Duke said: "Oh sure, you know Buddy Bolden. Buddy Bolden was suave, handsome, and a debonair cat who the ladies loved. Aw, he was so fantastic! He was fabulous! He was always sought after. He had the biggest, fattest trumpet sound in town. He bent notes to the nth degree. He used to tune up in New Orleans and break glasses in Algiers! He was great with diminished. When he played a diminished, he bent those notes, man, like you've never heard them before!"

By this time Duke had me psyched out! He finished by saying: "As a matter of fact you are Buddy Bolden!" So I thought I was Buddy Bolden.

On conclusion of the session Duke went to him and said "That was Buddy Bolden."'

Source: Crow (1990), cited in Weick (1999, p. 550).

This example prompts reflection on the non-rational but emotional way in which knowledge is transmitted through evocative expressive modalities which recall a state of mind by assonance. At the same time they construct a vocabulary with which to speak about taste, to share an experience, and to refine the taste of the practice intersubjectively. Thus, playing like Buddy Bolden becomes a shared code, a way to perpetuate a practice beyond the community of practitioners that originally produced it. Similarly cooking like Chef Passard, doing mathematics like Caccioppoli, or adopting the Old People Home's style express that taste is teachable and learnable.

Taste-making is therefore the process of giving voice to passion and negotiating aesthetic criteria that support what constitutes 'a good practice' or 'a sloppy one' and 'a beautiful practice' or 'an ugly one' within a community of practitioners. It is formed within situated discursive practices. The aesthetic judgement is made by being said – and therefore it presupposes the collective elaboration and mastery of a vocabulary for saying – and it is said by being made.

Practices are socially sustained through situated ways of learning the criteria for appraising, and situated ways of transmitting them and taste-making is an important activity in working practices for two main reasons:

- It makes evident and supports a conception of what constitutes a practice on the basis, not of the activities that compose it, but instead of its being socially sustained through criteria of normative adequacy ceaselessly discussed among the practitioners. Rouse (2002, p. 161) argues that practices are characterized in terms of normative accountability of various performances, rather than by regularities or commonalities among the activities;
- The constant negotiation of the aesthetic and ethical judgements on what is thought to be a correct or incorrect way of practising within the community of its practitioners makes possible the competent reproduction of a practice over and over again, and its refinement while being practised, or its abandonment. Refinement of a practice constitutes the specific dynamics of practice change.

These topics will be explored further in the chapters that follow. They have been treated in this chapter in relation to sensible knowledge and aesthetic judgements in order to show that working practices should be understood as a collective knowledgeable doing. But practices do not only involve production; rather, the reproduction of practices contributes to producing social order within working practices. I shall illustrate this point once again in relation to the body, to differently sexed bodies, and therefore to gender as social practice and situated practice.

3.4   GENDER AS A SOCIAL PRACTICE

How do we learn to embody and enact the gendered professional selves required by and considered appropriate to particular workplace situations? This question presupposes a conception of gender as situated performance and as a social practice (Mathieu, 2009; Poggio, 2006). In the early 1990s, many scholars started to conceive gender as a dynamic process, as practice, as what people say and do in addition to such static properties as an identity or social status. Patricia Martin (2003) argues that men and women socially construct each other at work: (a) by means of a two-sided dynamic of gendering practices and practising of gender; (b) that this dynamic significantly affects both women's and men's work experiences; (c) that gendering practices produced through interaction impair women workers' identities and confidence; and (d) that attention to the practicing of gender will produce insights into how inequalities are created in the workplace.

The philosopher Judith Butler (1990; 1993) showed the performative nature not only of gender but also of sex, thereby undermining the last essentialist buttress of the distinction between male and female. She maintains that 'gender is always a doing', but she stresses that it is not 'a doing by a subject who might be said to pre-exist the deed', because identity 'is performatively constituted by the very "expressions" that are said to be its results' (Butler, 1990, p. 33).

Identity can thus be analysed as the product, unstable and only partly under the individual's control, of what Law calls a 'heterogeneous engineering' which arranges human and non-human elements into a stable artefact. Following John Law we can assume that 'each one of us is an *arrangement*. That arrangement is more or less fragile. There are ordering processes which keep (or fail to keep) that arrangement on the road. And some of those processes, though precious few, are partially under our control some of the time' (Law, 1994, p. 33, original emphasis).

In order to understand *how* gender identity is generated as a social and organizational practice I propose to follow Omega, a young woman, 27 years old, recently hired by a consulting company, in her first day at work (see Box 3.10).

Omega has entered a male territory. Masculinity is apparent at the symbolic level and is practised and circulated in discourses, artefacts and in the physicality of the space. Consultancy work, with its characteristics of 'winning the client' is represented as typically male terrain. It is made explicit and justified by the categories of 'rationality', 'efficiency' and 'strategic acumen', 'killing the competition' and 'squeezing the others'. It is also reflected in material artefacts (as Omega explains, the 'briefcase' issued on the first day at Alpha contains corporeal constraints, a script which presupposes a male body), in verbal artefacts (the jokes among the consultants, the sexual innuendo and the sexual metaphors privileging men's bodies) and in the internal decoration of the organizational setting. In the advertising of Company Alpha, when the organization is in shape, it takes the form of a shark.

To be a man in such an environment yields rent from keeping all the previous elements aligned without putting much effort into aligning them. Masculinity constitutes 'a position rent' for the arrangements of all the masculine materials in a network that is male dominated. For a person of another gender or for non-hegemonic forms of masculinity such an environment is demanding in terms of legitimation and appropriate gender enactment. How did Omega learn to 'edit' her participation in order to support the mobilization of masculinity, how did she learn to handle her dual presence (as a woman and as a consultant) without losing face as a gendered person and as a competent professional?

BOX 3.10   THE CASE OF OMEGA GENDER POSITIONING

Together with an 'identification number', on the first day of work each consultant receives a large briefcase made of maroon leather with the Company Alpha logo gilded on the inside. Together with the portable computer, this briefcase constitutes the consultant's essential equipment. Each briefcase contains pens, pencils, stationery, a notebook and various documents. Omega only kept her briefcase for half an hour and then gave it to Delta, a senior male consultant, who wanted to have a new one. In any case, she did not like it because it was cumbersome, had little room inside, had to be kept away from the body because of its bulk and could not be slung over the shoulder.

On the first day, a male consultant comes into the staff room to advise Omicron (a male consultant, also just hired) to 'draw inspiration' from a presentation that he had just prepared for a project similar to the one that Omicron is developing. Omicron says that the consultant is highly qualified and also very likeable. Beside work information, in fact, he circulates games, files of images and porno clips.

After the lunch break, Omega again sits down at the computer to choose the colours to assign to concepts so that they can be differentiated in the questionnaire. In the afternoon, Delta calls her to finish the work to be presented. They go up to the first floor and sit around a table. [Omega notes an advertisement for Alpha published in *Sole 24ore* in 1996. The caption reads: 'Is your organization in shape?' and the picture shows a shoal of fish arranged in the shape of a shark.] Omega shows Delta what she has prepared this morning. She complains that she has too little information and, speaking about the forthcoming interviews, says, 'We've got to really squeeze them!'

A telephone call arrives to change an appointment fixed for the following day, which means that diaries will have to be rearranged. While Omega reports on Delta's appointments, she tells him: 'I feel like I'm your secretary.' He answers: 'In that case I'll feel you up [laughs].'

Source: Bruni and Gherardi (2001, p. 182).

In the course of the project, Omega's language gradually changes. In trying to mobilize a professional identity aligned with the material and semiotic practices of her community, and thereby proving to her colleagues her competence at doing it, Omega takes up a masculine discursive position: she produces double entendre and puns, and complies with their time requirements and male style. Let us follow her a couple of months later (see Box 3.11).

Omega's strategy is therefore to share the community's discursive practices and become an expert in gender switching. The term 'gender switching' denotes the dynamic by which Omega takes up a masculine positioning, acts from within it, leaves it and defends her gender identity when it is second-sexed by her colleagues, affiliates herself with other women or differentiates herself from them. The enactment of her professionalism is staged for the audience of her colleagues and it is discursively achieved by joining in a masculine positioning. On the other hand, membership

---

BOX 3.11   OMEGA LEARNING 'APPROPRIATE' DISCURSIVE PRACTICES

Omega and Delta are in the car on their way to the client. Delta asks what he should say if they ask whether this is the first time that they have done a project of this kind. Omega says that they could say that 'The individual parts we've already done, but we've never combined them in a single project . . . which is half true and half untrue.'

Delta: Meaning?
Omega: Well, this is the first form of integration, the perfect response to the client's needs. [They laugh.]

They have almost arrived, and Omega and Delta review the various stages of the project. Joking, Delta says that they could put together all the projects that they have prepared and presented in the past. Omega adds that 'Then we really would be whores [they laugh],' referring to the fact that they have always catered to the client's desires.

On arriving at the client company, Omega exclaims: 'Come on guys, let's go for it . . .!'

Source: Bruni and Gherardi (2001, p. 185).

of 'another' gender places Omega in 'another' community. And to some advantage: it is through Sigma, a female secretary (the gate-keeper of the community of secretaries) that Omega has obtained the keys for the basement where she stashes her tracksuit for after-work jogging, even though she is not yet a senior consultant. Her gender identity is recognized by the community of women, and this enables her to share a secret and to indulge in a non-canonical practice with another community.

The heterogeneous engineering of a professional identity is the effect of the action net which performs it. In the activation of the subject-network, Omega is only one of the actants[3] alongside other people and a set of artefacts which 'make' the consultant, like the computer, the briefcase, the projects developed by other consultants but which can be recycled and the staff room. Omega's professional identity is sustained as much by her colleagues as by Alpha's clients and its administrative staff. In other words we may say that gender is a social practice within a texture of practices.

3.5 TO SUM UP

This chapter has emphasized the centrality of the body in the analysis of situated working practices. We may therefore regard a practice as a situated seeing, saying and doing, thereby adding the dimension of seeing (which comprises a set of sensible capacities) to the traditional ones of saying and doing. Not only do people work through their bodies, they also know with their bodies; and the knowledge thus acquired is conserved in their bodies. Hence, if we want to consider the work of the body, we cannot ignore the fact that bodies are sexed and that in working we 'do gender' (Gherardi, 1995a; West and Zimmerman, 1987) and construct gendered organizational practices.

The gendered character of a working practice is the outcome of a process of alignment which holds together differently sexed bodies, artefacts which have different affordances in relation to bodies, gendered work settings, discursive practices which perform maleness or femaleness, and the power relationships between them and symbolic imageries of gender. Gender is an organizational practice, not just a social one, and in reproducing practices we reproduce gender. Sensible knowledge concerns what is perceived through the senses and what constitutes the object of the sensitive–aesthetic judgement.

The ability to use the hands to perform a set of activities, rather than the feet and the ability to use the senses of hearing, smell or taste, are acquired and developed during practices themselves. It becomes personal knowledge which distinguishes one individual from another, but which at the same time is inscribed in the collective knowledge of that community in the form of professional vision. To become a practitioner, it is therefore important to participate legitimately in a practice and thus be able to follow a learning trajectory (what Lave and Wenger, 1991, have called 'legitimate peripheral participation'). As a knowing-in-practice is developed, so too is a disciplined body (in Foucault's sense) which has learned to develop the senses in accordance with the 'feel for the game'. The identity of a practitioner is therefore a process of social learning performed through discursive capacities and interaction with the artefacts of the practice. The activities which stabilize a professional vision are processes enacted collectively in the cooperation among human, non-human and discursive practices. Listed briefly, they are: (a) coding, which transforms observed phenomena into the epistemic objects of an occupation; (b) highlighting, which gives salience to specific phenomena by marking them in some manner; and (c) producing and articulating material representations, which embed and structure the knowledge produced and transfer it through space and time.

In the next two chapters I shall explore the role of both artefacts and language. For the time being, I shall show how sensible knowledge and aesthetic judgement are intrinsically united in forming not only the professional vision but also the attachment of practitioners to the object of the practice and the normative accountability of that practice. The attachment that ties the practitioner to his/her practice and its object is a question of a passionate and pleasurable or painful relation both shared and collectively elaborated by the respective communities, that have developed vocabularies and specific criteria of taste in order to communicate, share and refine the ways in which such practices are enacted and reproduced or changed over time. Taste may therefore be conceived in terms of taste-making, as a situated activity that rests on learning and knowing how to appraise specific performances of a practice and therefore how to reproduce and change it through a dynamic of constant practice refinement.

Taste-making is a collective achievement realized through three processes: (1) the collective development of a lexicon of taste; (2) the formation of a sense of belonging to an epistemic community; and (3) the refining of performances through the negotiation of aesthetic judgements.

NOTES

1. A field of practices can be defined as composed of activities and practices interconnected in constantly changing patterns. My concern in studying a field of practices is to determine how connection-in-action comes about, how associations are established,

maintained and changed among the elements of a partially given form. I have called this connection-in-action 'texture of practice', my purpose being to emphasize the qualitative aspect assumed by the connection once the relations have been activated and the weaving together of the relations-in-act has begun.

2. This text derives from observation conducted by Laura Linetti, a nurse who watched the operation during a specialization course in managerial techniques at Mantua in 2010. I wish to thank Laura for permitting me to report this example.

3. Semioticians and Actor Network Theory (ANT) use the notion of 'actants' for all the elements which accomplish or are transformed by the actions through which the narration evolves.

4. Sociomaterial practices and technological environments

In this chapter we take a step forward in the empirical study of practices by considering the materiality of the relations which are woven together as a practice unfolds. In order to frame this way of looking at practices, we must take a step back and specify what is meant when practice is described as epistemological rather than as an 'object' or a privileged locus of learning and knowing.

To gain better understanding of the epistemology of practice – and therefore move away from analysis that privileges action as the product of actors in a given context – it is useful to recall how Ira Cohen (1996) distinguishes between theories of action and theories of practice. We may say that whilst the theories of action privilege the intentionality of actors, from which derives meaningful action (in the tradition of Weber and Parsons), the thoeries of practice locate the source of significant patterns in how conduct is enacted, performed or produced (in the tradition of Schütz, Dewey, Mead, Garfinkel and Giddens). Hence theories of practice assume an ecological model in which agency is distributed between humans and non-humans and in which the relationality between the social world and materiality can be subjected to inquiry. Whilst theories of action start from individuals and from their intentionality in pursuing courses of action, theories of practice view actions as 'taking place' or 'happening', as being performed through a network of connections-in-action, as life-world and dwelling (as the phenomenological legacy calls them, see Chia and Holt, 2006; Sandberg and Dall'Alba, 2009).

The adoption of an ecological model that gives ontological priority to neither humans nor non-humans nor discursive practices constitutes the fundamental difference between theories of action and of practice. It is in this interpretative framework that the difference can be grasped between the study of practice as an empirical object and the use of practice as epistemology. The difference is based on the attribution to practice of a realist ontology (that objectifies practices as primary units) and a social constructionist conception that does not distinguish between the production of knowledge and construction of the object of knowledge (between ontology and epistemology). From this derive different methodologies for the conduct of practice-based studies (Charreire-Petit and Huault, 2008).

Relational epistemology has only recently arisen in both organization studies and the social sciences in general; and it is yet to be consolidated, especially when it must descend from the epistemological level to that of methodology. To illustrate the difference between a sociology grounded on distinct 'entities' and a sociology grounded on relationships, Cooper and Law (1995) borrow the terms 'distal' and 'proximal' from anatomy in order to distinguish between two different epistemologies. In anatomy, the two terms are used to indicate closeness to, or distance from, a point of attachment or origin. Distal and proximal are two complementary but distinct ways of viewing human structures, just as a sociology *à la* Parsons is a sociology of being, while a sociology *à la* Elias is a sociology of becoming. In the former case, social elements are conceived as self-sufficient, in the latter as beginnings and transformations which constantly renew themselves. Distal thought prioritizes results and consequences, the products and finished objects of thought and action, everything that is pre-packaged. Proximal thought instead addresses what is continuing and incomplete, towards which it constantly tends but never reaches. The proximal view is always partial and precarious. The distal view highlights boundaries and divisions, distinction and clarity, hierarchy and order (relations of reciprocal determination); the proximal emphasizes implication and complicity, equivalence and ambiguity (relations of reciprocal determination).

In 'Manifesto for a Relational Sociology' Emirbayer (1997, p. 281) writes: 'sociologists today are faced with a fundamental dilemma: whether to conceive of the social world as consisting primarily in substances or in processes, in static "things" or in dynamic, unfolding relations'. While in the first option (substantialist epistemology) entities come first and relations among them only subsequently, in the second (relational thinking) social reality is depicted instead in dynamic, continuous, and processual terms.

The return of practice is part of the movement towards a relational epistemology, because practice makes it possible to see and to represent a mode of ordering the social in which doing and knowing are not separated and the knowing subject and the known object emerge in the ongoing interaction.

Not only do subject and object define each other within a context of interaction, but the relationship between the material and the discursive comes about as a single phenomenon in which not only is materiality social – as social studies on technology have shown (Law, 1994) – but the process of meaning-making encompasses material semiosis. In Law's

(1994, p. 24, original emphasis) definition, relational materialism is a process of 'ordering [that] has to do both with humans *and* non-humans'. The epistemology of practice is a post-human project in that it seeks to decentre the human subject and reconfigure the concept of agency within sociomaterial practices.

The term 'sociomateriality' has come into use after removal of the hyphen between the two terms (Orlikowski, 2007; 2009). And the term 'intra-action', coined by Barad (2003; 2007) to locate the relationship of mutual determination between subject and object, has also entered the lexicon of organization studies (Iedema, 2007; Nyberg, 2009) in relation to practice as epistemology. In other words, it is in the historically situated context of a practice that the knowing subject, the object of knowledge, and sociomateriality are involved in the processes of 'becoming' through which their identities are materially negotiated and (re)confirmed (Chia, 2003, p. 106). This focus on becoming thus conceives of organizations – and organizational practice as well – 'not as an ontological stable object, but rather something that exists only in its duration' (Clegg et al., 2005, p. 159).

The epistemology of practice makes it possible to articulate the dynamic that occurs between the becoming of a practice as a socially sustained mode of action in a given context and the 'given' sociomaterial context in which it develops. Practice is situated between the given and the emergent as an element in the sociomaterial ordering.

It is therefore within a framework of *constitutive entanglement* that I propose to read technological practices as the locus of organizing. In Orlikowski's words (2007, p. 1437): 'a position of constitutive entanglement does not privilege either humans or technology (in one-way interactions). Instead, the social and the material are considered to be inextricably related – there is no social that is not also material, and no material that is not also social'. We shall now see by means of an empirical example what it is to study technologies in use in light of sociomaterial practices.

4.1 TECHNOLOGICAL SOCIOMATERIAL PRACTICES

To provide an example of how constitutive entanglement characterizes sociomaterial practices, I refer to the research on communications practices conducted in the Plymouth company by Mazmanian et al. (2006) and summarized by Wanda Orlikowski (2007). In this company, the BlackBerry service was configured to continually push emails to handheld devices, and the professionals received email messages at any time of the day or night.

Even if the professionals could choose when to look and respond to the delivered emails, most reported that the scanning of their BlackBerrys was frequent, since the expectations of availability and accountability was generalized within that small community of information professionals (see Box 4.1).

This study shows how the communication changes that happened at Plymouth emerged from the performativity of the technology when involved in members' everyday practices. In fact, it was not that the material features of the BlackBerry (technology itself) had a social impact, or that the material affordances of mobile communication allowed more efficient communication. Rather, the performativity of the technology was sociomaterial, and it emerged when it entered into situated practices. As Orlikowski (2007, p. 1444) concludes: 'the "push email" capability inscribed into the software running on the servers has become entangled with people's choices and activities to keep devices turned on, to carry them at all times, to glance at them repeatedly, and to respond to email regularly'.

The concepts of technology-in-use and technology-in-practice (Orlikowski, 2000; Suchman et al., 1999) better represent the practice turn in the study of technology. When humans regularly interact with a technology, they interact with its material and symbolic properties, and it is through such repeated interactions over time that some properties become involved in a structuring process. It is therefore such recurrent practices which produce and reproduce a particular structure of the use of technology and, in so doing, give form to the set of rules and resources that connote those interactions. The conclusion is therefore that 'the practice lens' more easily explains the situated use of technology and the dynamic nature of the new technologies that take shape through their use:

> A practice lens more easily accommodates people's situated use of dynamic technologies because it makes no assumptions about the stability, predictability, or relative completeness of the technologies. Instead, the focus is on what structures emerge as people interact recurrently with whatever properties of the technology are at hand, whether these were built in, added on, modified, or invented on the fly. (Orlikowski, 2000, p. 407)

In fact – argues Orlikowski – we often conflate two aspects of technology: the technology as *artefact* (the bundle of material and symbolic properties packaged in some socially recognizable form, for example, hardware, software, techniques); and the *use* of technology, or what people actually do with the technological artefact in their recurrent, situated practices.

The expression 'technology as social practice' first appeared in an article by Suchman et al. (1999, p. 404). According to these authors, the design

BOX 4.1   THE CASE OF BLACKBERRYS

Within Plymouth, members stated that over time they felt a strong obligation to check incoming messages. Linda, a senior support member, explained: 'One of the things that I've noticed more and more is that people will BlackBerry me in the evening you know, after 8:30 in the evening. I'm pretty much settled in and people know that it [BlackBerry] sits next to me, my cup of tea is there, my knitting is in my lap, something's on television and I just take care of business.'

A system of expectations had reconfigured the communication practices of this community through their engagement with BlackBerrys, and as the members' communication became increasingly entangled with their BlackBerrys the distinctions between work and non-work, between public and private accessibility, became blurred. The professionals experienced both increased flexibility regarding their choice of when and where to work, and increased obligation to be constantly responsive.

In fact, this is what happened when somebody did not respond immediately to an email message: 'Well, you don't answer and you make them wonder why isn't he answering? And so being predictable all the time isn't good. But there's a new element in all this that never would have existed before these things were invented, especially when your counterparty is somebody that knows that you are looking at it a lot. The element is that there's an expectation on the part of the sender that what he's sending is being read immediately. Whereas in the old days before BlackBerrys, if you left a voicemail for somebody or if you sent some other message, a fax, you could never be sure that it got into the hands of the recipient, or when it got in. [Now] if you've sent a message to somebody who's a chronic BlackBerry user, I think you're pretty confident that person has seen what you said.'

The unintended effect of these collective sociomaterial enactments of the technology was an almost continual electronic communication within the firm and a feeling of compulsion (or addiction) within its members, since the individual desire to disconnect conflicted with the collective expectations of the sociomaterial network.

Source: Orlikowski (2007, p. 1442).

of technologies involves a practice of configuring new alignments between the social and the material: 'system development is not the creation of discrete, intrinsically meaningful objects, but the cultural production of new forms of practice. As practice, technologies can be assessed only in their relations to the sites of their production and use'. The importance of this statement is evident when one considers not only the context to which it refers – the participatory design of new technologies – but also the broader theoretical perspective which views working practices as activities situated and performed in the interaction between humans and non-humans. The former aspect implies that when new technologies are being designed, the designers must take account of (and inscribe in the artefact) the practices of use of the users, and in this sense it also concerns the *practice-based design* of information systems (Suchman, 2002). The latter aspect directs attention to the fact that the social and the technical form an ecology of knowledge, and that the introduction of a new technology produces a realignment of practices which is both material and cultural.

All practices are therefore sociomaterial, and 'what we call the social is *materially heterogeneous*: talk, bodies, architectures, all of these are implicated in and perform the social' (Law, 1994, p. 2, original emphasis). Paraphrasing Law, we may say that a practice is the effect of a process of 'heterogeneous engineering' which gives (relative) temporal and spatial stability to the organization of persons, texts and objects. Now discussed is how objects within practices exercise an 'affiliative power' (Suchman, 2005, p. 379): that is, they are not innocent, but fraught with significance for the relations that they materialize.

4.2   AFFILIATIVE OBJECTS

Material sociology has problematized the active role of objects in the construction of the social only recently, and two special journal issues (Engeström and Blackler, 2005; Pels et al., 2002) offer a good overview of the debate, partly linking it with the practice turn.

Within laboratory studies and social studies of science, sociomaterial practices have been studied in association with knowledge-producing practices, the purpose being to show another constitutive entanglement – of social relations and knowledge – or in Knorr Cetina's terms (1997, p. 8) of post-social relations or object-centred sociality:

> The traditional definition of a knowledge society puts the emphasis on the first term; on knowledge, seen as a specific product. The definition I advocate

switches the emphasis to society, a society that, if the argument about the expanding role of expert systems etc. is right, is no more inside knowledge processes than outside. In a post-social knowledge society, mutually exclusive definitions of knowledge processes and social processes are theoretically no longer adequate; we need to trace the ways in which knowledge has become constitutive of social relations.

We live in a world termed 'post-social' in order to emphasize that it comprises the objects of our mode of conceiving sociality. Consequently, objects and their material world can be construed as materialized knowledge (Knorr Cetina, 1981) and matter which interrogates humans and interacts with them. It is sufficient only to cite intelligent machines to demonstrate that the alleged superiority of humans over the material world is highly questionable. The Enlightenment faith in rationality was matched by an image of human beings who dominated nature and objects and were ontologically separate from the material world. In the post-social world, by contrast, human beings are constricted and made vulnerable by their humanity, and they use technology to create devices with which to extend their capacities to memorize, take action at a distance, see and feel. Instead of subjects and objects, there are quasi-objects and quasi-subjects connected in relational networks (Latour, 1993, p. 89), while objects take on the characteristics of humans, that is, they judge, they cooperate with other objects, they need to be socialized into already-existing practices and so on. The divide between human and non-human is blurred. By emphasizing the extent to which the social is ordered, held and 'fixed' by the material, new challenges are raised against traditional social theory, which until recently was only marginally interested in relationships between humans and non-humans, culture and nature, society and technology (Pels et al., 2002, p. 2).

According to Engeström and Blackler (2005, p. 309), three traditions of work have influenced the resurgence of interest in objects: a shift in cultural anthropology from rituals to everyday cultural and material practices (Appadurai, 1986; Ortner, 1984); the influence of social studies on science and technology (Latour, 1999b) and feminist studies (Haraway, 1997) stressing the hybrid character of people and things; and practice theories. In the special journal issue by Engeström and Blackler (2005), we can read about the difficulties of conducting research on the complexity of the material world, and we can follow what it means to conduct an ethnography on non-humans. Bruni (2005, pp. 371–2) describes how he shadowed an electronic patient record (EPR) within a hospital oncological ward and illustrates the necessity for objects to 'work together' (see Box 4.2).

BOX 4.2   AFFILIATIVE OBJECTS IN THE ONCOLOGICAL WARD

I observe Elisa (a nurse) at work in the infusions therapy section. She shows me how and where the drugs to be administered are prepared. While we talk, Elisa empties vials and fills syringes (almost without looking) and consults the printout of the day's appointments. Elisa notices that, strangely, one patient has two appointments that morning. This is odd because if the person logging the appointment makes a mistake when feeding in the data, the software should block it.

Then a colleague tells Elisa that the computer has printed out the wrong therapy! Gianna has noticed the mistake (before administering the therapy) because she knows the patient ('obvious things', they call them). For example it is always better to 'take a look' at the therapy (quantity, type, cycle) before administering it ('because the program is a bit rigid in its structure,' explains Elisa. 'When the cycle requires a particular order, a particular drug, and then for some reason it has to be reduced . . . you have to be very careful because he [the computer] always gives the same therapy at 100%. So that he [the doctor] often says "Reduce the dose" but he [the computer] doesn't reduce it, because you have to go into the first . . . first memory).'

Moreover, the patients are (usually) attentive to their therapy. They keep check on what the nurses are doing and call their attention to certain matters ('I realize from the patient,' continues Elisa, 'because when I've finished the examination, he says [the patient], "Ah, you know, the doctor said he'd reduce the dose this time . . . ". I see that the therapy sheet instead says it should be 100%, so that . . . prompted by the patient I can go to the doctor and ask about it, so we notice things.').

In addition, the Kirkner therapy (the one in question) is particularly 'difficult' because of the massive quantity of drugs administered and the complexity of the therapy cycle. So when they read KIRKNER on the computer printout, the nurses know that they must take extra special care.

The nurses 'know' that 'the computer makes mistakes with Kirkner' because it does not log changes in the therapy schedule and continues to impose the same sequence (Elisa says 'that the computer technicians have been told about the problem but they haven't done anything.').

Elisa adds that her greatest worry is that a problem of 'abbreviations' may arise, 'because we write . . . I mean, the computer gives us the therapy sheet but not the label.' She explains that the computer prints out the therapy prescribed by the doctor, but not the label which the nurses must attach to the drip-feed bottle (once they have prepared the therapy). As they write the labels, the nurses abbreviate the names of the drugs, so that Taxol becomes TAX, and Taxotere becomes TXT. Elisa says that all these 'passages' (the doctors who write on the computer, the nurses who read and abbreviate, the colleagues who 'decipher' the abbreviations) increase the risk of errors.

Source: Bruni (2005, pp. 371–2).

The account highlights what may happen when a clinical file is not 'controlled' and the objects of which it is composed interact with each other in an unusual manner unbeknown to the actors. The objects have multiple interrelations which may vary in space and time. At the centre of discussion is a particular object (the Kirkner therapy) defined (by the nurses) as 'difficult' because of the relations that tie it to different places and times of the organization, and which cause it to change. In fact, at a hypothetical 'time-zero', when the therapy is in the consulting room it is invariably itself, in the sense that it has a pre-established interaction with the other objects and it is therefore not necessary to verify its relations (the therapy associates standard quantities of infusion with a fixed administration schedule). But at a subsequent 'time-one', when the therapy is in the day hospital, it is susceptible to variations (according to how it has interacted with the patient and his/her haematochemical test results), and it is therefore advisable to check its relations with the quantity of the drug and the therapy cycles.

On the basis of the accounts given by the actors, the EPR commits errors in relating to this object because it is unable to take account of these spatio-temporal variations. The software is 'a bit rigid in its structure' (according to the nurses), although it cannot be blamed for this. Like any 'newcomer', the new technological object has learned experientially from the places and actors that it has encountered. Hence, whilst it has met other objects and experienced their behaviour in specific spaces and times, it is 'normal' for it not to know their overall behaviour within the organization. The actors are aware of the difficulty of this relation. They consequently activate a system of cross-checks. The spatio-temporal variation of an object is also responsible for the day-hospital head's 'greatest fear' that therapeutic objects may interact erroneously.

The researcher (Bruni, 2005, p. 374) observes that whereas it is usually the subjects observed that do not dutifully behave according to the researcher's expectations (emerging from the context to interfere with his/her action/observation), in the account set out in Box 4.2 above it is objects that cause this disturbance. Bruni offers a reflective observation on conducting ethnography of objects (see Box 4.3).

Through this research we have seen objects as actants in technological practices, and we have seen them act together with humans, exercising both a power of affiliation within a community of objects which may or

---

BOX 4.3   ON ETHNOGRAPHY OF OBJECTS

I realized that I could have described the reality confronting me by skirting round the actors, but I could not evade the objects. And this was because, as I have sought to show, in the organizational reality in question the (human) actors relied on the relational objects that embodied identity, power, risk, uncertainty, control and so on. Moreover, the (human) actors seemed much more attracted, intrigued, sometimes preoccupied, by the relations established among objects than they were by the predictable action of more 'canonical' subjects. By way of example, the nurses were so expert in finding clinical records that they were able to take account beforehand of errors committed by their colleagues, yet they were unable to cope with the relations among objects that obstructed their work. Likewise, patient-reception operations were unhinged by the fact that objects designed to follow a single, fluid and sequential trajectory often become entangled in ranges of action which call subject/object and activity/passivity distinctions into question.

Observing non-humans therefore requires one to plot the connections among different courses of action, and to determine how actions and subjects define each other in relations. From this point of view, shadowing non-humans requires the ethnographer to be able to orient his/her observations to the material associations that 'perform' relations, and probably also to devise new narrative forms able to make that performance 'accountable'.

Source: Bruni (2005, p. 374).

may not go together 'in the correct way', and a power to hold humans together within sociomaterial relations.

4.3 OBJECTS FOR LIVE MEMORIES

In the previous section, we saw how objects act by exercising an affiliative power. In this section we see how they act in relation to temporality and the process of organizational remembering. In working practices, as collective knowledgeable doings, the continuity among past, present and future action becomes an achievement made in the interaction between humans and non-humans, and through the delegation to non-humans of the distinctively human function of remembering.

The topic of organizational memory has been mainly addressed in terms of a stock of knowledge (Stein, 1995), a means to transfer knowledge from the past to the present (Walsh and Ungson, 1991), or technological systems to support the human memory. The image of the memory is primarily that of a large store (where the main issues are therefore the storage and retrieval of memory items), rather than that of a social and organizational practice. Nevertheless, there are authors who have focused on memory as a process, underlining the mobilization of memorized knowledge (Engeström et al., 1990; Orr, 1990) and the role of the cultural tools used for this purpose, such as orality in the form of both discursive practices and storytelling (Boje, 1991; Gabriel, 2000), writing (Ackerman and Halverson, 2000), the transmission of values and a moral order through organizational communication (Borzeix and Fraenkel, 2001) or inscriptions (Latour, 1987). Thus, in this area of analysis, study of the memory as an asset to be administered wisely has given way to study of organizational remembering processes in both relatively stable organizational settings and project-based organizations (Cacciatori, 2008).

There is a long tradition in technology studies which shows how artefacts play a more complex role than simply enabling the storage, retrieval and recycling of knowledge across different contexts. I shall now show their capacity to be actants that enact live memories, actualizing the past in the present and anticipating the future.

If we consider organizational remembering as a sociomaterial practice, we can examine how the translation process creates the links between human and non-human actors, and the connections among past, present and future. Actor Network Theory (ANT) (Latour, 1987) uses the concept of translation to describe the set of negotiations, calculations, persuasions and other devices mobilized so that authority and power can be exercised, and so that their exerciser can speak on the behalf of others (Akrich et al., 2006). It therefore concerns the operations whereby inscriptions are related to each other, and then with material elements, physical capacities, and rules and procedures (Latour, 1987). This formulation was at the basis of the research presented in the previous section; and it was also the basis of the research now described, the context of which was an emergency call centre in Canada (Grosjean and Bonneville, 2009, p. 320).

In their study on remembering processes and the role of objects in them, Grosjean and Bonneville (2009) identify three translations performed in order to trigger collective mnemonic functions:

1. Making past knowledge, decisions and events 'present' through statements or inscriptions. Through this activity the past is made present, and temporal continuity is not interrupted;
2. (Re)constructing or (re)creating the sense of a statement or inscription in the course of successive formulations. Through this activity, the present is constructed and made present in the sense of continuity (instantiation);
3. Relocating a statement or inscription in time and space. This is to make present what it is absent, acting at distance to deploy actants in different space-time frames.

Considering the processes and objects of the memory helps us discuss an important aspect of practices – temporality – and to do so in conjunction with materiality. It is for this reason that I have emphasized the process of anchoring collective practices in space-time frames which combine the sense of both the situated (*hic et nunc*) and the displaced (from the past to the present or future, or of acting at a distance).

We see a concrete example of this practice if we enter the emergency call centre studied by Grosjean and Bonneville (2009). The centre must manage a certain number of ambulances and their crews on the ground in compliance with the organization's rules on shift work. The personnel use tools ranging from telephones to computers, to a board showing the distribution of ambulances on the ground according to their service zones. The telephone operators have the task of taking calls, despatching ambulances and recalling them, but also the task of managing work shifts, breaks for lunch/dinner, and overtime for the ambulance crews. They must therefore be able to optimize both the rescue operations and the service schedules for the paramedical staff. It is therefore important that, as the operators do their work, there are no moments of memory breakdown as regards past events, decisions taken, actions already initiated, protocols to be followed, and occurrences that may have future consequences. To be noted is that these memorization needs are not exceptional, and that they recur in many other working practices where continuity between past and present is necessary and is normally achieved through a social and collective process of activating the memory and anchoring it in materiality.

The continuity of collective action is ensured: (a) by recreating the history of interactions in past events, which takes place, for example, at the moment (and through the activities) of shift changes and handovers from one operator to the other; (b) making organizational knowledge present, and therefore translating it into the present; and (c) by mobilizing different actants (embodied knowledges, rules, artefacts and texts) to support present action.

I shall consider handovers when I analyse discursive practices in the next chapter. Here I draw from Grosjean and Bonneville's (2009) study to show an example which concerns relocation (see Box 4.4).

R2 and R4 do not share the same decisional premises. Whilst R2 justifies his action on the basis of habit, R4 activates a previous situation.

BOX 4.4   LIVE MEMORIES AND THE RELOCATION OF THE PAST

Operator R4 comes into the emergency call centre to start his shift. He approaches the two operators, R2 and R3, present in the room. R2 is going off duty, and he summarizes the situation for R4 by showing him either his ambulance management sheet or the information visible on the screen of his computer.

R2: To tell the truth there aren't any overruns [of a crew's schedule]. The crew of vehicle 19 still have a couple of minutes. If you get a call to St-Andrè, pass it to them, let them overrun. That's what I've always done.

R4: Yes, but when we had the briefing, they said: 'ah, if there's anyone on the overrun line, don't let them overrun.' Okay, just as well I know, because at the briefing . . .

R3: Like, in this case here there'll probably be an overrun.

R2: Right, okay. [There follows a list of where the other ambulances are.]

Source: Grosjean and Bonneville (2009, pp. 327–8).

That is, he relocates the briefing made in the past so that it is present in the interpretative frame of the current decision. He thus actualizes an item of organizational knowledge (a decision taken in the past), and he acts as the mouthpiece for the people present at that briefing. He therefore does not grant authoritativeness to R2's justification. The example illustrates how an item of organizational knowledge is translated: that is, made present in the moment-now, interpreted and reconstructed, as well as being displaced in time and space during the work activity.

The operators place particular importance on the risk of overrunning because they rely on organizational knowledge concerning the contractual rules. These state that an ambulance operator who works twelve hours must have four additional hours off, but if it is not possible to give him those hours (overrun), then he must be given eight hours. This is an item of organizational knowledge inscribed in the organization's rules and shared by all its members. Nevertheless, in the exchange reported above, we see that the process which enables the mobilization of knowing and knowing what to do cannot be isolated from the practice and context in which that knowledge is actualized. In fact, knowledge relative to overrunning requires an effort of interpretation and translation so that it is actualized and recreated in relation to each new context. This point will be resumed later in regard to organizational rules and what is meant by following the rules.

I shall instead now return to the process of organizational remembering as a practical activity. This will become more complex when we see that it is pervasive in working and organizational practices, and that objects assist humans in the collective activity of giving temporal coherence to practices. Objects that incorporate representations of knowledge (procedure handbooks, drawings, mock models, software) are crucial in their capacity to travel and make associations within a texture of practices. Their capacity to translate knowledge also depends on how knowledge is inscribed in them (Carlile, 2002). A special case of this kind of knowledge consists in what Star and Griesemer (1989, p. 393) called 'boundary objects': objects which both inhabit several intersecting social worlds and satisfy the informational requirements of each of them. Since the term has been much misused, it is important to stress that in the first instance boundaries are not given but instead negotiated relationally, and second that different occupational categories collaborating 'across boundaries' traverse boundaries between educational and occupational backgrounds when they participate in common practices. Boundaries unite *and* separate. Boundary objects are not 'given'; rather, they become such within a situated practice. In fact, they operate as boundary objects (Carlile, 2002) when:

1. They establish a shared language with which individuals can represent their knowledge;
2. They provide concrete means for individuals to specify and learn about their differences and dependencies; and
3. They facilitate a process whereby individuals can transform the knowledge being used.

In the process of organizational remembering, the role of boundary objects in enacting live memories consists in temporality and in accelerating the process of meaning negotiation. We have already considered a process of relocation within a relatively stable organizational context. We may now move to observation of collaboration in project-based organizations as a case in which working between past and present and in collaboration across different occupational communities engenders the need to create and sustain new working practices. As an example I shall take the case of an engineering consultancy firm that developed an integrated procurement route to deal with client demands through a single point of contact (Cacciatori, 2008, pp. 1595–7). At the firm under study, a bid for a private finance initiative project usually involved four distinct organizational units, which over time developed various systems (manuals, checklists) to codify lessons from the past and make them available to the four units and the new people within each of them. Among the objects developed to render knowledge mobile there was one particular tool – an Excel workbook – whose role was different. It was employed to calculate costs across the life cycle (financing, design, construction and maintenance) of a building (see Box 4.5).

This example clearly demonstrates how a simple object like a workbook for the calculation of costs works both as a memory store of past experiences and as a boundary object between different occupational groups. Objects anchor memories in their materiality while enabling organizational remembering as a collective knowledgeable doing. In fact, Eugenia Cacciatori (2008) concludes her field research humorously by noting that there may be far less amnesia in project-based organizing than is commonly believed, because the mechanisms of knowledge transmission are

---

BOX 4.5   BOUNDARY OBJECTS AS MNEMONIC TOOLS

Initially, this Excel workbook was simply an assembly of individual worksheets produced by three different occupational groups: cost consultants (belonging to a traditional professional community);

facilities managers (a recent occupation not yet fully professional-
ized); and tax consultants. The purpose of this tool was to calculate the total cost of a building from the design stage to the end of
the project, the temporal profile of expenditures, and the most
convenient financial and tax arrangements. A change in the Excel
workbook started to emerge because of pressure to keep costs
low and take design choices involving a trade-off between capital
costs (sustained during construction) and occupancy costs (mainly
maintenance). Addressing these trade-offs in design choices was
difficult because the organizational memory of possible design
solutions (and associated costs) was heterogeneous and dispersed within and outside the firm. Moreover, the memory structure within the two communities was different. The professional
body of cost consultants maintained cost databases using the
standard classification of building elements employed in their profession. Facilities managers relied on the organizational memory
of costs, which were therefore not collected in the standard
manner and were dispersed among different offices within the firm.
They tended to express costs by square metres, and not on the
basis of building elements as the cost consultants did.

The Excel workbook initially reflected these differences in the
structure of memory and the practice of remembering between the
two occupational groups. It began to work as a boundary object
between them when its representation of knowledge started to be
changed so that it could be more easily manipulated. The Excel
workbook underwent several changes. A gradual project-by-
project enlargement of the information contained in the worksheet
of the cost consultants had the effect of shifting the Excel workbook from a tool representing a single building for the purpose of
its pricing, to a tool enabling comparison among potential building
designs, and therefore as a tool for off-line experimentation. As
cost information began to be perceived as an important part of
the process of managing collaboration among various professionals involved in bid preparation, more funding became available
to improve the tool, and more changes became possible. The
changes in how knowledge was represented and manipulated
increased the quantity of memory that was accessible, enhanc-
ing the tool's capacity to act across time, and not just across
groups.

Source: Cacciatori (2008, pp. 1595–7).

more subtle and less explicit, and therefore less 'docile' in the face of managerial action.

4.4   TECHNOLOGICAL INFRASTRUCTURES

We have just seen how a process of organizational remembering relied on a boundary object developed through cooperation between two communities of practitioners. I now slightly shift the focus and resume what for years was a research interest of Susan Leigh Star (2010) – as she expressed it in one of her last studies with a title paying homage to Magritte 'Ceci n'est pas un Objet-frontière [This is not a Boundary Object]'. This concerns understanding the nature of cooperative work in the absence of consensus. It is still commonly believed as well as assumed by numerous scientific models that consensus must be reached before cooperation can begin. Observation in the field of occupational groups which cooperate but do not agree is commonly reported both by Star and other researchers on working processes. How, therefore, can we explain the fact that, for example, multidisciplinary and heterogeneous groups cooperate but rarely reach consensus, and when consensus is reached, it is extremely fragile, yet the cooperation continues without problems? It is this dynamic that induced Star and Griesemer (1989) to define a boundary object in terms of the three following characteristics:

1.   The object is situated among different social worlds (or communities of practices), where it is ill-structured;
2.   When necessary, local groups work on an object, which preserves its vague identity as a common object while it is rendered more specific and better suited to local use within a community, and also more useful for work that is *not* interdisciplinary (Star, 2010, p. 22); and
3.   Groups which cooperate in the absence of consensus alternate between these two forms of the object.

An example is provided by an information system used by biologists and reported by Star (2010) in first person (see Box 4.6). How should we consider infrastructure? Again through the words of Star (2002) (see Box 4.7), we can understand how the term also covers what she calls 'tiny infrastructures'.

It is this that accounts for both the interest in cooperation in the absence of consensus and the birth of the concept of boundary object. Star introduced the concept of infrastructure as a relational concept (Star, 1999).

BOX 4.6   THE VIRTUAL LABORATORY

At the beginning of the 1990s, when the Internet was still in its infancy, I was working with a computer scientist to ensure that the Worm Community System (WCS), which should have provided a 'virtual laboratory' for data sharing, matched the needs of biologists. I would telephone a laboratory (I visited forty of them) and say something like: 'My name is S.L. Star and I am doing an analysis of the needs and usability of the Worm Community System. Do you use it? Can I come and see your work and ask you some questions?' The majority of the replies were of the kind: 'Yes, of course, we love it. Come along.'

Then, with paper and pencil ready to take fieldnotes, I would start by asking them to show me how the system had been installed and how it interacted with the work flow. The exchange usually went as follows:

Question: Can you show me how you use the WCS?
Answer: Ah, yes, erm, I know it's here somewhere. Wait while
                     I check. Ah, yes, there it is, a post-doc student uses it.
                     Pity he's not here today! [Then shouting] Does anyone
                     here use the WCS?

I would point out with great patience (at times I had travelled from England to Canada!) that they had told me they used it.

Question: Then where is it?
Answer: Ah, yes! We use it, but we've only just started.

Where did this contradiction come from, this strange amalgam of present and future? Were they trying to reassure me? Were they liars? Yet they did not hesitate to criticize the system and give me their opinions about it.

On looking more closely at communication between the system's developers and its users, I realized that it was paradoxical communication, in the sense of Bateson's double bind. What was obvious for some, was certainly not obvious for others. The users appreciated the system's interface when they sat down in front of it. But they did not know how to turn it into a functioning and reliable infrastructure. They asked the WCS team, which replied in terms that they found incomprehensible. And so I began see it as a problem of infrastructure.

Source: Star (2010, pp. 27–8).

BOX 4.7   TINY INFRASTRUCTURE

People often think of infrastructure as big, public, networked systems, such as electricity, plumbing and Internet services. Yet infrastructure has scope; it does enable action, and does have durability, but it may be quite small in scope. Consider the instruction manuals that usually come with chopsticks in a Chinese restaurant. Many restaurants no longer use these directions at all. What are they there for? Surely no one could learn to use chopsticks from either of these set of instructions. Rather, I suggest they serve as talking points for the (now rare) person who does not use chopsticks in the US, particularly in California.

Having a public inscription [the instruction leaflet] where one's ignorance can be discussed, as if it were common, forms a space at the dinner table that saves embarrassment and that sense of idiosyncratic shame.

The users of computer systems sometimes have these sorts of aids, and often do not. This is not necessarily a failure on the part of manual writers, but rather a failure to grasp the nature of legacy systems, and particularly, the invisible homes that accompany all complex work and play.

Source: Star (2002, p. 3).

Now summarized is the list of the characteristics of infrastructure drawn up by Star and Ruhleder (1996):

- *Embeddedness.* Infrastructure is contained, incorporated, in other structures, technologies and social arrangements. For instance, in the case of the WCS, the system incorporated a specific technological structure in the functionalities and the subcomponents of the software that the biologists had to use. This created problems when these functionalities did not reflect the operations to which the biologists were accustomed.

- *Transparency*. Infrastructure is *transparent* in the sense that it does not have to be reinvented for each task but invisibly supports it, and that its use is almost 'automatic'.
- *Persistence*. Infrastructure persists beyond a single event and/or situated practice.
- *Learned as a part of group membership*. Learning to do a job means learning to use the tools typical of that job, and acquiring familiarity with an activity means no longer paying attention to the tools necessary to perform it.
- *Linked with other conventions of the practice*. Infrastructure is contained and in turn contains the conventions of a community of practice. For example, the QWERTY keyboard has been learned by generations of typists, it continues in the computer keyboard and in the design of office furniture.
- *Embodies norms and standards*. Often modified by contradictory conventions, and having become transparent through use, infrastructure conditions other infrastructures or objects in a standardized manner.
- *Built on already-existing platforms and developed incrementally*. It is extremely rare, in fact, for infrastructure to be built 'from nothing' and independently from already existing platforms: optical fibres travel along old railway lines, and the most innovative software programs are always compatible with their predecessors. Technological infrastructure therefore inherits the strengths and weaknesses of the preceding architecture.
- *Being visible only when it breaks down*. Technological infrastructure is visible when it breaks down. Even when there are recovery devices, these only make visible what the infrastructure made invisible.
- *Being repaired by modular increments*. Often because of local features and meanings, changes in infrastructure take time, they require negotiations and adjustments with other aspects of the system.

Star and Ruhleder's (1996) study provides a first example of the 'how' and the 'why' of a situated approach to technology within sociomaterial practices. The 'how' consists in the prolonged ethnographic observation of the everyday work of actors and in the inductive procedure of the researcher. The 'why' resides in the pervasiveness of technologies in contemporary workplaces and their 'invisibility' when they function, but at the same time require a great deal of 'invisible work' (Star and Strauss, 1999) to make them function.

We have seen thus far how humans and non-humans work together in sociomaterial practices. But before concluding this chapter on materiality,

I intend to show the following: that physical space is a resource for practice; that working is a situated performance within a context equipped for the spatio-temporal conduct of practice; and that objects help humans to be competent. In this regard, the concept of improvisational choreography can help us analyse how a workplace is also a workspace – that is, the situational territory discussed in the first chapter.

4.5 EQUIPPED ENVIRONMENT AND IMPROVISATIONAL CHOREOGRAPHY

Returning once again to the metaphor of the climber and the co-production of handholds during a climb (presented in Chapter 1), we may imagine that the rock becomes somehow equipped to facilitate the climb if the climber regularly returns to the rock face or leaves pegs to help other climbers, or again, sets up a rock climbing gym. What I want to show with this shift of perspective is that when a practice becomes such – that is, it has become recurrent and coalesced into habits – the context of the practice is very probably an equipped context in which the main handholds for regular performance of the practice are known; they have been made familiar by repetition of the practice; they have been equipped so as to elicit their habitual use. It is now that artefacts, tools, objects and technologies come into play, and therefore the relationship with materiality (Svabo, 2009) which anchors relations and meanings and 'suggests actions'. Numerous concepts have been proposed to express this interpretative shift from the context as a 'container' more or less neutral and indifferent to the actions that develop within it to the context as a resource (Lave's 'arena' and 'setting'): the idea of instrumentation (Rabardel, 1995) as an arrangement to have a relationship of instrumentality (that is, that instruments are not such in themselves but become so in the relation with the action that they serve); the affordance (Gibson, 1979) of materiality that suggests its use to support a utilization; the intra-action of Barad (2003) which co-articulates meanings and materialities; the concept of 'jigging' (Kirsh, 1995, p. 37) as a way to prepare and structure the environment. The more completely prepared the environment is, the easier it becomes to accomplish one's task.

In other words, the recursiveness of practices establishes a relationship of co-production with the environment in which not only are the handholds for action discovered in the course of that action, but delegated to these handholds is the execution of certain operations of the same practice or certain functions, such as remembering (Grosjean and Bonneville, 2009), where helping not to forget is anchored in the materiality of signalling artefacts and technologies. Embedded in the theme of the equipped environment that anchors activities by suggesting to practitioners 'what next' in performance of the practice is the idea of improvisational choreography proposed by Whalen et al. (2002) when describing the arrangement of the objects and the gestures, as well as the body, of a call centre operator. Just as choreography is a matter of space and time – and a somewhat extemporaneous composition in this case – so the operator conveys to the caller that the latter's request is being handled fluidly – without impeding the interaction and therefore with competence – by skilful management of an equipped environment and with a cadence that does not leave gaps in the interaction (Whalen et al., 2002, pp. 245–53). The locally organized, improvisational choreography can be described as a kind of 'performance' (Goffman, 1959) which is shared by sales representatives, which is methodical in character, and which is grounded in the exigencies of their work. It is smoothly done by the representative when he[1] is on the telephone with a customer with his voice – in terms of the pacing and phrasing of talk – and, conjointly, with various artefacts and tools at his workstation (see Box 4.8).

BOX 4.8   THE OPERATOR AT THE CALL CENTRE

We are at the supply order centre (SOC), of a corporation that designs and manufactures office products. SOC representatives receive salaries, but they also are paid with commissions based largely on team performance. They work out of standard office cubicles set up as call centre workstations. Each cubicle contains various items of call centre equipment and many kinds of documents.

An especially important priority in the representatives' working practice is completing calls quickly and efficiently – within three or four minutes. A major reason for this concern is their expressed desire to take as many calls as possible in order to increase sales volume, which will then contribute to the pay of team members. Moreover, they do not want to keep other customers waiting on hold in the call queue for long periods, which would probably not be good for sales. At the same time, the sales representatives also stress that calls cannot simply be rushed through, and that their work is 'not just taking orders'. The representatives' concern is to have their calls go smoothly by minimizing any awkward moments as far as possible. One such awkwardness is a temporary halt in the conversation. They describe this phenomenon experientially: they do not have the information on their computer screen, or in some document that is readily visible, and they need to use it at that very moment in the conversation with the customer. They recognize that a customer's *only* access to their work is what he/she *hears* during the conversation. For the SOC sales representatives what is at stake is nothing less than *displaying professional competence in and through interactional proficiency*. The possibility of achieving this interactional proficiency depends on the representative's employment of various artefacts. The most important of these are: telephone headset; PC with a keyboard and mouse; software applications installed on the PC; the company network for entering all supply orders and retrieving information from the company's product and customer databases; paper documents of various formats and types that also contain information on products, customers, work processes and the like; paper and pen for writing notes. Each of these technologies implicates different means or modes of action, often in combination: talking; typing; writing; reading; lifting and turning or otherwise handling. In summary, achieving a hearably competent performance – organized around a closely interrelated set of practical concerns – requires an improvisational choreography of various means of action using different technologies and artefacts to carry off that performance.

The methodical features of improvisational choreography are four basic 'steps', as in a dance:

- *Arranging objects in the workspace and positioning the body in and for that arrangement.* To the right of the representative's computer monitor is a list of all the customers on his territory and their account numbers (very important when a customer cannot remember his or her account number). A small notepad and pen are placed to the right of the keyboard, where they can be used very rapidly by simply moving the right hand off the keyboard. A large flip-file of paper documents is positioned just to his left, and it is used to access pricing information and enter the product's number into the computer. The same information is available online, but the representatives prefer to have it on their left side, where it can be read simply 'at a glance'. The body and its positioning is part of this 'arranging of objects in space'. In fact, the representative has trained himself to use his left hand to manipulate the mouse. This is because he wants to be able to keep his right hand free to touch-type numbers on the numerical keypad area of his keyboard, which is located on its far right, and to write on his notepad, also placed to the right. These artefacts and his body have thus both been ordered and adapted for the choreography of action.

● *Counteracting problems generated by the immutable organization of the software.* For example, the computer software does not provide any way to record the customer's name immediately when the identification number has been entered; the system is insensitive to the basic social fact of talk-in-interaction. In order to keep the customer's name for later use, and thus preserve an important dimension of the social interaction, the representative uses his notepad and pen. This requires, once again, a close choreography of action. He begins to move his right hand and to shift his gaze away from the screen and keyboard towards the notepad at the precise instant when the caller says 'my name . . .'.

● *Anticipating events.* Sometime the representative furnishes the customer with information before he/she asks for it. This information comes from two different media: the flip-file of documents on his left and the SOC database on the screen. The representative carefully phrases his information delivery into coherent chunks, and pauses between these chunks, so that the customer has time to write down the pricing information. However, that phrasing and pacing of the representative's delivery is also organized so as to give him time to locate information on his computer, using his keyboard and mouse, *before* it has to be actually read and then 'placed' in his turn-at-talk. The representative closely coordinates the use of multiple means of action (reading, talking with the customer, typing) with multiple tools and artefacts. The problem, he says, is 'not running out of words before I get to what is needed for what I have to say next.'

● *Close coordination of multiple means and tools.* We have already seen this in the previous example. One should bear in mind that customers often require multiple items of information at the same time, and the representative has to anticipate the search for the next item of information at the same time as he is answering the first request.

Source: Whalen et al. (2002, pp. 245–53).

The concept of equipped environment enables us to see the spatio-temporal dimensions of a workplace, how it is sociomaterially organized into a workspace and a situational territory, and how performing a work practice may be seen as an improvisational choreography involving knowledgeable bodies in relation with a physical and discursive environment.

I draw from the study by Whalen et al. (2002, p. 254, original emphasis) a methodological reflection of relevance to the empirical observation of working practices. They write:

> If we had access only to the audio track for this call, with no access to the video and thus no *visual* access to the rep's actions that we have just described, we would be in the same position as the customer. . . . The result is a sales rep who is *hearably* in complete command of the information needed for the task at hand, with the crux of that performance – the actions needed to find, read, and fluently put that information into words – cloaked from view by both the limitations of the telephone channel and the rep's corporeal skills.

This observation highlights one of the main problems involved methodologically in the observation and representation of working practices. In fact, every way of 'seeing' is inevitably conditioned by the tools used to do it, and therefore every 'seeing' is also a 'non-seeing'.

4.6 TO SUM UP

In this chapter I have examined technologies, using this term to denote everything that elsewhere I have called non-human actants: objects, tools, artefacts, technological networks. I have done so from a relational epistemological position of constitutive entanglement between the technological and the social: that is, without giving prominence to either humans or technology, or their reciprocal relationship, but rather considering them as inextricably related.

The performativity of technology is sociomaterial, and it emerges when it enters into situated practices. In order to illustrate how this happens and how it can be studied, I have focused on objects and on the ethnography of non-humans. Within sociomaterial practices, objects may exert affiliative power in keeping together other objects and humans while shaping their associations; or objects may act as objects for live memories when they perform associations between past, present and future, and in so doing enact organizational remembering as an organizational practice.

Sociomaterial practices allow us to look at the context of working practices as a situational territory, an infrastructure and an equipped environment. Practising therefore may be seen as an improvisational choreography, as bodily (knowledgeable) movements within an equipped environment that connect and weave relationships both in a situated and extemporaneous way and as dislocations, coordinating multiple means and tools, counteracting problems and anticipating events.

In this chapter the theme of sociomateriality has been explored through the lens of technology and technological infrastructure. It has been illustrated with the following empirical examples:

- The case of the use of BlackBerry devices showed the performativity of technology when it enters into practice and it is entangled with people's choices and activities.
- The case of the hospital ward illustrated the affiliative power of objects in holding together sociomaterial relations.
- The case of memory objects and their role in relocating the past demonstrated the temporality of a practice and remembering as a practice phenomenon.
- The case of the Excel workbook continued the analysis of memory objects as mnemonic tools.
- The case of the virtual laboratory illustrated the concept of infrastructure and tiny infrastructures.
- Finally, the case of the call centre and the improvisational choreography conveyed the sense of how humans and non-humans dance within an equipped environment and enact knowing-in-practice.

NOTE

1. Since Whalen et al. (2002) have observed, recorded and analysed a phone conversation conducted by a male representative, I refer to their example and use only the male pronoun.

5. Learning to talk in practice and about practice

People work with their hands, arms, heads and bodies, but they also work with words, language and communication situated in interactions. Indeed, one may say that the more manual work diminishes in quantity and becomes immaterial and mediated by ICTs, the more communicative competence is important for efficient work and the prevention of errors and accidents. Moreover, in contemporary society, the expansion of services makes communicative competence of crucial importance, in that talk is not merely a way to communicate but, on the contrary, the principal ingredient of a service.

In work situations, talk is almost never talk for its own sake. Instead, as Boutet and Gardin write (2001, p. 97):

> Language is always directed towards an end, towards an action to be accomplished, a solution to be found, a damage to be mended, or a diagram to be understood. Moreover, language is rarely independent from the technical world of machines, utensils, and objects. This technical world shapes and even constrains the linguistic activities of operators.

In this chapter, therefore, we will analyse work as a discursive practice, that is, as a 'doing' and a 'knowing how to do' with words.

Just as the term 'sociomateriality' (without the hyphen) was used in Chapter 4 to make the entanglement between the social and the material graphically visible, so the aim in this chapter is to show that discursiveness is material (suffice it to consider that speaking requires a voice!). But it is also to argue that practices are 'materialsemiotic': I shall use this neologism with the hyphen between the two terms removed.

Describing the boundaries of discourse analysis and its inner connections (for instance among the anthropology of language, sociolinguistics and the ethnography of communication) would fall outside the scope of the discussion here. Nevertheless, following Boutet and Maingueneau (2005), we may say that the 1990s witnessed a general increase in attention paid to the uses of language in specific contexts and for particular purposes (Language for Specific Purposes, LSP), and that they also witnessed a growth of pragmatic interest in the use of language as a specific form of activity. Between the anthropology of language and sociolinguistics there lies the ethnography of communication (Gumperz, 1989; Hymes, 1974; Matera, 2002; Mondada, 2002). Moreover, there is a long tradition of ethnomethodological studies which consider the production of everyday organizational action through talk in interaction (Llewellyn, 2008).

Without engaging in subtle distinctions, we merely point out that contributions to discourse analysis have also been made by conversation analysis and the sociology of communication. Since language interests us as a situated form of linguistic mediation of work activities, we refer to this set of practices with the expression 'discursive practices'. They are practices because they are normatively sustained by a community of practitioners and are therefore learned and performed as an inseparable part of a practitioner's competence. Moreover, they are practices because they are collectively performed as an integral part of work: indeed, the organizing of the practices themselves comes about through discursive practices. Practitioners engage in conversations in practice and about practice not only to reach agreements but also to celebrate identity and the logic of the practice, and to participate in broader societal discourses.

We may conclude that discursive practices are the medium for the conveyance of knowledge, both for what language does and for the social relationships that it constructs. As we saw in Chapter 3, naming something 'knowledge' presupposes a coding practice within a domain of scrutiny, and the practice of coding is a collective achievement of a naming subject which, in naming knowledge objects, also names knowing subjects. Therefore, bearing in mind that, almost always, talk not only enables work but is also work in itself, we shall illustrate in detail how it is learned and how communicative competence is deployed in working practices. By 'communicative competence' we mean the knowledge necessary to use language appropriately in relation to specific cultural contexts (Hymes, 1974).

5.1   INSTITUTIONAL DISCURSIVE PRACTICES

The expression 'institutional conversation' essentially serves to distinguish talk-as-work from ordinary conversation. In work contexts, use is made of both ordinary conversation (which has crucial specific purposes, such as creating and recreating the work climate) and institutional conversation, whose purpose is to enable performance of the work and the reproduction of patterns of interaction which give stability to working practices.

A book considered a milestone in the analysis of discursive practices in institutional contexts is the collection of essays edited by Drew and

Heritage (1992). These essays analyse diverse work contexts and illustrate how, through situated discursive practices, some types of work are produced through the interaction between a professional acting as an institution's representative and the users of that institution. As the interaction between the professional and consumer proceeds, the institution is reproduced.

To give an idea of the contexts analysed in this book we may refer to Bergman's essay (1992), which describes the activity of a psychiatrist and his/her competence in asking questions to explore the patient's mental state. Bergman describes this linguistic competence in terms of 'discretion'. How do people 'do discretion' as a situated working practice? Bergman shows that discretion results from collaboration between patient and psychiatrist. It is produced through the choice of words and the management of turn-taking between the two people. A similar theme is that of 'cautiousness' between an interviewer and an interviewee, who may perceive the questions as hostile or invasive. Involved in both cases is an 'art' which consists in knowing how to ask questions, evaluate the replies received, create a climate which 'neutralizes' the asymmetry between the participants in such conversations, and avoid making overt judgements in regard to the replies.

One realizes from these two examples that, unlike ordinary conversations, these types of institutional conversation are real professional activities which activate a specific competence learned in different ways: through explicit training on the job and/or by simple imitation, watching and/or listening to experts as they perform an activity.

Another institutional context examined in Drew and Heritage's book (1992) is a small claims court (Atkinson, 1992; Button, 1992) where the arbitrator uses forms of interaction which avoid expressing any judgement on the statements being made. Again in regard to questioning, another essay (Maynard, 1992) focuses on the professional abilities of institutional actors in framing questions so as to collect raw materials for their specific work, and to produce the work context collaboratively with the user while the situated encounter produces and reproduces the institution.

Then considered is the activity of answer-giving. The essay by Gumperz (1992), for example, focuses on a multicultural context to show how the answers of people from other cultures are difficult to interpret in interactions with mother-tongue officials, and how prosody (accent, tone or intonation) plays a decisive role in these interactions.

All these examples show that there are institutional settings (for instance, courts or social-health services) in which conversation is the essence of the work, and they suggest other instances in which the management of relations with the client, the patient or the user is crucial for the production of a good-quality service and for management of interpersonal relationships. In fact, if we consider the previous examples, it is clear that both the parties concerned (whether the situation is an emergency call, a medical consultation, a deposition in court or a job interview) are oriented to the institutional task, to the goals established, to the resources that can be mobilized in the interaction, and to the parties' pre-understandings of the situation.

There are three main characteristics of institutional conversations (Drew and Heritage, 1992, p. 22):

1. The institutional interaction involves orientation by at least one of the participants to a goal, task or identity specifically associated with the institution concerned. This can therefore be described as an instrumental discursive practice, in that it is directed to a specific goal and is usually performed in a conventional way and/or with a communicative style determined by the conventions of a specific community of practice.
2. The institutional interaction may involve the presence of *specific constraints* on one or both the participants which they can use as *specific resources* in their interaction.
3. The institutional conversation may be associated with interpretative schemes and procedures specific to that particular institutional context.

There are then differences among institutional conversations due to the type of context. For instance, an emergency telephone call to the police is wholly directed to the despatch of a patrol car. Hence the telephone conversation will typically have a ('top-down' pattern). Conversely, a post-delivery examination by an obstetrician is generally a poorly defined task, and the institutional interaction will be mainly characterized by a negotiation to define the content of the examination. The conversation therefore will more likely have a 'bottom-up' structure.

We shall now discuss in detail a discursive practice that can be called 'giving bad news'. This may take place in numerous work settings, but it is more frequent in some professions than others. Clinical contexts furnish various examples. In fact, it is in one such context that Douglas Maynard (1992) analyses how a professional has the recipient participate so that it is the latter who verbally expresses the 'bad news'. We see how the practice of 'giving bad news' is reconstructed from the account of a mother who recalls how she received the news that she had given birth to a boy with Down's syndrome[1] (Jacobson, 1969, cited in Maynard, 1992, p. 333):

The doctor came in and he drew the curtains around my cubicle and I thought, oh no, you know. And he told me the baby was born completely healthy, but he's not completely normal. [At that moment the mother articulated aloud and in colloquial terms the fact that the baby was affected by Down's syndrome.] And I've never seen such a baby before in my life, but all of a sudden the flat features, the thrusting of the tongue, you know, just kind of hit me in the face. And that poor doctor couldn't bring himself to say a word. He said, it shouldn't have happened to you, not to your age bracket.

In this situation, the signals emitted by the doctor consist in his drawing the curtains around the bed to create greater intimacy for the interaction, and his allusion to an 'abnormality'. On the basis of her previous fears, and having noticed something odd, the mother guesses that her child is affected by Down's syndrome. This diagnosis the doctor indirectly confirms by saying that it is a rare event, considering the age of the mother. This exchange shows that the bearer of bad news has difficulty in expressing it directly. By not stating it and merely confirming the inference drawn by the recipient, he is able to manage transmission of the news as a collaborative activity, a co-production of the situation. This is called 'co-implication of the parties' in the breaking of bad news.

In clinical contexts – where this activity is a working practice – the professionals have developed a routine with which to co-implicate the recipient of bad news when the diagnosis is announced. This is the 'perspective-display series' a device that operates in manner to co-implicate the recipient's perspective in the presentation of diagnosis, and that consists of three moves:

1. The professional asks the patient (or the recipient of the bad news) a question or invites him/her to give his/her opinion or perspective display on the situation;
2. The recipient responds and/or expresses his/her assessment; and
3. The professional relates to the recipient and assesses.

Besides the above moves of clue-giving, guessing and confirming, the medical practice of communicating a diagnosis also includes the crucial move of 'perspective-display', which is a common feature of institutional interaction. One should also bear in mind that, in this type of interactive exchange, the recipients of bad news are not always ready to collaborate or to accept the professional's point of view.

For example, when Maynard (1992, p. 339, original emphasis) studied a centre for the evaluation of mental and behavioural disorders in children, he analysed how – when the doctors gave bad news – the problem might be denied by the parents. The following extract between a doctor (Dr) and a mother (M), illustrates how the doctors at the centre worked to create the conversational context in which they could break bad news:

Dr: How's Bobby doing?
M: Well he's doing uh pretty good you know, especially in the school. I explained the teacher what you told me that he might be sent into a special class maybe, that I was not sure. And *he* says you know I ask his opinion, an' he says that he is doing pretty good in the school, that he was responding you know in uhm everything that he tells them. Now he thinks that he's not gonna need to be sent to another school.
Dr: He doesn't think that he's gonna need to be sent?
M: Yeah that he was catching on a little bit uh more you know like I said I-I-I *know* that he needs a – you know I was 'splaining to her that he needs some special class or something.
Dr: Wu' whatta you think his *problem* is?
M: Speech.
Dr: Yeah, yeah his main problem is a – you know a *language* problem.
M: Yeah, language.

The example shows how delivery of the diagnosis is a negotiative process of confirmation, reformulation and elaboration. The two parties also begin to use a shared language, and the fact that the parent confirms and accepts the diagnosis is a collaborative outcome due to the fact that the mother, in responding to the invitation to state her point of view, furnishes discursive material which makes it possible to mark out terrain on which agreement on the diagnosis can be reached.

In conclusion, we see how, in discursive practices of institutional interaction constructed on 'perspective-display', the participants in the diagnostic activity are co-implicated in it. With this type of interaction, the professionals are able to do their work – that is, formulate a diagnosis and have it accepted – through conversation and an interaction which includes the point of view of the patient or the person indirectly involved. In this discursive practice, the purpose of inviting the patient to state his/her point of view is to elicit material on which to base a momentary agreement, produce confirmation of what the patient has to say, and progressively to construct confirmation of the diagnosis, with its subsequent reformulation, specification and other technical elaborations. It is therefore a process of alignment among the professional, the patient (or the user) and the clinical diagnosis.

Note that the effect of this discursive practice is also the production of situated social identities. The doctor does not put him/herself forward as someone whose evaluation of the situation is a scientific discovery; nor is the patient constructed as someone transported from a state of ignorance to one of knowledge. Instead, the interactional work of co-implication produces the patient as someone with imperfect knowledge, and the doctor as a professional who by modifying and adding something to what the patient already knows or suspects, ratifies and institutionalizes the point of view collaboratively produced.

Studies on institutional interaction are almost exclusively based on conversational analysis, and they are so precisely because their concern is to conduct comparative analysis of institutional discourse. They focus on the following elements in particular:

- Lexical choices, that is the way in which the speaker evokes the institutional context of his/her discourse. A technical (for instance) lexicon conveys specialized knowledge and an institutional identity. Often, when an institutional representative speaks, he/she refers to him/herself as 'we', because the institution is speaking through that individual. Likewise, institutional talk sometimes uses universalistic expressions in order to sanctify the institution's discourse, which is manifest in the specific situation but transcends it.
- The design of conversational turns. This comprises the twofold move of selecting: (i) the activity that the turn is intended to perform (confirming or defending the assertion made in the preceding turn); and (ii) the details of the verbal construct with which the turn will be performed.
- The organization of sequences. The question/answer sequence, for example, is common to numerous institutional activities in contexts such as schools, law courts, clinical practice or social work.
- The overall organization of the interactional structure. Emergency calls or teleconsultancy in medicine (Fele, 2008; Gherardi, 2010), for example, are structured by standard procedures and established sequences of phases. The same applies to education and class work.
- Social relations. The asymmetry of institutional interactions distinguishes them from ordinary conversations. Handling this asymmetry requires knowledge about how to manage the relation between discursive statuses/roles and rights/obligations, constructing 'situated identities' which respect the dignity of the person. For example, in relations between professionals and clients, the discursive rights of the professional derive from the institutional interaction (which steers the discourse), but the asymmetry also derives from the skewed distribution of knowledge between the participants in the interaction, and from the difference between the perspective of the institution, which treats the client as a routine 'case', and of the client, who sees his/her 'case' as unique and personal.

We may conclude that institutional interactions are interesting settings in which to examine work as a set of discursive practices which reveal new aspects of work through speech. We accordingly now examine a frequent and characteristic occurrence in many work contexts: the shift handover.

5.2   HANDING OVER AS A MATERIALSEMIOTIC PRACTICE

What is the principal difference between ordinary conversations and conversations in work situations? A first answer was given in the previous section, whilst in this section we start with the indications furnished by Goffman (1981).

Workplace conversations differ from ordinary conversations in two main respects:

1. The verbal exchange is subordinate to the work activity; and
2. The talk is open, in the sense that the speakers may suddenly start a brief exchange and then lapse back into silence with no particular conversational closure. They apparently do no more than add new items to an ongoing conversation.

Workplace conversations are therefore 'open' in the sense that they are largely unpredetermined and participation is fluid; but also in the sense that the 'spectators' (people present but not involved) may also participate in them, just as other participants may speak without addressing anyone in particular. It is as if conversations in workplaces are constantly ongoing and the participants 'log in' and 'log out' (for instance, when a task entirely absorbs their attention) and then return to full participation. We have already discussed these conversational patterns in the RER control room (Joseph, 1994; see Chapter 2 of this book). Léglise (1998) calls them *fluctuating configurations* activated by the progress of the interaction, by the actions that develop during the interaction, and by engaged participation in the interaction.

Focusing on these conversational modes raises various methodological problems. Principal among them is defining the indicators of participation in conversation so that it is possible to identify who is addressing whom, who is listening to whom, and who is present but not listening. There are indicators such as body posture, tone of voice, direction of the gaze and (obviously) turn-taking. For these reasons, it would be preferable to use video rather than just audio recordings or, if neither are available, to be able to annotate the progress of these fluctuating configurations and the fluctuations in the collective patterns of paying attention.

In France, the interdisciplinary studies produced since the second half of the 1980s by the *Langage et Travail* network have contributed greatly to bringing out the practical dimension of the use of language, especially in work settings (Borzeix and Fraenkel, 2001). They have raised new research questions, such as the role of temporality in speech processing, or the semiotic difference between oral and written discourse. A paper (Borzeix, 2003) on the specific contribution of this French network to the contemporary debate has emphasized that it is particularly attentive to the twofold nature of language as a working practice. The latter is valuable in promoting initiative, creativity, innovation and participation; but at the same time, the managerial use made of it may serve the purposes of normalization, standardization, codification and formalization.

We now consider – drawing on a study by Michèle Grosjean (2004) – how a very common practice where work is performed in shifts (with handovers from one shift to the next) constitutes a situation typical of work with words, as well as with specific artefacts.

With reference to shift handovers among nurses, one characteristic of this working practice is the absence of regulations, in that the procedures are dictated by the everyday functioning of the department. The only standardized procedure is the check conducted on the patients, which takes place in alphabetical order or ward by ward. Moreover, in interactive terms, the exchange follows a fixed and predictable pattern: the nurses going off shift are always those who initiate the exchange, even if other personnel are present and/or involved, and the talk centres on the patients and on equally predictable matters like therapies. Other topics to do with the organization – work schedules or the doctors – are absent or raised in relation to the patients' therapies. The verbal exchange of information is almost always accompanied by written messages, both in the nursing logbook and on other artefacts like whiteboards, cards or similar (which are updated before the shift handover and serve as prompts for subsequent actions). Although the script is almost invariable, its performance can vary greatly according to the habits of the specific department, the ways in which the participants take up their work stations, the 'dramaturgy' of the session, the use of written supports, the structuring of the discourses and the logistics of the place where the handover process takes place.

Dialogue between two people is the usual pattern of handovers, especially when they are made in a space specifically allocated to them and described as a 'monoactivity' place (that is, restricted to only that activity). Although this is a dialogue, it usually takes place in the presence of other personnel, like nurses and auxiliaries.

By contrast, polycentric conversation is the most frequent communicative mode in all other situations. Consider, for example, the handover now described in Box 5.1. We are in a paediatric department. The conversation concerns a small boy for whom, after many years, forced feeding has been suspended for some evenings a week. This means that the boy can eat with the other children in the dining room instead of having to remain alone in the ward.

BOX 5.1   HANDOVER AT A PAEDIATRIC WARD

N1 and CCA1 are respectively the day shift nurse and childcare auxiliary going off duty; N2 and CCA2 are respectively the night shift nurse and childcare auxiliary coming on duty.

N1:   No tube-feeding, no APC . . .
CCA1:   In fact we hadn't realized last Thursday that . . . there'd be a day without tube- feeding uh
N2:   . . . yeah
N1:   And since it's the first Thursday.
CCA1:   . . . he [the boy] obeys whatever you tell him – it's incredible – this evening, you say any little thing.
N1:   It's too much
CCA2:   . . . oh really
CCA1:   Oh yeah
N2:   I thought you were joking . . .
N1:   . . . you realize it's the very first night he has no treatment.

[The conversation splits into two parallel dialogues conducted in low voices.]

N2: Tomorrow, I said to C . . ., uh gotta do it early uh . . .
N1: Yes it's me tomorrow . . .
N2: . . . around 5 o'clock to give him his . . . [inaudible]
N1: Yes
N2: If it is possible . . .

CCA1: Usually we have to yell at them/with him it's upsetting for us
. . .
CCA2: Ah now that's good
CCA1: But now this evening say uh . . . I told him you read but you don't touch the games uh . . . you read . . .

[The conversation resumes in louder voices and with more assertive tones.]

N1:   It's unbelievable because I mean it was last Thursday in
           fact that it is prescribed we didn't realize we absolutely
           didn't realize, that one day . . . [a week] there'd be no
           tube-feeding and no APC . . .
CCA2:   We didn't realize, we were focusing on . . . [inaudible].

Source: Grosjean (2004, pp. 48–9).

Neither the nurses nor the childcare auxiliaries were aware of the change of therapy. They are excited and want to share their pleasure. The conversation thus becomes emotionally charged and, at a certain point, splits into two subconversations between the two professional groups: the nurses continue their conversation about therapies and the handover, while the two auxiliaries talk about the boy and their feelings for him. In fact, more than there being two parallel conversations, the same topic is treated more technically by the nurses and more emotionally by the auxiliaries. The shift from dialogue to polycentric conversation is marked by a lowering of voice tone and intensity, and the resumption of dialogue is marked by an increase in voice volume and tone.

Michèle Grosjean's (2004) study compares handovers in three departments of the same hospital. It describes how the same working practice is sustained by different communicative and interactive modalities according to the participants' ongoing activities, their professional and social statuses, the distribution of knowledge among the participants, the physical configuration of the place in which the handover takes place, and finally the habits and 'local' culture that have consolidated ritual and tacit forms of sharing. It would be excessive to provide a detailed description of these patterns here; suffice it to bear in mind that even a routine and simple working practice of this kind, sustained by an equally simple script, is enacted in very different ways. The example reported is intended to highlight the situated and open nature of conversation in workplaces, the duality of its purpose – instrumental and expressive at the same time – and the fluidity of participation in the conversation.

Finally, there is another aspect of talk in workplaces to be considered: it has to do with saying, not saying and camouflaging what is said.

5.3   CAMOUFLAGING CONVERSATION

Talk involves a delicate operation of assessing the situation in order to decide how to make speech appropriate to the situation, and how to use speech to change it. In other words, this concerns awareness that the context shapes discursive practices and that these in turn shape the context.

Let us therefore see how, in work situations, communities of practice configure and reconfigure their discursive practices according to the space, the time, and the actual or potential audience to the conversation. To illustrate this point I recall Goffman's (1959) concept of 'spatial region'. I shall, in fact, present a case which apparently challenges this concept and I illustrate the work of the anaesthetists in a hospital pre-operating room.

In order to distinguish between the forms of interaction that occur in places and at times accessible to the eyes and ears of 'outsiders', on the one hand, and those that occur in more private places and times on the other hand, Goffman (1959) uses the concepts of 'front stage' and 'backstage'. To employ a theatrical metaphor, social life can in fact be viewed as a stage on which the actors comply with what is prescribed by the activity and they enact a reality that does not present any oddity for the external observer as long as they are 'on stage'. But then, when the curtain falls, they criticize themselves, congratulate each other and talk about themselves in private. The same applies to a restaurant, where there is usually a door separating what happens in the kitchen ('backstage') from what happens in the dining room ('front stage'). In other workplaces, there are spaces not accessible to the public, or spaces accessible to one occupational community but not to others. In hospital departments, for example, there are frequently rooms or areas set aside for use by the nurses and where the presence of the doctors is not welcome. Spaces may therefore be created *ad hoc* to separate 'front office' activities from 'back office' ones, or which have been appropriated and marked out as territories belonging specifically to one group. Or, again, the separation between front stage and backstage is marked in temporal terms: the office of a manager (for instance) may be a backstage place where he/she can rest for a moment by taking off his/her jacket and putting his/her feet on the desk, but it then becomes the place where he/she wields authority and power.

In medical settings, it is interesting that the anaesthesia room (unlike the operating theatre, where the patient is unconscious, and the clinic, where the patient is perfectly conscious) is a situation in which the patient passes from one state to the other. For the personnel working in the anaesthesia room, transition from front stage to backstage is tied neither to the physical environment nor to the temporal determination, but to the patient's state of consciousness. To be noted in this case, too, is that the illustration which we provide is focused on a particular type of work, but the same discursive practice is common to almost all work situations. In fact, the presence/absence of the public (clients, users, students, patients) changes the relational and discursive situation within a group of colleagues. But it may happen that the group has to enact 'private' communicative forms also in the presence of the public. Let us see what happens in an operating theatre by recalling the description of Hindmarsh and Pilnick (2002) (see Box 5.2).

It sometimes happened that, during this phase of their work, the team had to talk together in 'private', or they had to discuss and negotiate matters not to be seen or heard by the patient. In other words, the team had to create a backstage while they were 'on stage', so to speak, and simultaneously with performance of their action.

BOX 5.2 DISCURSIVE PRACTICES IN THE OPERATING THEATRE

Hindmarsh and Pilnick (2002) analysed the discursive practices of a team of anaesthetists who often found themselves working with colleagues whom they had never met before. It was extraordinary, they wrote, to observe how interactive patterns change as the patient lost consciousness. Once the anaesthetist had checked (by lifting an eyelid and/or asking the patient a question without receiving an audible or visible reply) that the patient was unconscious, the team changed its mode of interaction. In fact, as long as the patient was awake, the ongoing discursive practice (of both the anaesthetist and the nurse) was directed at the patient. It focused on how he/she was feeling and on explaining the anaesthetization procedure, thus verbalizing the sense of the gestures being made. The behaviour of the personnel was sensitive to the presence of the patient as long as he/she was awake. But when the patient was unconscious, the conversation shifted to private matters, to work to be done, experiences with the surgeons, the agitated state of the patient, hospital politics, mutual acquaintances (if they did not know each other) and so on. Moreover, if junior doctors or trainee nurses were part of the team, they were not usually involved in the conversation when the patient was awake. But when the patient was anaesthetized, the experienced personnel attended to the training of the novices and 'put them to the test'.

Source: Hindmarsh and Pilnick (2002, pp. 153–6).

How was this separation and disconnection achieved? The work group engaged in a practice of camouflage. The need for this practice is well expressed by the words of Goffman cited by Hindmarsh and Pilnick (2002, p. 152): 'when one's activity occurs in the presence of other persons, some aspects of the activity are expressively accentuated and other aspects, which might discredit the fostered impression, are suppressed'.

The team thus avoided openly discussing their concerns in the presence of the patient, or asking for explanations that might cast doubt on their professionalism. Rather, a backstage was created in which they could interact non-verbally, using the part of the anaesthesia room which was not visible to the patient (usually the area behind him/her). Hindmarsh and Pilnick (2002) discuss one case of camouflage which exploited space, and then illustrate another case in which the camouflage was created within the conversation itself.

In the first example of exploiting space outside the patient's visual range, the team decided by means of gestures that they would use the anaesthesia with gas rather than liquid, which would have increased the influx of the gas. As the non-verbal exchange took place behind the patient, the senior anaesthetist talked to the patient about the odour that he would smell and about how he would feel, without the latter perceiving that the team had discussed and negotiated by gestures a change in the usual procedure.

The second example of camouflage shows how, while the anaesthetist talked to the patient, he sent messages to the nurse, transmitting information and instructions camouflaged in the ordinary conversation.

The fragment of conversation reported in Hindmarsh and Pilnick's article (2002, fragment 4, p. 156), accompanied by photographs, begins with the injection of the anaesthetic. Thereafter, some seconds pass before the patient becomes unconscious. In this lapse of time, the nurse must ensure that, as the patient slips into unconsciousness his arm does not bang against something, or that he does not hurt himself, and that the oxygen mask is beyond his reach. The nurse holds the patient's arm until the anaesthetic takes effect and the patient falls asleep. How long this takes depends on the type of anaesthetic and on the physique of the patient. In fact, the nurse is faced with a practical problem: when should he let go of the oxygen mask and grasp the patient's arm? The fragment shows that the anaesthetist is aware not only of the nurse's problem but also of the trajectory that the patient's body will follow in space. The anaesthetist gives the nurse useful information while apparently continuing to talk to the patient. I report the conversation with the anaesthetist (A) and patient (P) in a simplified form:

A: This is the stuff that's going to put you off to sleep . . . now sometimes this stings a little bit as it goes up your arm. How does that feel?

P: Okay.

A: Okay?

P: Hm-hmmm.

A: Right.

A: Now in just fifteen or twenty seconds you're going to start to feel very, very drowsy and you'll drift off to sleep . . . and the next thing you know it'll all be finished.

If we had a video recording of this fragment, we would also be able to observe how the verbal communication accompanies the non-verbal communication, how the anaesthetist and the nurse synchronize their gazes to ensure that both are focused on the few seconds left when the countdown begins, and how they move their bodies in space. Moreover, when the nurse raises his hand toward the mask as if *to* take hold of it and then rests his hand back down again, this communicates readiness for action to the anaesthetist. The video images would show us how the anaesthetist's body and attention are first directed to the patient's arm and the syringe, and then shift to his face, where the effects of the anaesthetic will be first apparent. The images would also show how the anaesthetist's bodily orientations are matched in space and time by those of the nurse. When the nurse puts his hand on the oxygen mask, the anaesthetist says 'fifteen to twenty seconds' to the patient, and the nurse can be seen removing his hand from the mask. In fact, the information is not directed at the patient, but at the nurse, to whom the anaesthetist signals awareness of his action and collaboration.

Medical teams have been much studied in order to demonstrate that its characteristic collegial activity relies on an ecology of different types of knowledge. These studies show that group work is a practical outcome of interaction which is obtained despite the fact that the participants are unequal in terms of power or status. However, this particular example of how interacting in the presence of a watching and listening audience while colleagues engage in coordinating the work or negotiate the course of action, commonly occurs in many workplaces.

For example, Marjorie Goodwin (1995) describes how airport workers camouflage their conversations in the presence of a listening and watching audience by using slang, abbreviations or codewords to exchange information without it being understandable to the audience. That is to say, they employ an 'elliptical code'.

These various examples of discursive practices show that workplaces are situational territories, ecologies of interactions, which simultaneously involve several workers in diverse theatres of action. In particular, they prompt reflection on how speech, once uttered in such territories, confers (in one way or another) the status of the participant in the conversation to all those within earshot.

Finally, discursive practices combine to shape, disseminate and stabilize a more or less shared understanding of the situation. We now describe the process by which the situation is constructed and interpreted.

5.4   TALKING IN ORDER TO UNDERSTAND

To work, therefore, is also to enact competent discursive practices: that is, ones appropriate to the task-in-situation (as commonly understood in the profession or occupation), to the organizational role that a person intends to interpret, as well to the formal and informal rules of the organization where that person works, to public/private boundaries, and to interpersonal relations with colleagues. How does a work group produce this 'appropriateness'?

We shall focus on the process of 'sensemaking', using this term in a broad sense as a process of situation-building.[2] We therefore propose to explore sensemaking as a social practice concomitant with work and as a collective outcome obtained mainly through material-discursive practices. We start from the apt definition of the concept provided by Taylor and Van Every (2000, p. 275): 'Sensemaking is a way station on the road to a consensually constructed, coordinated system of action'.

Taylor and Van Every (2000) describe this 'way station' as the place or moment in which circumstances are put together and transformed into a situation which is (or may be) verbalized and can be used as a springboard for action. This definition enables us to concentrate on the reciprocal relations among words, interpretations and actions, and to use language and interpretative categories more complex than a scheme of linear causality.

Researchers, like other workers, are faced by the problem of making sense of what they are doing. In order to illustrate how sensemaking may change research questions, I take an example reported by Weick et al. (2005, p. 410) and taken from Snook (2001). It concerns an incident of so-called 'friendly fire' during the Iraq War of 1994, when the pilots of an F-15 fighter plane shot down two 'friendly' helicopters and killed 26 soldiers. Was a wrong decision taken? As Snook (2001) says, this is not an incident where the F-15 pilots 'decided' to pull the trigger. Snook could have asked, 'Why did they *decide* to shoot?' However, such a framing leads straight back to the individual decisionmaker and away from potentially powerful contextual features. In fact 'Why did they decide to shoot?'

quickly becomes 'Why did they make the *wrong* decision?' In Snook's words (2001, p. 207, original emphasis):

> Such a reframing – from decision making to sensemaking – opened *my* eyes to the possibility that, given the circumstances, even *I* could have made the same 'dumb mistake.' This disturbing revelation, one that I was in no way looking for, underscores the importance of initially framing such senseless tragedies as 'good people struggling to make sense,' rather than as 'bad ones making poor decisions.'

This methodological reflection by a researcher on his research practice is illuminating from various points of view. First, it directs attention to the technical issue of how sociologists should put their research questions both to themselves and to their interviewees. It is evident that the choice of words and the initial framing (organization) of the problem can be used to direct the replies and their subsequent interpretation. We may therefore enquire as to the roles performed by the researcher's emotion in regard to a sudden reflection and his/her empathy with the research object (or subject) in the production of scientific knowledge. Finally, we can evaluate the productivity of this reflection in terms of its capacity to offer alternatives with respect to a first interpretative category perhaps unconsciously inherited from previous studies. Then, if we were particularly critical, we could consider the researcher's reflection as a text, and observe how the rhetoric with which it has been constructed is of narrative type – that is, it recounts a story 'from the field' to introduce a methodological discussion – unlike the majority of texts on research methodology, which use a prescriptive rhetoric.[3]

This example has the merit of embedding the researcher in the research process itself, and of suggesting an analogy between the difficulties encountered by the researcher in understanding a situation and representing it to others (his/her readers, for instance) and those encountered by people who work together when they grapple with the question of 'What's happening now?'

The interactive practice of mutual checking and questioning has been observed and related to the development of a reflective capacity within a community of practice, both in a novice's introductory period and later in acquisition of the occupational culture. Jordan (2010, p. 398), while shadowing novice nurse anaesthetists, noticed the interactive practice of mutual checking and questioning between nurses and doctors, with the use of phrases like: 'Have you already . . .?' 'Shouldn't you first . . .?' or 'Do you know how . . .?' Novices acquired these practices of informing and questioning as part of their socialization. The difference between such an 'interactive learning practice' and a checklist or a standard operating procedure

is that, while the former aims at producing specific answers, the latter aim
at discovering something unexpected, since 'they imply "I might be wrong
somehow" and thus further sensitivity towards perceiving surprise' (Jordan,
2010, p. 398, original emphasis). In fact, in the specific circumstances of
constantly changing work teams, a culture of asking questions and an
attitude of 'not-to-be-taken-for-granted' can be regarded as a collective
capacity to engage in reflective practice, and as a willingness to engage in it.

Talking to understand is indistinguishable from talking to negotiate,
and more generally, from talking to exercise power. I take an example
from 'strategy as practice' studies, since the field of strategy lends itself
very well to analysis of the discursive structures of the process of strategic decisionmaking. Dalvir Samra-Fredericks (2003; 2005) conducts
such analysis by mobilizing a theoretical approach which draws on both
Habermas (1979) and conversation analysis. There follows an extract
from the field accompanied by the interpretative theoretical scheme, which
may prompt interesting methodological considerations.

A group of six white male strategists are occupied with an ongoing strategic investment programme, as well as exploring future possibilities. They
are convinced that their major competitors are installing sophisticated
IT systems deemed to yield 'cost savings' and secure 'shorter innovation
lead times'. To be in a position to acquire other companies, they need to
be competitive, and to secure 'competitive advantage' one critical success
factor is perceived to be a sophisticated and integrated IT infrastructure
for cellular manufacturing. Strategists A and B have a short exchange
(Samra-Fredericks, 2005, p. 820, original emphasis):

> Extract 1
> St A: Well in fact I would have argued that cost should never have been a
>   criteria if our strategy and policy was to run cross company modules on
>   mainframe . . . cost should not have entered into the discussion
> St B: Well (I think where accountants are making decisions its got (unless
>   unless it not not
> St B: To . . .
> St A: Well, I I don't think accountants cannot make decisions even account-
>   ants cannot make decisions which *contradict* company policy.

According to Strategist B, when accountants take decisions, 'cost'
should enter the discussion: this is deemed to be correct behaviour and a
'fact'. Yet this focus on cost is interpreted by Strategist A (given his/her
utterances here, the reference to 'company policy', and the use of 'even'),
as neglecting a long-term perspective where investment requires suspen-
sion of a short-term focus upon costs.

In this company, and following encounters of this kind, Strategist A is 'taken' to be the more 'valid knower' in terms of truth/facts and correct-ness/rightness, so that he/she effectively redeems the validity claims on 'facts' (truth) and on correct behaviour, and also on being taken as sincere.

In regard to extract 1, what happens next is that the talk revolves around establishing the 'contents' of the company policy and further identifying how accountants' practices departed from it, and who seems to condone this departure (that is, who is to be blamed). Unfortunately, Strategist B is aligned with the accountants, and subsequent interactions continue subtly to deprive Strategist B of 'resources' so that he/she is unable to assume a viable position as a 'strategist' or maintain his/her prerogative to strategize the next time.

Although brief, the above extract is sufficient to introduce the analyti-cal framework that Samra-Fredericks (2005) develops from the speech act theory of Austin (1962), Searle (1969) and Habermas (1979). This last divides performative verbs into four classes, each producing distinctive 'worlds of actions' sustained by appropriated validity claims. Samra-Fredericks builds on Habermas's classification in order to focus on four forms of knowledge concerning:

1. 'The' world of external nature, which is performed by constative speech acts (asserting, describing and so on) and is sustained with validity claims based on 'truth'. The external world is deemed to encompass established ideas and knowledges (such as 'competitive advantage' in the example presented) which are asserted or described in such a way that they are 'taken' to be facts.
2. 'Our' world of society, which is performed by regulative speech acts (norms that can be obeyed or breached) sustained by validity claims regarding correctness or correct behaviour (in the above example, what accountants can or cannot do).
3. 'My' world of internal nature, which is performed by representative speech acts using verbs like 'to admit', 'to conceal' and so on. The speakers thus disclose aspects of their subjectivity in terms of their attitudes, feelings and emotions. The associated validity claim con-cerns issues of sincerity which can be verified or questioned.
4. Language, which is sustained by communicative speech acts and validity claims based on intelligibility. This last category is the most comprehensive because the previous three are considered to be ele-ments in communication.

Whenever we speak, all four validity claims are made. Nevertheless, a speaker may 'thematize' a particular claim by emphasizing a 'domain of reality': representation of facts, establishment of legitimate social

Table 5.1   Typology of worlds of action and associated validity claims

Domains of reality	Types of speech-act	Validity claims
The world of external nature	Constative (verbs asserting or describing facts)	Truth
Our world of society	Regulative (establishment of legitimate social relations, norms that can be obeyed or breached)	Correctness
My world of internal nature	Representative (verbs disclosing the speaker's subjectivity)	Sincerity
Language	Communicative	Intelligibility

Source: adopted in simplified form from Samra-Fredericks (2005, p. 814).

relations, or disclosure of subjectivity. Although Table 5.1 simplifies the analytical scheme proposed by Samra-Fredericks (2005), it can aid understanding of how research can be conducted on situated discursive practices in order to determine the interactional constitution of power effects.

Samra-Fredericks (2005) shows how discursive practices produce an intersubjectivity on which reciprocal understanding relies, but also the negotiation of power positions, and the formation of a subjectivity as a discursive and interactive effect.

A Habermasian approach is not widespread in practice-based studies, with the exception of Geiger (2009), which adopts Habermas's conception of practice in order to distinguish between talk in practice and talk about practice. Habermas (1984) distinguishes between life-world practices, to which corresponds a narrative mode of communication, and discourses which are argumentative in nature. The distinctive feature of Habermas's approach is that the questioning of validity claims requires an argumentative mode of communication which differs significantly from the narrative mode used in life-world practising. When problems occur in the everyday mode of practising (for example breakdowns), validity claims are no longer simply taken for granted but are discussed in an argumentative mode of communication aimed at reaching an intersubjective agreement on how the problem can be remedied. Or, as Habermas (1984, p. 18) puts it, a switch from a mode of unreflective practising to a reflexive mode of communication occurs when validity claims 'can no longer be repaired with everyday routines and yet are not to be settled by the direct or strategic use of force'. In those cases, the validity of a claim is explicitly discussed. According to Habermas (1989), life-world practices and discourses do not exist in isolation and manifest separate, independent 'worlds'; rather, they form a mutually *interactive relationship*. How can a Habermasian approach benefit practice-based studies? Geiger (2009, pp. 139–40) writes:

> This perspective – which directs our attention to communicative actions – reveals that shared modes of life-world practicing are continuously pervaded by modes of explicit contestation and reflection. Practicing and reflection/communication on practice are therefore interrelated modes of practical understanding. Discursive modes of reflection upon practice are embedded in the everyday mode of practicing (Habermas, 2003, p. 53). This way practitioners ensure that practices continue to be practiced, although in a revised mode. Practicing and contestation/disagreement therefore go hand in hand.

When engaged in the knowledgeable collective action that we call a practice, practitioners talk *in* practice, in life-world communication style, and they switch to an argumentative mode of communication by engaging in an intersubjective reasoning process enabling them to talk *about* practice.

5.5   TALKING IN ORDER TO OVERCOME ABSENCE AND DISTANCE

Thus far, we have discussed discursive practices in situations of co-presence and interaction. But talking at a distance and talking in order to work at a distance raise specific problems that enable us to see, amongst other things, how a single practice links a series of spaces and times together. ICT technologies have made distance work commonplace, and study of the discursive practices which connect and coordinate at a distance demonstrates that the locus of the organizing is situated in a rarefied space and operates at a distance. We now consider the case of telemedicine and show how the discursive practices of cardiological teleconsultancy make present what is absent and make close what is far.

Teleconsultancy may be defined as a collective action performed through discursive practices within a virtual encounter. The form of the interaction is highly standardized, owing to the protocols used in cardiology (and which standardize the data and the criteria to which a cardiologist (C) and a general practitioner (GP) refer), and owing to mediation by ICT, which requires cardiologists to compile a patient file for each electrocardiogram examined, and therefore to ask the GP standard questions in a largely standard sequence.

Telecardiological consultation is much used to certify good health. This situation configures very brief telephone calls, in which the interaction is confined to the context of practice; and all opening and closing moves

---

BOX 5.3   THE CASE OF A TELECARDIOLOGICAL CONSULTATION

GP: Hi, it's me.
C: [Gives his surname.]
GP: How, how are you? Hi . . .
C: Fine.
GP: Good, listen, I don't know if the ECG arrived properly because it's a seven-year-old boy.
C: Yes, everything's fine.
GP: It's only . . . he . . . he wants to join a football club.
C: Everything's okay, physiological sinusal arrhythmia, everything's okay.
GP: Good.
C: I'll send it to you.
GP: Yes, thanks, bye.
C: Bye.

Source: Gherardi (2010, p. 510).

---

dictated by courtesy (that is, by a general social practice) are removed and contextualized in the 'colleagueship' relationship between doctors. An example[4] is shown in Box 5.3.

The duration of this call is 43 seconds, and the exchanges are reduced to the minimum. Also the forms of knowledge mobilized are simple: the GP brings to the interaction his/her knowledge of the 'patient-as-child' and of the technology, which may not produce a good-quality trace when the electrodes are attached to a small thorax. The cardiologist contributes his/her expert knowledge by reading the trace. The outcome of the interaction takes material form as a certificate signed by the cardiologist. He/she therefore materializes professional competence in signed form by assuming responsibility for statements concerning a third party. We may imagine how the certificate, as a materialsemiotic artefact, enters a wider field of practices and what it 'does' as an affiliative object (Suchman, 2005) that associates humans and non-humans.

The certificate activates the relation between family and GP, and between the former and the football club, which requires a medical certificate before it will accept a new member. We can conclude that the football club is more reassured about the admission of its new healthy member, and more accountable in case of an incident, if it can prove its thoroughness. Further relations are established with institutions: for example the local health authority, or the body which supervises the administrative practices of sports clubs (which may take the certificate as an accountability standard) and which may also provide them with funding. The availability of telecardiological consultation changes not only clinical practices but administrative ones as well. This example shows that a practice is always inserted into a 'texture of practices'[5] (Gherardi, 2006) by a system of referrals and connections in action which also activate network learning.

When situations are not problematic, the interactions follow a pattern in which the GP first constructs the scene, almost simultaneously introducing, and in an interwoven manner, both the patient and the reason for the telephone call. What the GP does through his talk-in-situation is to perform a narrative that presents to the expert the absent patient and the context of the interaction. This story becomes the affiliative object (the intermediary) between the two clinicians and associates with the graphic representation of the patient, who thus becomes disembodied and also invisible.

If we analyse the telephone call in terms of discursive practice, we can distinguish among what is said, what is meant, what is done and what the doing does (see Table 5.2). A useful methodological suggestion, in fact, is to pay attention to what is said (the textual level of analysis) what is meant (the interpretative level), what is done through words (the production) and what the effects of the saying/doing are (the reproduction of practices generates social effects).

In the following turns, what the cardiologist does in the interaction is to read the ECG aloud so that the artefact representing the absent patient is made present in the interaction. The invisibility of the ECG to the GP is replaced by a vocal intermediary. When the cardiologists were asked why they thought aloud while reading ECGs, they replied that the reason concerned the social sustainability of the relation in the distance interaction: whilst physical co-presence makes what is being done reciprocally visible, in the absence of visibility the co-presence must be maintained through the voice (we saw this in Chapter 4 in the case of the call centre). Even if the verbal exchange may have an informative purpose, the GP is unable fully to understand the sense of the fragmented reading made by the cardiologist.

Finally, there is a further element of invisibility in this virtual encounter, because when the GP leaves the conversation, it continues between the cardiologist and the operator at the coordination centre to whom he is dictating the report, which will then be faxed to the GP. Invisibility assumes several forms in these three settings where the virtual encounter takes

How to conduct a practice-based study

Table 5.2   An analytic schema for interpreting a discursive practice

What is said	What is meant	What is done	What the doing does
GP: . . . I don't know if the ECG arrived properly because it's a seven-year-old boy.	The transmission of the data may be unclear when the patient's thorax is narrow.	Representing the absent patient in a clinical narrative.	Objectify the patient. Make the infrastructure supporting the interaction visible.
GP: It's only . . . he . . . he wants to join a football club.	The patient is a healthy seven-year-old boy. The reason for the GP's call is to obtain a certificate.	Activating a relationship between institutions.	Legitimize professional authority and its accountability.
C: Everything's okay, physiological sinusal arrhythmia, everything's okay.	I do not see anything suspicious.	This is a 'thinking aloud' performance in which C reads the inscription of the patient into the artefact representing him.	Produce a professional judgement and assert jurisdiction over the knowledge thus produced.

place: the patient is not visible to the cardiologist and is made present by an intermediary – the ECG; the latter is not visible to the GP and is made present by the thinking aloud of the cardiologist; doctors and patients are invisible to the coordination centre operator, and they are made present, besides the ECG, by another affiliative object, a form on which the cardiologist and operator collaboratively inscribe the reason for the call and the actions undertaken following the consultation. A final kind of invisibility is given by the technological infrastructure which materially anchors the interactions, both making them possible and restricting their expressive forms, but which is transparent when it works and conceals the collective and cooperative work necessary to make it function. This is the articulation work (Strauss, 1985) necessary both to understand 'work that gets things back "on track" in the face of the unexpected' and to understand when information systems work or do not (Schmidt and Simone, 1996, p. 158).

As a practice, a teleconsultation weaves together a texture of organizational relationships and acts as the virtual encounter where the spatiotemporal dimensions are blurred. Through discursive practices, what is absent is made present, and what is far is made near. Visibility and invisibility are connected in a reciprocal game.

5.6   TELLING STORIES TO BUILD A COMMUNITY

Thus far, we have discussed the instrumental use of talk and discursive practices as work instruments and as means for the collective interpretation (and construction) of work situations. But the treatment would be inadequate if it were not accompanied by reflection on discursive practices as expressing collective identities and as celebrating the life of a community. In all workplaces, stories are told, organizational sagas are recounted, knowledge about the past is transmitted through folklore, and the organizational culture is preserved and changed through myths which pass by word of mouth. Narratives have recently been greatly revalued as means to analyse everyday life in workplaces (Boje, 2001; Czarniawska, 1997; Poggio, 2004). The reason resides in the rediscovery of narrative knowledge.

The psychologist Jerome Bruner argues (1986) that narrative knowledge is complementary to paradigmatic knowledge, which serves to specify the flow of experience, to distinguish, individualize, calculate and make comparative assessments. Whilst the paradigmatic mode allows only one representation of reality at a time, because its validation criterion is truth (true/false), the narrative mode allows a plurality of simultaneous reconstructions/representations of the world because its validation criterion is plausibility. In fact, it is through narrative that a situation acquires meaning for the self and for others, because it is narrative which constructs the categories that give names and meanings to the events narrated. The extraordinary power of narrative knowledge therefore resides in the connection that people establish through narratives between the exceptional and the ordinary when they attempt to explain, justify and interpret common everyday facts.

Narratives are therefore ways to create and negotiate meanings, identities and temporal continuity (Jedlowski, 2000). At the same time, they are important resources with which to maintain, develop and distribute practical knowledge within work groups. Numerous studies have analysed narratives in specific communities of practice, such as police officers who, at the end of their shift, drink beer together and, by recounting the events of the day, contribute to maintaining, transmitting or changing a code of behaviour and a professional competence. The best-known study is that by Orr (1990) on photocopier technicians, who by swapping 'war stories' about the malfunctions of the photocopiers, how the problems were diagnosed and the tricks used to solve them rapidly, created a 'community memory': that is, a repertoire of practical knowledge which was kept alive and transmitted. Situated narratives not only accumulate, preserve and transmit a community's skills; they also celebrate its identity and the attachment of its members.

Moreover, knowing the stories of the community distinguishes the expert from the novice. While recounting them enhances the former's reputation as an insider, listening to them provides the latter with important access to forms of tacit knowledge transmitted indirectly. Stories are often ways to communicate allegorically or indirectly a message that cannot be, or is not wanted to be, transmitted directly. Let us consider an example drawn from an ethnographic study on the transmission of safety knowledge on a building site (Gherardi and Nicolini, 2002b, p. 203). Interested as the authors were in knowing how novices entering the community of practices learned about on-site safety, they were more concerned by the organization's silence in regard to such an important matter. The story that is presented in Box 5.4 was recounted by one of the workmen. It helps shed light on the question.

Telling this story to a novice amounts to transmitting an admonition and a warning. The moral of the story, in fact, is that a 'smart' worker would leave the firm unconcerned with safety and look for a job with a more careful and responsible one. A social dynamic of mutual choice between firms and workers is implicitly signalled to the novice. In the labour market for building workers, the best firms will attract the best workers. Conversely, the weakest firms, which invest least in safety, will attract workers with less bargaining power, poorer qualifications and lower costs, and who are more likely to have accidents. The organization's silence on safety had a precise meaning; but this meaning was transmitted through a story, and it was up to the novice to grasp its meaning and relate it to his own situation.

Telling 'war stories', regardless of whether or not they are true, whether or not they really happened to the protagonist, or whether or not he/she is repeating them second-hand, is the means and the form of the knowledge by which a novice accesses professional expertise safeguarded within the community, and transmitted and constantly elaborated by the latter. Stories 'make' communities both for those who tell them and for those who listen to them. The stories recounted in workplaces are studied because of their symbolic value as artefacts which give access to deeper-lying and hidden meanings. The myths and stories thus collected can be interpreted as symbols of control, adaptation, imprisonment or renewal.

BOX 5.4 STORYTELLING FOR THE TRANSMISSION OF KNOWLEDGE

'One of my mates told me this story. He'd gone to work for one of those firms that build the piers for motorway viaducts. They were working on an enormous overpass on the *** ring road, you know, one of those really high flyovers. They work like this in that firm: they have scaffolding all around the pillar, mounted on rails, which extend bit by bit. Every day they'd bolt together, say, thirty meters, and then they'd pour the concrete. You know, they use special prefabricated panels. The next day they come back, unclad the piece, extend the rails, climb the stretch that they'd done and then start again. You begin at the ground, but after a week you're 150, 200 meters high . . .

Anyway, my mate was up there on the scaffolding and he saw that down in the yard, slightly apart from the others, there was a hut which no one ever entered. He was curious, and a few days later before he knocked off, he went to the hut, without anyone seeing him . . . who knows what was inside. So, he went to the hut, and he saw that it wasn't even locked. He opened the door and went inside. In the middle of the room he saw two coffins. Yeah, two brand-new coffins with their lids propped against their sides. Ready and waiting. He went straight into the office and quit.'

Source: Gherardi and Nicolini (2002b, p. 203).

5.7 TO SUM UP

Language is an important mediator in working practices. The use of language in situated communication is an activity able to produce tangible effects. Practical knowledge therefore presupposes communicative competence: that is, the knowledge necessary to use language which is appropriate to specific operational contexts.

In contemporary society, in which around two-thirds of the labour force is employed in services, communicative competence is the core of the capacity to supply a service. When we go to a computer technician, diagnosis of the problem is co-produced through the questions put to us and the answers that we give. As the technician asks questions, he follows a consolidated and professionally learned practice. Likewise, many of the professionals that we encounter in institutional settings enact discursive practices which, with our collaboration, produce the service and reproduce the institution.

Institutional conversations have specific features. Besides speech, they use artefacts, gestures, predisposition of the environment and enactment of the user's point of view. In general, talk in work settings has two distinctive aspects: it is subordinate to the work; and the conversation is open, so that also participation in the conversation is fluid and equally open. Moreover, discursive practices in workplaces mark out public and private spaces, and the respective communicative modes are learned as competence in speaking, in remaining silent and in camouflaging the communication by using an 'elliptical code'.

Working together presupposes the construction of a shared space of mutual comprehension and agreement on the methods with which to understand power relations but also to negotiate them. The distinction between talking in practice and talking about practice has been introduced in order to differentiate between discursive practices contextualized in doing, on the one hand, and reflexive and argumentative discursive practices on the other.

Numerous discursive practices are situated in contexts of face-to-face interaction, but others take place within virtual encounters. In the latter case, performed within the conversational space is a delocation between what is absent/present and what is distant/close. The network of connections woven together by discursive practices is the locus of organizing.

Discursive practices are functional to the performance of work, but they are also symbolic because they 'do' community and indirectly transmit profound meanings.

In this chapter discursive practices have been brought to the attention of the reader through the following case studies:

- A couple of examples of institutional work illustrated how an institution is embedded in practitioners' talk, and how working is talking.
- The case of handover at the paediatric ward showed the polyphony of talk.
- The case of the operating theatre was paradigmatic of situated talking and saying and not saying.
- The case of the managers engaged in strategizing illustrated how discursive practices produce an intersubjectivity on which reciprocal understanding relies, but also the negotiation of power positions,

and the formation of a subjectivity as a discursive and interactive effect.

● The case of the teleconsultation demonstrated the mobilization of visible and invisible 'objects' of discourse.

● Finally, storytelling as a mode of talking in practice showed how sensemaking is accomplished and meaning transmitted in an indirect mode of communication.

NOTES

1. I have simplified the transcription of the telephone call, but one should bear in mind that conversation analysis pays maximum attention to all pauses, overlaps among words, hesitations, repetitions and so on, in talk, and that it has developed an elaborate notational system to reproduce them in writing. Our reason for simplifying these features is our predominant interest in talk as a specific 'doing' without engaging in technical analysis of the conversation.
2. The concept of sensemaking was used by Karl Weick (1995) to describe and interpret the processes by which groups and organizations rationalize what they do, have done or are doing. Weick is a social psychologist, and the success of the category of sensemaking has led to its use in cognitivist terms, although this was not Weick's intention. However, although situated knowledge (Rogoff and Lave, 1984) and distributed knowledge (Hutchins, 1995) are phenomena widely studied in relation to work-in-situation, and although cognitivist cultural psychology has contributed to developing knowledge on the relation between knowledge and ICT, I do not intend to venture into this terrain here. Rather, I want to offer a complementary reading which, without denying that work also involves knowledge, foregrounds the relational and social dimension of socially producing sense and meaning.
3. On the other hand, the fact that methodology texts are more comprehensible to those who already know how to do research, compared with those who read such texts to learn how to do it, is well known but rarely taken seriously. The alternative suggested is to furnish narratives of the research process so that the practices of doing research are reconstructed (Roth, 2005). It is this awareness that has induced me to write a book which gives space to narratives from the field, so that substantive knowledge of the subject is combined with methodological awareness.
4. The examples provided have been translated from Italian, and unfortunately prosody is lost in translated texts. For this reason, the transcripts do not comply with the conventions of conversational analysis. There are numerous methodological problems relative to translation from one language to another when discourse analysis is to be conducted. I do not discuss these problems here, merely pointing out that I am aware of them and that I analyse conversations mainly for the purpose of analysing discursive interactions.
5. A field of practices arises in the interwoven texture that interconnects practices. This texture is held together by a certain number of practices which provide anchorage for others. Texture is a strongly evocative concept which recalls the intricacies of networking but at the same time furnishes an analytical, qualitative framework (Strati, 2000). The key to understanding texture is the idea of 'connectedness in action', an endless series of relationships which continually merge into each other.

6. On rules, on knowing the rules and on ordinary prescription

A perspective of analysis proposed by practice-based studies – but which has a tradition within the sociology of work – is exploration of the gap between what organizational rules prescribe and what people actually do in their situated working practices. A classic study on this theme is the organizational ethnography carried out by Julien Orr (1996) on photo-copier repair technicians and commented on by various authors in a special issue of *Organization Studies* celebrating the decennial of the publication of Orr's book (Tsoukas, 2006).

This chapter examines the normative infrastructure of practices: that is, how rules are resources for practical activities; and it does so by starting from the dual nature of rules. These, in fact, are stated in decontextualized and universal terms, but they are sustained and translated into practice in a situated manner so that they interweave with discursive and techno-logical practices. To resume the metaphor of rock-climbing, rules are the handholds for the performance of practical activities, and they are practi-cal accomplishments in the course of their application.

The chapter also discusses the artefacts (protocols for instance) which give material form to rules, as well as the media – like speech or script – which mediate the maintenance and transmission of rules.

6.1 RULES AS *LANGUE* AND *PAROLE*

The previous chapter dealt with language, communication, narrative and discursive practices. From that discussion an analogy can be extracted which will enable us to focus on rules. The linkage is provided by linguistics and its distinction between *langue* and *parole*. The former term refers to the grammatical and syntactic rules that describe and prescribe the correct use of a language, and relate to a set of conventions which slowly change with the usage of that language. The latter term instead refers to the everyday and situated use of a language, to the variations that use introduces into it, to local and specialist uses, to the 'living' language. The analogy enables us to conceive rules – norms, laws and organizational rules in general – as a structured set of prescriptions structuring situations (*langue*) and at the same time as a normative corpus which is changed, sustained or allowed to lapse through use-in-situation (*parole*). This analogy also makes it possible to show what constitutes 'competence' in the case of *langue* and in that of *parole*. An utterance may be correct grammatically and semantically (and therefore demonstrate the linguistic competence of the speaker), but at the same time it may be inappropriate to the situation and therefore demonstrate the speaker's incompetence in situation.

A similar way to understand processes that account both for structure and action and for stability and change is Feldman's (2000) theory of routine as practices. The epistemological position that links the analysis of practices with the analysis of routines is adopted by Feldman (2000) and by Feldman and Pentland (2003), who propose a reading of routines as practices in order to move from the analysis of routines as programmes of action to that of routines as performances. In order to explain the dynamics of routines, Feldman (2000) uses the distinction between their ostensive and performative aspects. The performative aspect refers to the mutually constitutive and recursive interaction between the actions people take and the ostensive aspect refers to the patterns thus created and recreated. The ostensive aspects are called 'routine' in principle but their normative character is poorly represented by written rules or formal operating procedures, since the performances of routine (their 'situatedness' as I called it in Chapter 1) modify the ostensive aspects. The mutual constitution of ostensive and performative aspects of routine enables inquiry into power asymmetries and how they play out in specific contexts.

Feldman's theory of routines as practices concerns both stability and change: 'theorizing routines as practices emphasizes the consequentiality of the actions that people take while they are enacting routines and both the potential for change and the work that goes into stability' (Feldman and Orlikowski, 2011, p. 1245).

In these studies, the tradition of inquiry into routines initiated by March (1988) overlaps with a new research programme concerned with the dynamic aspect of the recursiveness of organizational actions, although it maintains the function of routines and practices as uncertainty reduction devices.

Traditional sociology identifies a normative structure in the social order's maintenance (which implies that actors attribute the same meanings to the same norms), whilst ethnomethodology affirms that norms are constructed (so that they are understood in different ways by different actors). It also maintains that, in any case, rules do not specify the interpretative procedures with which people decide on their applicability to the situation. In this regard we may recall what Garfinkel (1967, p. 9) described as the distinctive feature of rules: that they are always applied 'for another first time'.

A rule's range of application is always constituted by a number of different situations undefinable a priori. Hence rules always have a margin of ambiguity and non-specificity – as also argued by the branch of neo-institutionalism (March and Olsen, 1989) which emphasizes the incompleteness of rules. Consequently, it is analysis of how rules are interpreted and negotiated which yields understanding of what rules are expressed in practices and what rules are sustained by those practices.

The twofold nature of rules directly entails that order is negotiated (Strauss, 1978): that is to say, it is a fluid process which springs from interactions and is contingent and non-generalizable. When one speaks of rules and a negotiated order, one is therefore referring to an emergent order, not to a static product. Analytically, the focus is on order as a process or, as John Law (1994) puts it, on the 'modes of ordering'. Viewed in these terms, rules assume a temporality: their situatedness involves their being in history as they reflect the historical experience that has produced them. The duality of rules means that they produce conformity; but they also produce deviations, standardization and, simultaneously, variability.

According to the notion of negotiated order, rules are socially sustained, and the network of rules and the relations that these rules define is supported by trust and by the sense of appropriateness. As the philosopher MacIntyre (1988) points out in fact, situations comprise a logic of consequentiality (which connects choices with predictions of their results) and a logic of appropriateness (linked with the action deemed normatively suitable). When a person thinks in accordance with the logic of appropriateness, he/she asks the following question: in this situation, to what extent are the possible actions appropriate to me and my position (social, organizational, occupational and so on)? March and Olsen (1989) argue that actions are associated with situations according to their appropriateness. This is what we saw when discussing communities of practice and how practices are normatively sustained by rules of appropriateness. March and Olsen (1989) also describe the processes which adapt rules to situations and situations to rules. They explain changes in rules on the basis of the following processes:

1. *Variation and selection* (rules develop through experimentation, competition and survival);
2. *Problem-solving* (solutions to problems generate new rules);
3. *Learning from experience* (that is, through trial and error);
4. *Conflict* (among individuals or groups pursuing different interests);

5. *Contagion* (rules spread from one institution to another because of fashion or by imitation);
6. *Turnover* (that is, a change in personnel and/or beliefs).

Note that the interpretation of the processes which, in following and applying the rules, change those rules is also applicable to the problem of how working practices change, how they are repeated and how their repetition[1] always involves their re-specification.

I now examine the role of rules in structuring practices in light of production games – a classic theme of the sociology of work (Burawoy, 1979; Roy, 1952; 1953; 1969; 2006; Turner, 1971) – in order to illustrate the negotiated ordering and joint regulation of organizing. In fact, one should bear in mind, that working practices are not regulated through a prescriptive process which exercises organizational control 'from above'; but nor are they regulated by control exerted 'from below' and which expresses both the autonomy of the work collective and the social space that I call ordinary prescription. It is for this reason that the concept of joint regulation of practices best expresses normativity as a practical accomplishment with respect both to the dichotomy between formal (prescribed work) and informal (real work), and the dichotomy between control (prescription from outside) and autonomy (prescription from within).

6.2   NEGOTIATING THE AMBIGUITY OF RULES: PRODUCTION GAMES

The daily quantity of output to achieve is what is at stake in the so-called 'production games'. In principle, it is the management's responsibility to set the production quota, and it is the workforce's responsibility to fulfil it (and, if possible, exceed it). What happens instead is that the quota that for the management represents the minimum quota below which production must not fall, is for the workforce the maximum quota of daily production. The production game (in its various forms) consists in this covert, never explicit (though known to both parties), negotiation. It is a conflictual and cooperative game repeated day after day, and which is therefore a good example of how working practices are jointly regulated.

Factories and blue-collar work are the main frames in which production games have been empirically studied, but one should bear in mind that – as Crozier (1963), Friedberg (1993) and the French school of strategic analysis point out – 'strategic games' take place among and within groups in all kinds of work because conflict gives rise to relatively stable interactions which do not destabilize cooperation.

The expression 'game of the parts' aptly expresses the mix of cooperation and conflict among and within groups, amid relations well known to the parties but not immediately visible to outsiders, nor easily accessible through *parole*. Box 6.1 presents an example of how production rules are negotiated in the workplace.

The example (Box 6.1), concerns a factory manufacturing batteries (Gherardi, 1995b) where the management has decided to raise productivity after a period of plant upgrading and a long battle waged by the workers on the shop floor against lead pollution ten years before. Although many years have passed since that struggle it has left a cultural legacy in the form of a production rule. In fact, the workers in the assembly department have been awarded an hour of 'free time' during which, once they have fulfilled their production quota, they can reduce their work rate, play cards or chat. This tacit rule has long been respected, but now the management is no longer willing to tolerate it. In the meantime, moreover, numerous workers have left the factory and been replaced by younger ones, for whom the rule does not have the same meaning because they have not shared the struggle experience. As we shall see, this production rule has become a cause of conflict, both within the group of workers and between workers and management.

We are in the assembly department, where the workers fit the battery components – positive and negative plates – together. The plates are of varying consistency, and this variability affects the speed of the work, and therefore the number of batteries completed. On the end wall of the department, written on a blackboard so that all can see it, is a number representing the day's quota to fulfil. The number is an unambiguous indicator, objective and easy to verify, but the quality of the material is less easy to determine objectively. 'Today the plates are soft' is the expression used by the workers to announce a restriction of the quota. But how soft are the soft plates? And to what extent will the number of batteries produced decrease? The ritual of the production game is described in Box 6.1.

Thus far we have considered the mobilization of power and the negotiation of the social order that sustain production rules. But also to be discussed is a more hidden aspect: the role played by ambiguity in fostering production games and in producing and coordinating collective action.

It is crucial for this community of practitioners to maintain the ambiguity of the relationship between the quality of the material and the fulfilment or non-fulfilment of the quota. Disambiguation of this relationship is necessary for action. At the same time, however, no decision on 'reducing the quota' can be taken in ambiguous conditions. Ambiguity enhances the flexibility of action; it enables one course of action to be chosen depending on whether the definition of the situation resolves its ambiguity by

BOX 6.1   TODAY THE PLATES ARE SOFT

The announcement 'today the plates are soft' sometimes assumes the form of a self-evident truth; at other times it is greeted by a chorus of denials; finally, there are occasions when the announcement resembles a start button which must be pressed several times before the ritual is triggered. In fact, not all the voices in the department enjoy the same authority in proclaiming that 'today the plates are soft', so that the softness of the plates also depends on the voice that announces it. The ambiguity of this measurement is therefore resolved within the department's network of power relations, in which tacit negotiation takes place on what is 'soft' and what is not. But what does this signify for the situated action?

The practice begins when one of the workers goes to the department supervisor, persuades him to inspect the material, gets him to agree that it is impossible to produce the quantity established, negotiates a reduction and orchestrates the chorus of support. Also the supervisors are aware of the ritual, and they act their part: they try to be invisible, to involve the head of quality control, to minimize the event, and, when necessary, to concede with dignity.

It may seem that the announcement 'today the plates are soft' is simply a device to reduce the quota and to exercise social control over those who might exceed it, and simultaneously over the managers and supervisors. This is a correct but reductive interpretation, however. Consider the power dynamics that pivot on the degrees of softness of the plates:

1. Individual reputation, the esteem of workmates, the workers' competence and the celebration of personal skill are at stake;
2. Such interpersonal relations as status difference between young/old workers must be maintained and reproduced;
3. The safeguarding of the work group as a collective actor must be maintained and reproduced. In fact, within the group, the conflict between the world-vision of those who want the free time zone and those who want to 'take it easy' (or work at what they regard as a steady pace) is legitimate, but it has its limits in that both groups of workers recognize that the group is a resource and a collective good;
4. The counter-power against the supervisors and management

must be maintained and balanced as the right to co-determine the quota and, when this has been accomplished, the right to treat the remaining work time as free time, worker time, time appropriated from the boss.

Thus when the signal is given but the above-described ritual does not take place, the inaction may have various meanings. First of all, unless the raw material is obviously impossible to work with, in which case anyone is entitled to define the situation (and it is usually the first worker to lose his temper and is willing to fetch the supervisor that does so). Or, unless the announcement is made by the one or two undisputed leaders of the workers, prior to the 'official' announcement, there is a muted operation of testing the ground to see who agrees and whether the operation can start. When the signal fails to start up with the script, the atmosphere may be one of horseplay and teasing, with dirty jokes and puns on the term 'soft'. Or else the atmosphere may be tense because the two groups are assessing which of them is entitled to define the situation, or because they are calculating how many times that week the quota has been met, or not, and therefore negotiating whether to reduce the quota or to give up their free time.

When the group has decided that 'today the plates are soft', then the external interlocutor is called in; an external interlocutor who does not necessarily figure in the hierarchical order. The supervisor is sometimes called in because he is the spokesman for the group; sometimes he is considered an opponent; and sometimes a 'hierarchy leap' occurs. The rationale for the choice of the interlocutor lies in the 'objective' conditions of the material (the less ambiguous the task of establishing the degree of hardness/softness, the more the supervisor is an ally), in the person of the supervisor (as more or less a class ally), and in the personal relationship between the shift supervisor and whoever goes to fetch him.

The choice of which manager to call follows the same logic, but interestingly the group does not always take the soft option but may decide to pick a quarrel. Picking a quarrel, expressing hostility, the flexing of collective muscles is one of the non-explicit goals of the negotiation over reducing the quota. Regardless of whether agreement that the quota cannot be reached is achieved, and whatever reduction is decided, the collective argument, heated disagreement, the expression of hostility is cathartic. It leaves the group feeling satisfied whether it wins or loses. This, in fact, is a ritual within a ritual which reproduces the group's identity on a routine basis; it is what Durkheim (1912) called a positive ritual which confirms a value and facilitates its expression.

The managers' interpretation of this situation confirms that the group reinforces its collective identity through this dynamic. The managers react to the altercation with boredom and apathy: for them it is 'the same old story'. They report, in fact, that they constantly 'have to find the energy to argue' while the workers emerge from the encounter refreshed, and the researcher suspects that it may sometimes be a game played for its own sake, purely for the pleasure.

Source: Gherardi (1995b, pp. 14–20).

replacing a polysemic term with a univocal one. When a course of action is chosen, ambiguity has been reduced but it does not necessarily disappear. Just as a culture requires a minimal sharing of values and meanings, collective action requires the sharing of a minimum set of univocal meanings.

Observation of how this community resolves semantic ambiguity in order to initiate action (and vice versa) provides a decision model of more general applicability. The significance of the micro-decisions which enable this occupational community to handle the ambiguity of the soft plates is a three-stage process of negotiation:

1. Coping with the ambiguity of interpretations: the decision to call the plates 'soft' is taken individually and collectively.
2. Coping with the ambiguity of implicatures: the utterance 'today the plates are soft' may have many meanings. It may be a way to start a conversation, to express tiredness or boredom, a statement of fact, an ironic joke, a secret code and so on. But when an authoritative voice makes the announcement, the other workmates know the relation between 'soft plates' and 'reduce output' and decide that the one implicates the other.
3. Coping with the ambiguity of implementing the action. Who initiates the 'reducing output' script and how? It may be the worker who made the announcement, or it may be a chorus of two or three people. Alternatively, the process may involve some kind of turn-taking. In any case, rapid tacit coordination takes place, and action rather than inaction is chosen.

This occupational community therefore follows a script which relates the quantity of output to the quality of the materials, and which directs individual and collective behaviour. This script – which interweaves with other strategies of action, such as 'you work calmly and steadily all day' or 'you step up the work rate at the beginning, you slow down towards the end and the last hour is sacrosanct' – is not necessarily shared by everyone, and not all the time. It is not the sharing of a cognitive schema that triggers the action, but the decisionmaking process which dissolves the ambiguity that suspends will and selects a course of action.

We have illustrated a type of rule which is made explicit, legitimated and materialized in a production quota written on a blackboard and sustained by a network of tacit rules which are unwritten, shared and contested at the same time. This example not only enables us to see an organizing process based on conflict and autonomous regulation, and therefore intended to change the rules of organizational control; it also lets us see the dynamic processes by which the everyday stability of rules is established and therefore reproduced.

We now illustrate another case of rules – protocols – and discuss the relationship between oral and written expression in sustaining them.

6.3 WRITING AND ORAL EXPRESSION TO SUSTAIN RULES

In Western culture, the written form of rules enjoys a reputation encapsulated in the Latin dictum *'verba volant et scripta manent* [spoken words fly away, written words remain]'. This is a brief reminder that the written form enjoys an aura of certainty, and that common sense expects activities – especially in complex organizations (from hospitals to nuclear power stations) – to be expressed in written form so that that they can be consulted at a distance, will persist in space and time, and will provide reliable referents if criminal liability or the correctness of behaviour must be adjudicated. Moreover, information systems, together with forms of certification (for instance on quality or safety), have contributed greatly to the proceduralization and formalization of working practices in written rules.

The dream that it might be possible to state in written rules the knowledge necessary to standardize work behaviour, and to crystallize the knowledge optimal for executing a certain operation into rules, has a long history in Western culture. It ranges from the birth of bureaucracy (Weber, 1922) and administrative law to the most recent movement of so-called 'best practices', which implies that a 'good practice' can be made explicit and formalized so that the knowledge contained in it can travel across time and space and be applied in contexts other than those in which it originated. This laudable aspect of learning by imitation (and the belief that the goodness of an item of knowledge is so self-evident that any reasonable person would want to adopt it) may obscure the relationship between decontextualized knowledge frozen in rules and the knowing-in-situation kept alive through its everyday reproduction and by the working practices that renew it by repeating it. Organizational contexts are rendered complex not only by the incompleteness of rules but also by their heterogeneity; and identifying what rule can be applied in the actual situation is a problem that is anything but banal.

The use of rules requires expert knowledge; and work also entails knowing how to use rules and maintain their efficacy. Competence in handling rules therefore relies on speech as an active mediator between the community which maintains those rules and their formulation in writing.

Before introducing the reader to a further story gathered in the field, we shall provide some theoretical indications on how and where writing has been studied in relation to speech in working practices.

The anthropology of writing (Goody, 1993) has traditionally focused on the relationship among writing, thought and social organization. From this area of inquiry has developed a strand which, in analogy with 'ordinary conversation', studies 'ordinary writing' and analyses the pervasiveness of script in the relational fabric of society (Fabre, 1997). The reference is to the network of French researchers denominated *Langage et Travail* (see Chapter 5) which studies specific types of written text produced by work practices: letters of complaint to public services (Borzeix et al., 1995); maintenance service reports in the IT sector (Fraenkel, 1993); and forms used in the public administration (Pène, 1995). Finally, in studying healthcare contexts, Cicourel (1982) pointed to the difficulty of interpretation of a fragment of script or speech eradicated from the domain of its production since the ecological validity of clinical data is achieved through the connection of writing and speaking.

These and other studies are based on empirical observation of what texts 'do', not just of how they are constructed. They highlight an activity that almost always goes unobserved in work contexts and is taken for granted: writing is a specific work activity which has different pragmatics in different contexts, so that writing is a work technology.

As a classic example I take that of protocols (also in order to indicate an area of inquiry which could be further developed in the future). The use of protocols has become pervasive both in scientific research and in hospital settings. Protocols today constitute the idealized image of what certification and/or the dissemination of good practices should achieve.

The term 'protocol' originates from the ordering of presences and places in official contexts (who comes first, who must stand next to whom) so as to ensure the orderly progress of a ceremony and express agreement on its conduct. In a broader sense, a protocol provides guidance to one or more operators so that they can exercise continuous control over the order to be respected – whether this concerns people and the consideration given to them, or whether it concerns priorities among the things to do and the initiatives to be taken (Joseph, 1994). Protocols may vary in their degree of formalization, but they are generally produced in written form.

An outstanding contribution to this area of inquiry has been made by Michèle Grosjean and Michèle Lacoste (1999), who pose the following significant questions. When a new script enters a work context, what new tasks does it entail? What relationship does it establish with the oral communication which previously prevailed? What are the prerequisites for its use? What relationships does the new script establish with the other objects, tools or technologies already being used? Finally, how can the effectiveness and efficiency of written rules as 'work instruments' be evaluated?

The following case (see Box 6.2) reported by Grosjean and Lacoste (1999, pp. 453–5) shows what is entailed by following protocols, what the limits of written procedures are and what invisible work is necessary to make a protocol effective.

BOX 6.2   FOLLOWING A PROTOCOL

The setting is the paediatric department of a hospital. Aurelio is a six-month-old baby boy with growth difficulties, who has been hospitalized to restore his nutritional balance, and who must undergo a series of clinical examinations, among them a fasting test. During this test, blood samples are collected at regular intervals. But, during one sample collection, a discussion starts among the nurses about which protocol to follow. In effect, although a protocol is designed to be a reliable reference frame for action, it must be aligned with the context so that the situation is not ambiguous.

Charge nurse: Is it a new protocol?
Nurse 1:   No, it's still the same one.

Charge nurse: Ah, it's still the same one . . . we've always done it another way . . . but he [the doctor] has just written another one. Should we follow this protocol? We'd better look at the one he's [the doctor] just written.

Nurse 1: Ah, right.

Nurse 2: Ah, if this is the one . . . we should ask him [the doctor].

Which protocol is valid, therefore? How does the new protocol differ from the previous one? What is the doctor's intention? One difficulty arises for the nurses because protocols do not state *the conditions for their application*; another difficulty concerns *comprehension of the content.*

Nurse 1: What do you understand from there to there? If it's hypoglycaemia, do this?

Nurse 2: Yes, if there's hypo . . . wait . . . if you look, you do it if there's hypoglycaemia. Otherwise you do it at the end of the test.

Nurse 1: But do you think that even if there's no hypoglycaemia, it should be done anyway? At the end of the test?

Nurse 2: Ah, certainly! We always do it this way!

Nurse 1: Right! It's because there was all this written, so I said to myself . . . it may be that the protocol needn't be followed.

It seems that the nurses are trying to follow instructions whose logic they fail to understand. They do not draw on medical knowledge, but rather on habit and previous experience ('We always do it this way!').

Nurse 1: The last time he [the doctor] kept him [the boy] twenty-four hours without doing the hypoglycaemia. The fasting test was a bit tricky. In fact, he [the doctor] didn't do the glucagon, and he [the doctor] waited for the hypoglycaemia to be done . . . to see how long he [the boy] could go without eating.

Source: Grosjean and Lacoste (1999, pp. 453–5).

This fasting test – a difficult and 'aggressive' procedure, especially when applied to an infant – was also a test for the entire team. The uncertainties concerning application of the protocol caused the nurses considerable emotional pressure. The protocol, which was supposed to guide their work, produces a discussion which did not lead to any solution except that of asking the doctor.

We may therefore reflect on how following a protocol entails evaluation of the conditions of its applicability, as well as the assumption that it is unambiguous in stating the procedures to follow. However, the above example shows that both processes are collectively constructed by the work group through successive corrections and adjustments.

Some work settings have seen a proliferation of protocols introduced in order to support routine work. However, it does not seem that due account has been taken of the fact that protocols subject work groups to an additional task which increases the 'invisible work' necessary for them to do their jobs. The limitations of proceduralization are well known in the industrial sector and International Organization for Standardization (ISO) certification, which presupposes that the principle of 'write down everything that you do' prevents numerous errors. At the end of the above example, Grosjean and Lacoste (1999) point out that phenomenological and ethnomethodological studies have amply documented that situated experience cannot be entirely proceduralized. In the above example, the written text was based on assumptions which if not shared by the reader prevented his/her understanding of that text. By contrast, it is shared experience, the habitus of the occupation or profession, which confers a practical meaning on written protocols. It is therefore oral communication which determines how a written text is to be interpreted. This occurs in numerous organizational situations: consider work meetings, during which the rules are not only 'interpreted' but also 'created' *ad hoc* and entrusted to the understanding of those present.

Many lessons can be drawn from the foregoing discussion on how to write protocols which support tasks, and how to introduce them into work groups so that the regulatory aspect is not imposed from the outside and top-down but reflects a shared way to regulate activities, so that the rules result from joint regulation. To refine the analysis, now discussed is how so-called 'prescriptive relays' subvert the dichotomy between top-down and bottom-up rules.

6.4 PRESCRIPTIVE RELAYS

Consider the following question: how do novices learn the organization's rules, given their heterogeneity, and given that employment conditions are increasingly marked by precariousness so that a novice remains in a job for a brief period of time? It is evident that in situations of this kind the hierarchy on its own is unable to regulate the work either through written rules or through their verbal communication. Hence, workers must have other ways to learn how to apply the appropriate rule to the given situation. The concept of prescriptive relay (Denis, 2007, p. 504) enables us to see how prescription is effected through non-hierarchical channels: for example, by asking a more experienced colleague for advice; by being shown how something is done; by asking for confirmation of what one has done; and so on. When by means of speech and gesture one operator shows another how something is done, and why it is done in that particular way, he/she becomes a link in a prescriptive chain, but his/her words and gestures do not transmit orders. On the contrary, they are devoid of hierarchical authority and are therefore perceived within an interactional context in which the indexicality of the situation is completed to acquire a practical meaning. A prescriptive relay is a colleague who lends a hand, who points out an error, who responds to a request for help. His/her work of transmission and connection is invisible work not part of his/her job and of which the management is not aware. This is therefore the 'ordinary' type of prescription which consists in showing what must be done and why it must be done in a certain way. Box 6.3 shows the example of two film editors working on the production of commercials for a television chain.

The example illustrates how prescription, whether written or oral, is present in the workspace but in order to be effective requires a series of intermediaries that transmit what is to be done, when it is to be done and why it has to be done. This is accomplished in a situated way and by anchoring knowledge in gestures, in artefacts (note that the film editors use the cut and paste commands to mobilize elements which already incorporate the organization's production rules) and in the workgroup's memory. We may therefore say that the transmission chain of prescription comprises a series of relays which convey the organization's rules while translating them into technical prescriptions and freeing them from the direct chain of command. This process takes place both within an individual organization and in interorganizational networks responsible for application of the rules. This point is now illustrated by an example (see Box 6.4) which refers to the application of safety rules on a construction site during an inspection.

As the site foreman tries to negotiate the meaning of the rule, he is also

BOX 6.3   A PRESCRIPTIVE RELAY

Jean, a film editor, is showing José (another film editor) how to insert a 'post-packshot' (a sequence which shows some minutes of the film or the broadcast after the sponsor's sequence). He is seated at the computer and explaining to José what he is doing:

Jean: It's simple: you import the plan. If it lasts less than three seconds, you directly attach the chain's logo. Otherwise you pull it up and then down. But there must be enough time. The aim is to install this signal everywhere, so if the announcement is too short, you put it in directly without editing it.

José: And the post-packshot, how do I attach it to the billboard sponsor?

Jean: You do 'cut'. You don't have to do anything else, just paste it later. It's very important: you should never put a sponsor at the end. The principle of this montage is that the sponsor and the chain are kept very distinct. So there's always 'cut'.

It was said during the meeting when the new montages were explained that each sponsor had to be clearly separated from the others by a separation announcement. If these were sponsored, they in turn needed a 'post-packshot'. But it is at the editing table that Jean translates these principles into concrete operations, when he shows the manipulations that each rule involves and anchors the new prescriptions to technical gestures that will very soon become ordinary.

Source: Denis (2007, pp. 503–4).

learning the logic of the inspector's practice so that he can make use of it when the next inspection is made. For his part, the inspector constructs both the situated meaning of a rule and the practice of its implementation, since it is probable that on the next occasion the site foreman will point out that the parapet is of regulation height. The competence deriving from this type of interaction with the control authority is described as 'learning to get ready for an inspection'. This involves the ability of the site foreman to identify the aspects on which the inspector will focus and that should therefore comply with the regulations. Interestingly, 'getting ready for the inspection'

BOX 6.4   THE INSPECTION IN A BUILDING SITE

The inspection is the means with which the regulatory agency translates and imposes its decisionmaking premises, seeking to anchor them in building site safety. What happens during an inspection is more similar to a negotiation than the simple imposition of orders. In this case, the attention rules are manifest in what the inspector decides to see or to ignore, and in what he decides to report or to let go:

Inspector: If the earthing hasn't been done properly, or if anti-fall barriers haven't been installed, then we report it . . . but it's obvious that if I find a plank with a nail sticking out of it on a site which is generally in order, then I let the matter drop.

During a spot check, the site foreman accompanies the inspector, seeking to negotiate the meaning of what the latter sees:

Inspector: This parapet is out of order.
Site foreman: You must be joking, it's standard workmanship.
Inspector: No, no, it's too low.
Site foreman: Aw, come on, it's five centimetres.
Inspector: No, I must be strict about this.

Source: Gherardi (2006, p. 199).

includes a deliberate decision to neglect certain details so that the inspector can write a 'minimum' report. All inspections, in fact, usually conclude with a fine. Consequently, the organizational actors help the inspector in his work, directing his attention to some minor irregularity so that he is distracted from looking for other, more serious breaches of the regulations. Once this competence has been acquired by the foreman, it is transmitted to the occupational community together with implicit fragments of 'practical wisdom' on how to cosmeticize a building site so that it looks safe. But at the same time the inspector and his community are aware of the game.

Prescription relays are therefore reticular in form, and they include both cooperation and conflict.

6.5   ATTENTION RULES

We have seen that the possibility of understanding, negotiating, maintaining or changing rules resides in situated interaction and in sociomaterial relations. We may now ask whether the new information and communication technologies, which modify workplaces by introducing physical distance among workers and channelling communication through technological mediation, also influence the ways in which the interpretation and regulation of behaviour take place. The discussion will centre on attention rules and how these relate to the understanding and performance of working practices.

The concept of attention rule derives from decision theory. March (1988) used it to describe how attention is a scarce resource which cannot be devoted to everything all at once. The object and time of the attention determine how the situation is interpreted, and they define the work task and the implicit and formal rules which regulate it. Attention and definition rules can be described as mental and interpretative schemas (thereby emphasizing the cognitive aspect of the mental representation of the task and its embedded rules. But they can also be described in pragmatic terms as the social construction of the rules that regulate a task while the activity of understanding and performing that task is in progress. Both these aspects should be remembered while focusing on how an action and its rules reciprocally constitute each other, rather than engaging in arid discussion on whether or not schemas of thought precede action.

The first case discussed (see Box 6.5) concerns a project to develop an e-business for teaching purposes which involved 45 geographically dispersed work groups.

It is often emphasized (and this example provides confirmation) that one of the main difficulties in contexts of computer-mediated communication consists in the construction of a mental representation of the partners' situations and updating it as and when new information arises. In the case just reported, because the differences between the local rules defining the task remained hidden when the collective work was being planned, the attention rules of the two groups of students conflicted when they identified what should be the aim and meaning of their joint task.

The expression 'local knowledge' has been used by the anthropologist Clifford Geertz (1983) as the title of one of his books. He employs it to discuss the relation between the particular and the universal. The expression is often used synonymously with contextual or situated knowledge, in that it denotes the knowledge (often non-verbal) based on experience and repeated interactions in particular contexts. Drawing subtle distinctions would be out of place here; it is more appropriate to adopt the adjective

BOX 6.5   DEVELOPING AN E-BUSINESS PROJECT

Among the work groups involved in the teaching project, there arose a conflict between the students at George Mason University (GMU), who did not want to use an online chat room to discuss the project and who proposed the use of telephone conversations; and the students at Texas Christian University (TCU), who strongly pushed for the use of computer-mediated communication. The latter were involved in the project because it was part of their course on the organization of information systems, so they were required to use the online chat room as an intrinsic component of the course. Conversely, the students at GMU were attending a course on organizational behaviour which did not prescribe any particular type of communication medium. Unfortunately, these distinctions had not been communicated between the groups, and the group leaders regarded them as details of little importance.

In describing this conflict, Cramton's intention is to emphasize that problems of this kind are very common in ICT-mediated work contexts, because knowledge about the local rules of the nodes in the network is deficient, and especially because the local rules are rarely discussed (or even remembered) in other locations.

When the two groups met to discuss the problem of the online chat room, they discovered that the nature of the task had been constructed differently in the two local contexts, and that this local knowledge was segregated. The GMU students interpreted the problem as resulting from the 'preferences' of the TCU students, who underestimated the difficulty of organizing online chat room meetings. In their turn, the TCU students thought that their colleagues at GMU did not care about the project and simply wanted to follow the simplest path. In short, what for one group was the choice of a communication medium (as a means to an end), was for the other group a rule constitutive of the task. Misunderstandings of this kind show that interpretation of the overall task interacts with the local context, creating (local) knowledge which is unlikely to be held in common.

Source: Cramton (2001), cited in Elsbach et al. (2005, p. 427).

'local' to refer to contexts of interaction consisting of multiple places, whether interrelated or unconnected. As shown by the above example, and as characterizing of many of the problems that arise in distance work using ICT, the distribution of knowledge among all the nodes of the network gives rise to an equivalent number of local knowledges pertaining to particular situations and experiences. Hence, different attention rules construct different local knowledges.

A second example of how physical distance interacts with the rules regulating the task, as well as the formation of specific occupational and professional skills, is provided by cooperative work for the development of technological innovation. This area of inquiry (von Hippel, 1994) has made a notable contribution: first to the understanding of situated knowledge (showing that knowledge is 'sticky' and therefore not easily transportable from one context to another); and second to the study of innovation as a process of co-construction in which both the final users and the producers themselves participate. Box 6.6 shows an example of how the producers (the engineers working in the laboratory) and the users (the operators working with the new machine) developed different understandings of their shared task according to their respective attention rules.

These two empirical examples, illustrated in Boxes 6.5 and 6.6, show that ordinary prescription is also inscribed in the understanding of a work task and in the assumptions that govern it: that is, the attention rules that result from the interaction between the context of the task and its abstract representation. These two examples also illustrate the problems typical of working at a distance (whether it is a significant geographical distance or separation in the same space). They specifically show that communication between physically distant contexts involves problems whose solution requires overcoming the boundaries of locally produced knowledge.

6.6   TO SUM UP

The specific contribution made by practice-based studies to the analysis of rules consists in its focus on the dynamics that converts them from 'norms' to 'resources' for action. Practices therefore rest on a normative infrastructure that can be defined – using a spatial metaphor for the locus of joint and distributed regulation between organizations and institutions, human and non-human actors – in terms of a space of ordinary prescription.

Situated work is regulated by rules that contribute to the shaping of situations, yet those rules are the effect of a negotiated order. They are 'given' and 'emergent'; they are expressed in explicit and universal form; but they

BOX 6.6   THE REPRESENTATION SCHEMA

A new machine for the automatic assembly of circuit boards was being tested (Tyre and von Hippel, 1997, cited in Elsbach et al., 2005, pp. 427–8). The users in the production department observed that the machine had started to place the components slightly out of tolerance. They informed the engineers so that they could find the cause of this technological 'drift'. Divergent conjectures on the nature of this drift arose between the engineers (in the laboratory) and the users (in the production department). They originated both from the ideas that the two groups possessed of what constituted the machine's 'normal operation' and from their location in physically distant contexts.

In the case of the users, 'normal operation' meant the 'precision processing of high-quality parts'. Their attention was therefore concentrated on the fact that the components were not being positioned exactly. When this information reached the engineers, they surmised that there was a programming problem, and they asked the users to check whether they were carefully following the programming rules. Only after the engineers had been reassured that the machine had been correctly programmed did they go the production department and inspect the machine. Once in the department, one of the engineers immediately noticed a loose screw on the camera which guided the placement of the components. The problem therefore lay with the machine.

While the engineers were in the laboratory, they had been unable to understand the problem because their representation of the machine's 'normal operation' was centred on specific expectations about how the machine should behave while in operation. Therefore, in trying to understand the problem, they employed a schema of inquiry which centred on what the machine 'did'. But being in the laboratory prevented them from seeing the machine, so that they had to rely on the descriptions of it given by the users. The latter, focused as they were on the final result and not on the machine, did not provide information about the machine's operation, but only about the incorrect placement of the components. Only when the engineers' representation schema came into contact with the machine's context of use did their representation of the problem become more accurate.

Source: Elsbach et al. (2005, pp. 427–8).

are also sustained through practices and in practices. This twofold nature of rules confronts communities of practices with the problem of understanding and negotiating what rule is constitutive of the situation, given the heterogeneity of rules. In fact, there is always a margin of ambiguity and incompleteness in rules which is contingently specified.

In pragmatic terms, a large part of actions and interactions in situation are not based on agreements, but rather on a set of tacit assumptions neither explicit nor fully explainable, and which are taken for granted. Rules, therefore, instead of being the causes of concrete actions, are future ideals to be achieved – or better, to be used retrospectively to legitimate what has been done and simultaneously to give it order and meaning.

Thus rules cease being normative of actions and become constitutive of their intelligibility. Both for ethnomethodologists and for phenomenology *à la* Schütz (1962), in everyday life 'following a rule' does not simply mean complying with it; it also means acting 'as if' one is following it: that is, constructing it, reconstructing it, rationalizing it and rendering it observable in particular contexts.

Production games exemplify how some working practices are socially sustained by models of interaction implicitly negotiated through conflict and cooperation. In the space of ordinary prescription, therefore, a (top-down) regulation of control and a (bottom-up) regulation of autonomy encounter each other, and in mobilizing their mutual power resources give rise to a joint regulation. However, it would be simplistic to think that this joint regulation is the outcome of two opposing logics, because joint regulation involves numerous human and non-human actors, some of which act as prescriptive relays. A prescriptive relay consists of the actors which (internally to an organization or within interorganizational relations) translate the rules (written or oral) within operational prescriptions which state what to do, when to do it, why it should be done, and possibly anchor these translations in sociomaterial artefacts.

Rules are sustained by diverse technologies which reinforce their prescriptiveness. One of the most important and pervasive of these technologies is writing. Indeed, the spread of written rules engendered the birth first of bureaucracy and then of protocols. Protocols are the contemporary expression of an endeavour to augment the proceduralization and standardization of work activities, and they have been accompanied by the spread of accreditation processes. The protocols and writing used to support prescriptiveness and strengthen the universality of rules are limited by their necessary relationship with speech and with negotiation of the ambiguity that arises in situated practising.

Finally, a particular case of context-creating rules consists in attention rules. Deciding what should receive attention, and when, is a process which structures how the situation is interpreted and shapes the definition of the work task and the implicit and formal rules that regulate it. Different attention rules may characterize different communities of practices or nodes in a network of distributed collaboration, thus giving rise to different local knowledges, at times connected, at times disconnected. We can grasp in these interactions the social construction of the rules that regulate a practice as the activity of understanding and performing as that practice proceeds.

The normative infrastructure sustaining a practice has been illustrated in this chapter with the following cases, which with their interrelations point to the specific aspect of practice as ordinary prescription:

- Production games and the case of 'today the plates are soft' allowed the reader to consider the ambiguity of rules and their situated enactment. In production games both aspects of work regulation are present: managerial control and the workers' autonomy and compliance together produce a pattern of co-production of situated rules.
- The case of protocols illustrated another duality: that between the inscription of a rule within the materiality of a written tool and its interpretation in situated oral discussion of its prescription.
- The concept and the example of a prescriptive relay illustrated how prescriptions are practically accomplished and assume a normative character within a chain of transmission – using a plurality of tools – of what should be done, how should it be done and why. There is not only prescription from the top and prescription from below. Rather, the field of ordinary prescription constitutes a net of normative links.
- The case of the inspection at a building site illustrated how situated prescriptions are inscribed within a wider net of institutional and organizational prescriptions, and how in encounters between different organizations the meaning of a rule is negotiated, and in negotiations a process of learning across organizational borders takes place.
- A less visible case of rules is represented by attention rules. The example of how to develop an e-business project showed how rules operate in relation to coordination at a distance and in the process of maintaining or disrupting a sense of the situation.
- This argument was developed further in the case of the misfit between the production department and the engineers' representation schema. The negotiations of the point of view, organizational rules and situated rules for the conduct of action constitute a space

of power enactment where both the change and the stability of practices are at stake.

NOTES

1. Repetitions are never without variations. Bernstein (1996) has defined this trial 'a repetition without repetition'. By being repeated, an operation becomes a new activity and the sequence of a series of repetitions fuels the functional repertoire (Clot, 2005).

7. Representing the texture of practices

Going to the cinema is an example of a social practice familiar to us, and which we perform with greater or lesser frequency. Let us use Garfinkel's (1967) technique to defamiliarize this practice by asking ourselves: when does the practice 'going to the cinema' begin? When we enter the cinema, when we buy the ticket, when we arrange with our friend to go and see the film? And does it finish with watching the film? Or is talking about the film afterwards over a beer, or some time later with a group of friends, part of the practice of 'going to the cinema'? The pleasure of going to the cinema continues and is renewed through discussion of films that we have seen. Going to the cinema is therefore connected with other sociability practices which form the texture of 'being together' and link with identity practices to show others that we are 'abreast with the facts of the world'. Talking about the films that we have loved or hated, discussing the reasons and the aesthetic categories that account for our cinematic tastes, associating ourselves ideally or materially with others who express appreciation similar to our own, becoming collectors of a certain genre of film and calling ourselves 'amateurs' of a cinematic genre, are all activities that we recognize as being part of the same social practice. This social practice is founded on a set of activities, on the processing of an individual aesthetic experience, on its discursive sharing within social settings – and therefore on the development of aesthetic categories that enable its communication. It produces specific subjectivities (for instance 'fans of police thrillers') within a broader community of 'film buffs'. We can continue our reasoning on the institutional and organizational level to stress how film clubs are organized, film libraries are formed and university courses on cinematography are institutionalized. From the individual aesthetic experience to the institutionalization of cinematographic representation as a socially legitimated form of production of knowledge about society, there extends a field of practices connected together and sustained by connections in action.

I shall resume the idea that one of the greatest theoretical and methodological opportunities offered by the concept of practice resides in the fact that practices rest on other practices: that is, they are interconnected and their interconnection makes it possible to shift the analysis from a practice to a field of practices which contains it, and vice versa. The concept of 'texture of practices' conveys the image of shifting the analysis to follow the connections in action and investigating how action connects or disconnects. Hence, in this chapter I shall start from the texture of practices in order to address the question of how practices are represented to their practitioners, and therefore of why and how to study the minutiae of practices in order to improve them. I shall then illustrate how the texture of practices connects situated work with social practices. As I do so, I shall discuss, more openly than in the previous chapters, a number of methodological issues concerning the empirical analysis of practices, my intention being to answer some questions current in the literature: whether the minute study of practices is an end in itself?; whether description is the sole purpose of the analysis of practices?; and if and how management studies profit from practice-based studies? I shall provide some examples from research to give my affirmative answer to these questions in regard to practice-based studies, but the reader will draw his/her own conclusions.

7.1   INTERWOVEN PRACTICES AND THEIR TEXTURE

How can a 'practice' or a 'field of practices' be isolated? Are all practices equal? Do some practices anchor other practices? How are practices interwoven to form a texture?

To give a concrete example, before introducing the concept of texture theoretically, I shall borrow an example provided by Ann Swidler (2001, pp. 89–90) in order to show how some practices anchor, control or organize others (see Box 7.1).

The example is a telling one for it raises the question as to whether in a field of practices the researcher should abandon him/herself to an endless deferral of nested practices, or if he/she can detect any practice that could anchor, control or organize others. In the case of the building of houses, practices associated with capitalism, such as paying for a house or owning it, are more enduring and powerful than others. In analysing practices, therefore, we may ask which practices are more important in shaping or constraining other social arrangements.

The methodological principle of 'follow the practices' acquires concrete meaning when the researcher observes a situated practice and moves up from it to the institutional order or conversely moves down from it to the individual-in-situation. Or in other words, when he/she explores a connective web which branches in all directions and traces the social connections among individuals, collectives, organizations, institutions, the situated contexts in which these connections take specific form and all

BOX 7.1   PRACTICES THAT ANCHOR OTHER
            PRACTICES

Take a hypothetical architect's plan for a house. Long before the
architect can draw up plans for the house, constraints on its possible design are built into taken-for-granted practices which involve
standard kinds of materials (bricks, door frames, steel girders and
so on). Like composers who cannot write music for which there are
no instruments (Becker, 1982), architects assume the standard
kind of materials that are available, and ignore the potentially infinite set of materials that are unavailable.

The plans that architects draw up are inevitably incomplete.
Even when the competence of a contractor or a builder is brought
in, the plan for a house leaves most of what will be required to
build it unspecified: the skill of the crafts workers, the ways in
which different workers with different specialities coordinate their
activities, what they consider to be the appropriate uses of standard objects and materials.

Behind the plan lie other, almost invisible, practices. The architect's knowledge of what a house is, how people use one, whether
sleep should take place in a room different from those reserved for
eating or washing. Numerous cultural differences are inscribed in
such a common, universal activity as living in a house.

Also lying behind the plan is the set of professional practices
against which the architect's aesthetic judgement is compared
and which furnishes the vocabulary of meanings with which he/
she works in order to produce the aesthetic effect valued by his/
her professional community.

Another set of practices links the architect to the client: who
decides what payments should be made and how, who owns the
house and how. A broad set of practices then link both the architect and the client to the capitalist market economy, mobilizing the
work of other persons and institutions.

Source: Swidler (2001, pp. 89–90).

the intermediaries utilized by them – intermediaries that may be physical objects or artefacts, discourses or texts. And his/her analysis is conducted, not statically with description of a structure of connections, but dynamically as the constant becoming of a form which self-reproduces but is never identical with itself in that practices are incomplete and indeterminate until they are situatedly performed.

My concern in studying a field of practices is to determine how connection-in-action comes about, how associations are established, maintained and changed among the elements of a partially given form. I have called this connection-in-action 'texture of practice' (Gherardi, 2006), my purpose being to emphasize the qualitative aspect assumed by the connection once the relations have been activated and the weaving together of the relations-in-act has begun. Not all 'theoretically' possible connections are established 'in fact' and then endure. Hence power is the power to connect (or not to connect) and it results from the texture of the field of practice. Associated with power is knowledge, with the consequence that 'knowing-in-practice' acquires more definite meaning, the more its embeddedness in a field of practices defines the spatiality, facticity and the weaving-together of the connections that constitute the texture.

Emery and Trist (1965) introduced the idea of 'texture' into organizational studies in order to stress the connectedness between an organization and the environment. And they used the term 'causal texture' to highlight the dynamic interaction among environmental parts, as opposed to the conception of parts as relatively independent subsystems. Emery and Trist (1965) borrowed the idea from earlier psychological studies by Tolman and Brunswick (1935) and the philosopher Stephen Pepper (1942). The philosophical referent for the concept of texture is contextualism[1] as a root metaphor for seeing the world. For Pepper, texture is not only connectedness, it is also fused with action: 'It is doing and enduring, and enjoying: making a boat, running a race, laughing at a joke, solving a problem, communicating with a friend' (Pepper, 1942, p. 232, cited in Cooper and Fox, 1990, p. 575). These acts consist of interconnected activities with continuously changing patterns. In other words, we may call them practices.

Cooper and Fox (1990, p. 576) offer the following definition of the texture of organizing: 'The key to understanding texture is the idea of "connectedness in action"; this phrase brings out the definitive features of texture, its endless series of relationships which continually move into each other'. The woven text has a texture that stretches and shrinks, and 'to follow the pattern and interlacing of the composition requires the weaver's art of looping and knotting' (Brogan, 1989, p. 12, cited in Cooper and Fox, 1990, p. 580).

Texture is a strongly evocative concept which recalls the intricacies of networking but at the same time allows for an analytical, qualitative, framework (Strati, 2000). The texture of organizing can be conceived as:

> An imaginary territory, a circumscribed domain marked out by a plurality of organizational actors which comprises ideas, projects, emotions, that subjects assign to their organizational behaviour. . . . It is the symbolic territory of policies, conflicts, negotiations and exchanges, but also of reciprocal socialization by organizational actors to the diverse rationalities of their own activities. (Gherardi and Strati, 1990, p. 617)

The texture of organizing is not something that is explicitly linear, and the mental images best able to grasp it are a crossword puzzle (Cooper and Fox, 1990), the metaphor of flux and transformation (Morgan, 1986), the view of becoming (Clegg et al., 2005), the idea of tacit knowledge (Polanyi, 1966) or the 'et cetera' problem in Garfinkel and Sacks (1970), where any attempt at literal description simply multiplies the task in an infinite regress.

As Polanyi (1966, p. 5, added emphasis) wrote '*there is always more than we can say*'. For example, legal knowledge (and indeed any form of practical knowledge) is rooted in tacit knowledge, so that what laws actually means is subject to subsequent persuasive interpretation in the courts. A lawyer's competence is simply one version of a glossing process general in social life, and it is a process that copes with the excess of 'open texture' in everyday life. In fact, there are two basic ways to approach social life as 'text': glossing and weaving. Glossing is a socially controlled way to fix the mobile, and the gloss itself is meant for 'instant consumption': its fixed meaning implies that the reader is external to it, he/she is positioned in such a way that he/she believes the glossed text to be already constituted and beyond his/her influence. Weaving implies the tendency of an open text to transgress its socially contrived meaning: 'the woven text opens in a centrifugal way and can only be experienced as an activity of creative production, in which the agent/reader is caught up as an active element in the ongoing, unfinished movement of the text' (Cooper and Fox, 1990, p. 578). The reader is in the text, and in a very similar way knowing-in-practice presumes a subject who is inside the knowledge production process and abandons him/herself to the centrifugal connections of meanings/actions.

The framework that I propose for analysis of the texture of a field of practices is therefore indirect and metaphorical, since although texture can be shown or demonstrated, it can never be defined. Explanation risks losing the very nature of what it seeks to elucidate. Weaving, that is, following the multivalent process that constitutes texture, is the analytical metaphor most appropriate for its understanding (Brogan, 1989).

Nevertheless, this is not to imply that texture is a hidden object that cannot be grasped; rather, we should develop a style of thinking and doing research that enables us to show the relevance of connectedness in action and its continuing deferral.

At this point we may say that the texture of a specific field of practices is shaped by the processes of alignment of material, semiotic and normative elements within the field and the modes of alignment are the effect of local connectedness in action. In order to conduct empirical investigation of the qualities of texture and the processes of its weaving, we must define and circumscribe some units of analysis within a seamless web. The units of analysis are not pre-given, nor do they rest on any natural distinction; they are arbitrary choices made by the researcher on the basis of a theoretical scheme, or the researcher may choose to take as 'a' practice what the practitioners define as practice (Bjørkeng et al., 2009; Carlsen, 2006).

7.2   REPRESENTING PRACTICES TO EMPOWER PRACTITIONERS

Actors often employ ambiguous vocabulary to justify a social practice obeying rather different principles. They do so to disguise the true nature of their practical knowledge as '*docta ignorantia*' (Bourdieu, 1990), that is, a mode of practical knowledge unaware of its own principles (Gherardi, 2012). Whether we refer to Polanyi's tacit knowledge, whether we refer to Bourdieu's '*docta ignorantia*', or whether we recall the sensible knowledge discussed in Chapter 3, we are faced with the following methodological problems: the opacity of practices (an opacity shared by both practitioners and researchers); how to render explicit and state in 'objective' language what does not often pass through language; and finally not only how to do so but also why. In methodological terms, the problems are how to conduct the data gathering; how to interpret the data collected; and how to report and represent practices, for what audience and for what purpose.

Within a workspace, a stabilized way of doing things becomes a practice when it is institutionalized and made normatively accountable both to its practitioners and those who view it from outside. For the empirical analysis of a practice we may choose three levels of analysis (Gherardi, 2010), the first two based on the distinction between objectivism and subjectivism (Bourdieu, 1990), or in Evered and Louis's (1981) terms between 'inquiry from outside' and 'inquiry from inside', and the third one based on the distinction between production and reproduction (I shall analyse this third level in Section 7.3).

When practices are read 'from outside', the inquiry concentrates on their regularity, on the pattern which organizes activities and on the more or less shared understanding that allows their repetition. The recursiveness of practices is the element which enables both practitioners and researchers to recognize a practice as practice, that is, a way of doing sustained by canons of good practice (a normative accountability) and beautiful practice (an aesthetic accountability). Therefore a practice is such when it is socially recognized as an institutionalized doing (Gherardi, 2008).

For example, we can go back to the research on telemedicine illustrated in Chapter 5. When a cardiologist tells a colleague that from 10 to 12 o'clock he/she will be 'doing telecardiological consultancy', the expression is intersubjectively meaningful as a specific work practice which is different from others not only because of the use of an ICT technology but also because of the set of relations activated to produce that practice and to sustain its legitimacy and value. When I read teleconsultancy practice 'from outside', my knowledge interest will be driven by the following question: how does the object of the 'telecardiological consultation' practice emerge from the recursiveness of the activity? I shall assume that the goal, or the object, of a practice is not a *telos* which exists prior to that practice. It is not an end that directs the practice to itself. Rather, the object of the work, of every working practice, is emergent, and it is constantly defined and redefined during the activity.[2]

To understand practice 'from outside', the researcher may draw on and analyse a number of 'repetitions' of the same practice, with the purpose of constructing a typology of activities within the practice and, on this empirical basis, deduce what are the objects of the practice and the organizational logic that governs the enactment of organizing networks. In fact, a reading of a practice from outside will enable the researcher to compare the rhetoric of its use (the field of prescription) with the situated interpretations that emerge from its being practised (see Chapter 6 for the difference between prescribed and real work). Nevertheless, an analysis of practices 'from outside' may be useful for familiarizing the researcher with the activities of the practitioners, for understanding their vocabulary and for writing the presentation of the practice as the background of his/her study; but it is a rather limited use of the potentialities of the practice lens.

A second reading can be conducted 'from inside', that is, from the point of view of the activity which is being performed, with its temporality and processuality, as well as the emergent and negotiated order of the action being done. In fact observation of practices enables simultaneous analysis of the reproduction and change of the social order.

Seen from the inside, practice is a knowledgeable collective action that forges relations and connections among all the resources available and all the constraints present. We saw how doing telecardiological consultation requires knowing how to align two kinds of knowledge: medical knowledge, an artefact (the ECG) representing the body of an absent patient; and technological knowledge, a system that receives and transmits communications. We saw how doing telecardiological consultation also requires knowing how to align the action-net (Czarniawska, 2004) which is interwoven and deployed so that every element has a place and a sense. From this definition it follows that knowing is something people do together, and it is done in every mundane activity. To know is to be able to participate with the requisite competence in the complex web of relationships among people, material artefacts and activities (Gherardi, 2001). Acting as a competent practitioner is synonymous with knowing how to connect successfully with the field of practices thus activated. Whilst an inquiry from outside focuses the researchers attention on 'doing', an inquiry from inside focuses on 'knowing' as a collective doing.

I do not wish to discuss all the methods for conducting inquiries from inside, rather I shall limit myself to a research technique which I have found very useful for eliciting knowledge from inside and for re-presenting this knowledge to practitioners within an action research framework. I shall now illustrate the interview with the double, which was the method that I used to gather the descriptions of the production game 'today the plates are soft' (see Chapter 6).

The interview with the double has a twofold origin simultaneously in Italy (Gherardi, 1990; Oddone et al., 1977) and in France (Clot, 1999), where Oddone et al.'s book was translated in 1981. The interview with the double first arose in social psychology in a cultural context which valued worker experience as source of anti-capitalist knowledge, and in a context of adult training. I then resumed the technique in the 1990s as a means to elicit the knowledge situated in micro-decisions and subsequently as a type of ethnographic interview (Bruni and Gherardi, 2001) and as an action learning tool (Nicolini, 2006; 2007). A detailed description of the merits and drawbacks of this method has been provided by Nicolini (2009), to which the reader is referred, while here I shall restrict my treatment to the logic and further applications of the method.

I developed a technique of projective interviewing – the interview with the double – to gather further data while I was doing action research in two productive contexts, a battery manufacturer and a publishing house.

The interviewee was asked to perform what was described as a 'bizarre' task:

> Now that I have analysed your job, I want to understand it even better. I want to imagine what it would be like to do it myself. I want you to imagine me as your double, completely the same as you, and that tomorrow morning I shall

be going to work in your place. How should I behave, what should I do so that no one discovers the switch?

I then checked that the interviewee had understood the situation. To do this, I exchanged roles and gave the interviewee the example of my own job. I would begin more or less as follows:

> Tomorrow you'll go into the university, but not before 9.30 because everyone will be surprised to see you, since I'm not a morning person. Instead, I tend to stay on in the evenings, sometimes till 8 o'clock. Say good morning to everyone but don't stop and talk, because I'm crotchety in the mornings.

The example contained an implicit invitation to focus on the minutiae of everyday life, on relationships and feelings, rather than on the technical aspects of the job. The interviewee was given all the time that he/she needed, and was told that the interviewer would not intervene 'so as not to interrupt your train of thought'. At the end of the interview, the interviewee was asked for a list of instructions arranged in order of importance. This request was made in order to prompt a moment of reflection on what had been said.

From a theoretical point of view, this technique rests on a number of assumptions:

- On reciprocal knowledge between interviewee and interviewer (the in-the-field work lasted on average two years) which, in principle, should encourage a trust relationship and therefore increase the implication of accountability in the conversation with the interviewer (Antaki, 1985).
- On the principle that the interview is a social interaction, and not an 'objective' collection of data. This implies three premises: the social construction of the topic of discourse, of the speaking subject and of the interaction; the contextuality both of the interlocutory situation and of the broader context in which the interview takes place; the medium of the interaction, that is, language. Language, in fact, does not describe an objective reality to which it corresponds; rather, it organizes a discourse on truth in a partial and partisan manner.
- On the assumption that the interviewee is willing to accept the projective technique, that is, the interviewee commits him/herself to a participative research relationship.

The main advantage of a projective technique is that it overcomes the barriers of self-consciousness and rationality, of social influences and of unconscious repression. A projective interview elicits imaginative and unusual associations, and hypothetical 'as if' conjectures, and therefore it yields interpretations that reflect the respondent's interests and preoccupations. Projective techniques give the researcher access to the interviewees' modes of imposing order on reality. These modes render ambiguity into something that the interviewer can grasp while simultaneously preserving it in order to conceal contradictions and secrets, should they be unable or unwilling to disambiguate. Consequently, 'the proper perspective for evaluating projective tasks is a tool for the researcher to increase his/her contact and insight into the problem at hand' (Branthwaite and Lunn, 1985, p. 114). One should bear in mind that the expression 'projective technique' subsumes a variety of procedures which share the common feature of a highly ambiguous, novel and sometimes even bizarre task, the meaning or interpretation of which is determined by the respondent who must structure it and render it meaningful (Branthwaite and Lunn, 1985). The interview with the double is therefore one of the many techniques that can be used, such as an ambiguous drawing, a story that must completed, a visual or acoustic stimulus with which to make associations or, as we shall see, video clips of work situations.

A warning is in order concerning the use of interviews with the double. It should always be remembered that the interview, and therefore the use of explicit language in the description of a work practice, is a blunt instrument because the researcher mainly accesses what the interviewee thinks about his/her doing, what he/she can and wants to say, but not the complexity, the situated and tacit knowledge, and the collective dimension of practising. Hence the interview with the double is a fruitful means to elicit tacit and sensitive knowledge (Vermersch, 1994) when it is combined with other techniques, such as participant observation, narrative analysis, shadowing and other methods of qualitative analysis (Czarniawska, 2007).

I shall not go into details on how to conduct the interview (on this see Nicolini, 2009), but I want to give an example of the beginning of the interview (see Box 7.2) which enabled me to understand the production game related to 'today the plates are soft' (see Chapter 6) when I was conducting participant observation in the assembly department (Gherardi, 1995b).

The numbers against the instructions derive from the categorization that I drew up when analysing the interviews on the basis of grounded theory as a codification technique, and which I subsequently used to describe the process of situated decisionmaking. This type of projective interview has the advantage of rendering the work 'visible' by making it 'tellable'. Yet it also has the second advantage of making accessible to the researcher the moral order which presides over the practice by giving instructions on what to do and what not to do, what is right and what is

---

BOX 7.2   THE INTERVIEW WITH THE DOUBLE

[1]   You are a worker in the fitting shop of a firm making batteries. You must report for work at 6.00 in the morning and work non-stop until 9.15.

[2]   When you enter to take my place, the first thing you must do is check on the large board at the end of shop to find out what type of battery is being assembled today and what the quota is.

[3]   Then you go and meet your workmate. You'll be taking turns with him to weld the terminals onto the batteries and beat the plates.

[4]   When you are the beater, lay the separators on the bench, put the negative plates on the left, the positive plates in the centre and the separators on the right. Then lay the separators on top of the negative plates and then the positive plates on top of them. Repeat the action several times to build up the units. Then put the units on the bench for your mate to pick up and weld the terminals.

[5]   As the beater or the welder you will notice that the quality of the materials is highly variable; for example, the plates can be stiff or too soft.

Source: Gherardi (1995b, p. 12).

---

wrong, what is subject to dispute and different interpretation. The normative infrastructure of the practice is thus augmented by prescriptions 'from outside' and 'from inside' the community, and it is imbued with moral order that enjoins what is to be done, what is not to be done, what cannot not be done and what need not be done.

Thus far, I have argued that it is necessary to describe practices 'from inside', and I have provided an example of how to access the collective knowledge contained in practice. But the purpose of the analysis of working practices is also to create collective awareness of the stock of knowledge which the work collective possesses, develops and may change should it consider this opportune. Hence the accurate description of the working practice by the researcher becomes an input to group discussion both to gain awareness of how it works as a group and to sustain the analysis and revision of working practices with a view to professional and organizational development. This is the logic which regulates the representation of practices as a process of their re-presentation that enables the practitioners to introduce distance between the self and the work, and thereby open space for reflection on the practice and its critical reappropriation. What for the researcher is a process of representation of the practice for interpretative purposes, is for the practitioners a process of re-presentation – that is, a moment when the researcher reflects practice back to its practitioners. Both processes have methodological difficulties that I do not intend to discuss here. I shall instead merely give an idea of how the analysis of practices has numerous applicative goals:

- Oddone et al. (1977) made use of such analysis with the evident Marxist intent of empowering workers in their capacity to act on the surrounding world. Their interviews were structured on four main categories with which to organize the instructions: the task, the comrades, the factory hierarchy and the trade unions or other workers' organizations. The aim was therefore emancipatory.
- In my research, it was a heuristic tool and an occasion for a collective reflection through group feedback for the development of professional knowledge.
- In the research by the French school (Clot et al., 2001) consisting of social psychologists and ergonomists, and using activity theory, the method is aimed at a 'clinic of activity'. It is on this research that I shall dwell here.

It can be deduced from the above that when I talk about the representation of practices to their practitioners, I am proposing an 'engaged' inquiry (Eikeland, 2008; 2009; Eikeland and Nicolini, 2011). This philosophy is well visible in the French school's methodology based on the techniques of *autoconfrontation* (self-confrontation) and *autoconfrontation croisée* (crossed self-confrontation).

The methodology has been developed within the clinical approach to activity. That is to say, the researchers start from a request by their interlocutors to analyse working practices in order to modify what they perceive to be degraded work. The assumption and the dynamic on which the researchers concentrate is that of the psychological experience of the work group, which through the dialogic method, establishes contact between external conflict and internal conflict. This therefore requires finding and proposing to a group of 'knowers' a moment or an element or a gesture of the practice (what is called the link-object) which is controversial, and that by arousing debate and discussion establishes a multilingual community in which the dialogue takes place. The researchers may use various means, from the story of a worker (which becomes the subject of comment/comparison by a second 'expert') to video recordings. The purpose is to stimulate discussion within the community about its work and trigger curiosity and enthusiasm which leads to appropriation of the work and a desire for change and improvement. For example, the researchers start from an exploration of the work in its natural setting. They extract a small sample which is video recorded and shown to the worker appearing in it, who is asked to describe what he/she is doing and how he/she is doing it (this is simple *autoconfrontation*). Then – still in the presence of the researcher and the first worker – a second worker is asked to comment on what the first one is doing (this is *autoconfrontation croisée*). Also this sequence is recorded and subsequently shown to the work group as a whole. A cycle builds up around what workers do, what they say they do and finally around what they do about what they say. The purpose is therefore to arouse the unforeseen, curiosity and comparison between what is done implicitly and the personal knowledge that each has developed unconsciously. The dialogue thus develops around the 'ways of doing' developed to achieve the same objective.

To conclude, we may say that there are numerous methods to extract a representation of practices 'from within'. The researcher's imagination must be stimulated to develop yet others, while the purpose of representing practices to the practitioners in general is to isolate practices from their context so that discussion and negotiation can take place on how they are practised and on how they can be changed.

When we study practices 'from within' and when the aim of the study is to empower practitioners, they are seen as the active agents of change in practices and reflection on the personal, collective and organizational development of practices. However, practices have lives of their own, in that they produce social effects in their being practised. Hence there is another analytical level for the study of practices, and it concerns the social and historical reproduction of practices.

7.3 THE REPRODUCTION OF PRACTICES

One characteristic of practices is that they are institutionalized but open to the dynamic of continuous refinement that takes place in both everyday and long-period reproduction. Recursiveness shifts the researcher's attention from practice as production to practice as reproduction. I use the expression 'recursiveness of practices' to illustrate their reproduction, and I reserve the expression 'reproduction of practices' to denote the process which, through the everyday recursiveness of practices, ensures that their being practised produces longer-period social effects. This distinction allows me to pose the following (theoretical and methodological) question: what are the effects produced by the fact that certain practices continue to be practised? At this analytical level the researcher asks: what is the 'doing' that the practice does?

This third reading of practice – beside readings 'from outside' and 'from inside' – relates to the reproduction of society and considers the social effects of a single practice in relation to its being practised within society. Ethnomethodologists talk of the inevitable reflexivity of practices to show that every practice creates its context. Bourdieu (1972) speaks of 'circuits of reproduction', that is, the reciprocal, cyclical relationships through which practice creates and recreates the objectified social structures and the conditions in which it occurs. An effective way of expressing this concern has been formulated by Schultze and Boland (2000, p. 195), who draw on Barbara Townley (1993), who in turn paraphrases Foucault: 'People know what they are doing, they know why they are doing it, but they don't know what doing it does' (Foucault, 1982, p. 787). And it is this level at which ethical questions can be asked and at which the emancipatory or exploitative effects of a social practice may be questioned. Therefore it is at this level that the researcher can look for the power effects enacted by the reproduction of practices.

It is therefore necessary to analyse the circuits of reproduction of practices, and I shall do so in order to consider practices in their 'doing' of society. Returning to my research on telemedicine (Gherardi, 2010), I shall ask: what is the social effect of telecardiological consultation? And I shall integrate the two previous readings of practices viewed objectively and subjectively with reflection on the circuits of reproduction of the social in order to argue that telemedicine engenders mainly a reassurance effect. I shall start from the encounter between two logics of practice in the patient/doctor relationship (see Box 7.3).

Therefore a sociological and organizational definition of reassurance sees it as the effect of a situated activity, a collective accomplishment achieved within a network of personal, organizational and institutional relations which mobilize people, technologies and knowledge in response to a demand – individual and collective – for the exclusion or amelioration of a justified fear. Reassurance can therefore be seen as something that is 'done' within a sociotechnical ensemble,[3] and the availability of a new technology redefines the previous sociotechnical network. Paradoxically, as Illich (1982) noted, the availability of diagnostic instruments increases demand, with predictable increases in health service costs. The new technologies in health care, among them telecardiological consultation, may feed into this simple dynamic between the doctor's and the patient's expectations and give rise to unexpected consequences. One of these is that, as

BOX 7.3   A SOCIOTECHNICAL REASSURANCE PRACTICE

When someone goes to a doctor they usually have a simple expectation: they hope that the doctor will tell them that they have nothing to worry about, that their symptoms are not alarming; or if they have some form of chronic disease, that it is manageable. The expectation of being *reassured* about their health not only affects the state of mind with which patients contact the health professionals, but it is also a macro-social factor in the growing demand for health care in the Western countries. A health professional, on the other hand, has been trained to formulate diagnoses according to the principle that it is worse to declare a sick person healthy than the other way round. Although they have an interest in common, the logic of practice of the patients is informed by a need for reassurance, while that of the doctors is more concerned with a search for proof; and if instruments or tests are available to bear out the initial hypotheses, they will presumably be used in the search for confirmation/non-confirmation of the disease.

Health professionals see reassurance as involving a minimization of the problem, a distortion of information, a 'mother/child' maternal relation, so that it pertains to the private rather than the professional sphere. They prefer the concept of information to reassurance because unlike reassuring, the action of informing establishes an adult/adult relation and inserts distance – and therefore professionalism – into the relationship with the patient. The negative image is also extended to the patient 'who needs to be reassured'. In this case, he/she is defined as either a hypochondriac or troublesome.

Owing to their professional training, it is not easy for clinicians to see reassurance as a social practice in its material and organizational manifestations, and not as a feeling or a pathology. On the contrary, I conceptualize reassurance as a social practice performed through situated interaction involving not only persons but also a technological and a normative infrastructure.

Source: Gherardi (2010, p. 518).

the telecardiological consultation enters into use, it is inscribed more in the sociomaterial practice of reassurance than in the medical practice of preventing and coping with emergencies.

The case of telemedicine shed light on the social effects of a new practice once a technological practice had changed the texture of practices from inside. While within practice-based studies, most studies have considered mainly endogenous changes emerging from the community of practitioners under study, it is important also to keep in mind that practices may change from outside. In order to see how an exogenous change has effects on the emergent relations that stabilize a provisional new practice through negotiations within an institutional context, I illustrate the case of medically assisted reproduction in Italy after the introduction of a new law (Perrotta, 2010; Gherardi and Perrotta, 2011).

Medically assisted reproduction in Italy is a practice field subject to strong institutional pressures (a recent Italian law limits medical practices) which change the technological practices of the professions involved. In 2004, Law 40 forbade surrogate motherhood of any kind, the insemination of homosexual couples and singles, insemination after the partner's death and of women in non-precocious menopause. It also prohibited heterologous fertilization (that is, with gametes from donors external to the couple), the production of more than three embryos per cycle, the cryoconservation of embryos and the performance of pre-implant diagnosis. And it ordered that all the embryos produced must be transferred to the uterus even if they were potentially malformed. Moreover, by equating the embryo with a person, Law 40 made its rights prevail over those of the mother. The limitations introduced by law were widely discussed and criticized in regard to both its ethical and clinical aspects, since medical procedures were paralysed, while the clandestine market and the search for assisted reproduction in other more permissive countries were stimulated.

Nevertheless the restrictions introduced by Law 40 were incorporated into the complex texture of the working practices of assisted reproduction centres. The spread and the stabilization of the new practice is the effect of a distributed agency which seeks to impose a change in practice by mobilizing resources of power, coercion, authority, legitimation and jurisdiction over knowledge (see Box 7.4).

On the basis of the foregoing case study it is illustrated how enactment of a law restricting medical practices in Italy has exerted coercive power on organizations and professions and how a new practice has become stabilized within a texture of social practices. Therefore I propose to study practice as an order-producing device, integrating the *what* it is that is done (the activities performed within the practice), with the *how* it is done

BOX 7.4   THE STABILIZATION OF A NEW
          PRACTICE

The stabilization of the new practice took place through three different mechanisms – *limitation, rhetorical closure* and *anchorage
in materiality* – which are now described:

- *Stabilization by limitation.* When Law 40 came into force, it
  forbade the freezing of embryos and required the transfer of
  all the embryos produced, defining a maximum number of
  three transferable embryos. These restrictions entail the
  impossibility of fertilizing more than three oocytes so as not
  to produce more than three embryos. Stabilization by limitation has not only restricted the field of what can or cannot be
  done; it has also given rise to negotiation among professionals, and between these professionals and their organizations, which has become visible in the production of a new
  practice standard: the fertilization of three oocytes (and
  three embryos implanted on average) per treatment regardless of possible multiple pregnancies (and their effects on
  women' health).
- *Stabilization by rhetorical closure.* The prohibition on cryo-
  conserving embryos meant that patients had to undergo
  ovarian stimulation for every cycle of treatment. To avoid
  this restriction, in the first months after enactment of the law
  the operators at the reproduction centres, and their professional associations, tried to redefine the categories of their
  practice. They questioned the notion of 'embryo': when can
  a fertilized oocyte be considered an 'embryo' and therefore
  as constituting life and a person? Some scientists, drawing
  on their professional authority, proposed an intrinsic distinction between embryo and pre-embryo. Mobilizing their professional authority, they thus proposed not a legal, but a
  medical interpretation of the law which enabled them to cir-
  cumvent its provisions. In other words, it was not technically
  forbidden to freeze pre-embryos. The professions thus tried
  to assert their jurisdiction and tried to oppose the coercive
  pressures from the state. Nevertheless, the attempt by the
  professions to overcome the restrictions imposed by the law
  through defining work failed because the coercive pressures

of the state, allied with large part of public opinion and contrary political parties, were able to operate a rhetorical
closure of the debate around the beginning of life and therefore pre-embryos constitutes life.

- *Stabilization by anchoring in technology.* The prohibition on
  inseminating more than three oocytes interweaves with the
  choice of the type of technique to use. And one of the most
  striking effects of the new law has been the induced change
  in technological practice and the enhancement of the professionalism of the biologist vis-à-vis the gynaecologist. In
  the case of *In Vitro* Fertilization (IVF) the biologists use the
  morphological appearance of the cells, their arrangement,
  and their colour, to obtain information on their state of maturation, but they do not have certainties. In the case of ICSI
  (Intracytoplasmic Sperm Injection), the cleansing of the
  oocyte instead enables them to be more certain about an
  oocyte's state of maturation, and therefore select the best
  oocytes. In so doing the law allies itself with this technique
  and becomes another contextual reason for preferring ICSI
  to IVF in an increasing number of cases. The new technique,
  in fact, has not been adopted because of its superiority or
  greater efficiency in terms of results (pregnancies), but
  instead in response to institutional pressures. The indis-
  criminate use of this technique has a serious impact on the
  work schedules of laboratories and on medical resources.

Source: Gherardi and Perrotta (2011, pp. 602–7).

(the subjective and situated meaning of the practice for its practitioners),
with the *power effects* generated by its circuit of reproduction.

Since power and knowledge operate in a mutually generative fashion,
we may see practice – following Messner et al. (2008, p. 71) – 'as the interface between power and knowledge. Practice is where a certain way of
doing things and a certain way of acquiring knowledge collide'. The circuit
of reproduction of the new stabilized practice thus allows us to connect
processes of stabilization with the power effects generated by it:

- The use of coercive power – obtained through political mobilization
  and the production of a law – not only institutionalizes a change
  in a field of practices but also de-institutionalizes the previous
  practice.

- The anchoring of the new practice in technology entails not only that one technology is progressively supplanted by another, but also that scientific and technological research develops in an unexpected manner as it explores and improves techniques previously little used, thus advancing scientific research.
- The third unexpected effect of the new practice's circuit of reproduction is the marginalization of couples, from that taking away of decisions which directly concern them. Beyond the rhetoric on 'patient-centred' medicine, in this field of practices the power of expert knowledge is further strengthened by a restriction which increases the practice's uncertainty.

In conclusion, we may say that the negotiation among several competing rationalities which weave the texture of practices produces both intended and unintended consequences, but that the stabilization of a practice is always temporary and it is open to further re-negotiations. Considering the institutional environment and the institutional forces surrounding a texture of practices enables us to better link the micro-analysis of practising with the macro-analysis of the circuits of practice reproduction and the power effects generated by practising.

7.4 THE SPIRAL CASE STUDY FOR MAPPING A TEXTURE OF PRACTICES

Isolating a practice within a texture of practices is a heuristic operation by the researcher who, depending on his/her research interests, delimits a field of analysis. However, one of the main methodological opportunities connected with the use of a 'practice lens' consists of being able to move within the texture of practices from any point of entry.

I now provide an example to illustrate the research method that I have called a 'spiral case study' (Gherardi, 2006, p. 55; 2009c). Figure 7.1 graphically depicts how it is possible to conduct a series of linked case studies which start from a research situation and interest more focused on the micro-level and then shifts to more macro-levels, and vice versa.

The object of the research to which Figure 7.1 refers was safety as a social practice. The construction industry is well known for its high accident rate and for the importance which society attributes to safety. I can confidently claim that safety is a social value, a body of institutionalized knowledge, and a field of situated practices that involves all levels of society and is supported by a set of legal precepts. Therefore safety may be defined as a property emerging from a texture of situated practices in an

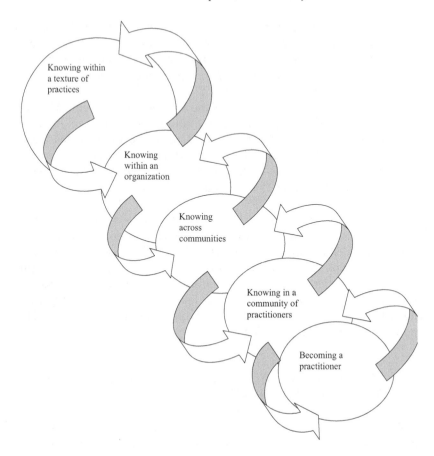

Figure 7.1   A graphic representation of the spiral case study

industry. I drew up a research design which enabled me to conduct empirical analysis of how safety knowledge is formed and transmitted within a
texture of situated practices and within courses of action that integrate
those on the construction site with an institutional context comprising all
safety-engendering practices. The base assumption was that society as a
whole can be studied within situated interactions construed as the fragments of a hologram.

   The units of analysis were selected so that attention could focus on the
process by which practical knowledge is institutionalized – that is, the
moments when and the processes whereby knowing-in-practice becomes
'knowledge' – and simultaneously on the manner in which the 'known' is

enacted in actual 'knowing'. The image is that of a spotlight trained on the scene of an action (becoming a practitioner) which then moves to the next one. Hence, the scenes presented in each case study are these:

- A young assistant building site manager begins his/her new job by flanking the site foreman. How does he/she learn safety, and how does the community of practices that he/she is now joining teach him/her safety? A ethnography of the work entry process recounts the development of a knowledge base and an occupational identity, as well as the practical acquisition of a situated curriculum (Gherardi et al., 1998a).
- Several communities of practice perform interdependent tasks in the same construction company and are therefore co-responsible for the production of safety. How do the engineers, the site foremen, and the project managers explain the causes of accidents and how to prevent them? A causal analysis of their accounts sheds light on practical reasoning processes, and an analysis of their discursive practices shows that as diverse communities 'talking *in* practice' they sustain their respective identities and socialize each other into their respective logics of action (Gherardi et al., 1998b).
- Accidents represent breakdowns in practices; they are moments when quotidian 'normality' disintegrates and must be reconstructed. Can these moments occasion organizational learning? How is the texture of a field of practices repaired? Comparative analysis of the organizational processes enacted after a serious accident was the methodology for this case study (Gherardi, 2004).
- Within a circumscribed territory, construction companies and institutions with competence for safety encounter each other and come into conflict. The interactions in which they negotiate their power relations give rise to a local safety culture. How are interorganizational relations woven together, and how is the learning network constructed? Qualitative network analysis will answer these two questions (Gherardi and Nicolini, 2000).

These four case studies represent therefore four points of observation: individual, collective, organizational and societal. But they focus on the fact that the field of safety practices is a single seamless texture, and that all the levels of reality are interwoven and co-present in the texture of practices.

The spiral case study in my research on safety began with situated practices. However, as the study on the practices of assisted reproduction illustrates, the inquiry can be conducted in both directions. For mapping the texture of practices, we began from the institutional change brought about by the enactment of a new law that restrictively regulated the types of intervention possible in assisted reproduction. The exploration continued on how individual laboratories (different from an organizational point of view) applied the law in their practices of fertilized embryo implantation, and how they sustained a culture transmitted to novices as 'the correct way' to perform practices of assisted fertilization (Perrotta, 2010).

This case study is interesting because it considers – contrary to my treatment in Chapter 3 – the change that takes place in practices following an external event disruptive of their everyday reproduction. Whereas in Chapter 3 I described how practices change as an endogenous dynamic sustained by the process of practice refinement, in this research study I illustrated how practices also change through an exogenous dynamic when other practices (for instance, the institutional framework) transfers constraints and limitations. A texture of practices in fact may be explored following all the directions and all the connections between practices.

7.5   TO SUM UP

The chapter began with an example of a mundane practice: going to the cinema. From this example we may start to explore the texture of this practice with a case study focused on individual strategies of practicing 'going to the cinema', then shift the focus on the organizational implications of people 'going to the cinema', then shift again to the production/consumption industry and maybe we wish to finish with a focus on the institutionalization of the values and policies supporting the individual practices of 'going to the cinema'.

While traditional sociology treats this process as a matter of social levels – individual, collective, organizational, interorganizational and institutional – the aim of a practice-based approach is to understand how all of them are connected in action and how a texture of practices links individuals and institutions at the same time and within the same practice. Therefore we can define a practice-based approach as a research *strategy* which focuses on understanding the dynamics present within interconnected settings of situated practices. It follows an understanding of practice-based research as a way of organizing social data so as to preserve the *unitary character* of the social object being studied. In this chapter I was interested in exploring some of the applications of practice-based studies and the methodological choices they imply.

Hence, a first field of application has been examined in relation to how the process of analysing individual and collective working practices and presenting them to practitioners can be a methodology aimed at the empowerment of those practitioners through the construction of arenas for collective reflexivity and negotiation on practices, as well as being aimed at a 'bottom-up' change in organizational practices. From the methodological point of view, this chapter has discussed the use of projective techniques: in particular, the interview with the double, and the self-confrontation and crossed self-confrontation methods.

The interconnectivity of practices and their intrinsic incompleteness are the elements that make it possible, from the methodological point of view, to start with analysis of a highly circumscribed practice and explore how this connects with increasingly broad and interconnected practices so as to form the texture of society; or, vice versa, start with analysis of a social macro-phenomenon and explore how this is rooted in routine and situated ways of doing and relating. As a methodology for the analysis of the texture of social practice, I have proposed the spiral case study, and I have illustrated its logic in the case of workplace safety as a social practice, and in the case of an institutional change pertaining to assisted reproduction, to show the effects of a new law on the situated practices of the professionals and the couples that resort to this medical service.

Finally, one should bear in mind that this chapter has more explicitly addressed problems of methodology concerning practice-based studies, but it has not sought to conduct either an exhaustive or explicitly methodological reflection. My choice has been to speak constantly of methodology in this book's various chapters, but illustrating it through examples of empirical research and not discussing it explicitly. In the next chapter I focus explicitly on ethnographic methodologies in order to answer the question concerning possible fields of application for the knowledge produced by practice-based studies.

NOTES

1. Pepper's (1942) characterization of contextualism is the absence of distinctions between up and down, inside and outside, big and small and so on; they simply merge into each other, they are implicated in each other (and not assuming for example that the big contains the small).
2. Activity theory has made a major contribution to the conception of the object of activity as an emergent object (Engeström, 1999a). As conceptualized in cultural-historical activity theory, objects of activity are simultaneously: given, socially constructed, contested and emergent (Blackler and Regan, 2009).
3. Bijker (1995, p. 274), states that whenever we consider a 'sociotechnical ensemble' we should be able to spell out the technical relations that go into stabilizing that institution', that is, the construction processes of artefacts, facts and relevant social groups.

8. Ethnography for the practice-based design of information systems

It is undeniable that applicative interest is one of the main reasons for studying work as a situated set of practices. The development of new technologies (especially ICT), the increasing complexity of work environments and the dematerialization of work, have focused attention on the question of how to technologically and socially support cooperation in knowledge-intensive jobs. This question also concerns how an accurate description of work-in-situation and in natural settings can contribute to developing competence in collective work and to changing work practices in the spirit of action research. Finally, given that society does not consist of sealed compartments, working practices and social practices are closely bound up with each other. The effects of society on working practices, and of working practices on society, constitute a challenge and an opportunity to explore the continuity of the interweaving between the micro-level and the macro-level of analysis of practices.

There is a particular community of researchers, around information systems, which is interested in practices to develop and support technologies, since the developers of technologies to support practices need to understand the knowledge embedded and embodied in the practices. This is not the only applicative context for the description of working practices, but I want to refer to this body of studies because of their extended use of ethnography at the service of interventions in organizations (Anderson, 1997; Østerlund, 2003; 2004; Schultze, 2000; Schultze and Boland, 2000; Schultze and Orlikowski, 2004).

The practice-based design of information systems (Suchman, 2002) has developed from dissatisfaction with technologies constructed as commodities and using 'design from nowhere'. The latter expression, which illustrates a certain conception of the design very well, has been widely used. Design from nowhere conceives technologies as produced exclusively from the vision of their developers. They are therefore products which can be transferred to any place whatever, and to which the users must adapt if they are not sufficiently strong to reject them and not use them, or use them only partially. Closing this gap between design and use requires that the validity of other forms of knowledge be recognized, and particularly the knowledge which is embedded in working practices. The condition for reconciliation between designers and users is therefore 'that developers give up control over technology design (which is in any case illusory), and see themselves instead as entering into an extended set of working relations, of contest and alliances' (Suchman, 2002, p. 142).

The expression 'design from nowhere' recalls the feminist critique of knowledge 'from nowhere', of those forms that Donna Haraway (1991, p. 193) calls 'ways of being nowhere while claiming to see comprehensively'. It is therefore necessary to replace this claim of universal knowledge with 'views from somewhere', with a located accountability (Suchman, 1994) and with partial, locatable and critical knowledges. The advantage of a 'partial perspective' – the term is Donna Haraway's (1991) resumed by Marilyn Strathern (1991) – is that knowledge always has to do with circumscribed domains, not with transcendence and the subject/object dichotomy.

Therefore, the consideration that the context of development and use of technology is a highly politicized context, in which the voices and forms of appropriation of technology by its users and their development of a design-in-use are made silent, has generated an intellectual movement which asserts the need for mutual learning and partial translations. This is an area in which, from a methodological point of view, the anthropology of technology makes a significant contribution when developers realize that their usual methods (usability tests, technical requirements) are increasingly ineffective. In describing her own experience in the field, Lucy Suchman (2002, p. 143) argues thus for an alternative understanding of change and innovation in the workplace: 'this alternative view rests on the premise that innovation and change are indigenous aspects of technology-in-use, work practice, and organizational life'. Corporate innovation initiatives are directed towards the intensification of ongoing activities and the extension of existing activities into additional or new markets, but local improvisational activities are the generative practices out of which innovation comes about as artful integration: 'a frame of artful integration emphasizes the ways in which new things are made up of reconfigurations and extensions to familiar environments and forms of action' (Suchman, 2002, p. 144). This is therefore the field in which change and innovation take place as the refinement of practice.

In their 1994 article, 'Moving out of the Control Room: Ethnography in System Design', John Hughes and colleagues identified four ways in which ethnography contributes to the design of information and communication technologies:

1. *Concurrent ethnography*. The ethnographic description of the work practices becomes an input to the design process, and this in turn asks questions and requests knowledge for further descriptive study of the work and for interaction with the participants. The two activities are therefore conducted in sequence and feed into each other. The researchers expect this procedure to improve the degree of acceptance of the new technology by its future users.
2. *'Quick and dirty' ethnography*. This pejorative expression has become widely used, supplanting that more neutral expression of 'rapid ethnography' proposed by Donald Norman (1998). It refers to one of the most controversial requirements of the ethnographic orthodoxy: long-term observation in the field. Ethnographers of work ask the 'purists' how long should this 'long-term observation' be? When does the ethnographer know that he/she knows enough about the field of study? Shapiro (1994) advises those who conduct ethnography of working practices in connection with the new technologies to adapt the sociological and anthropological orthodoxy to the object of study and the topic that they want to investigate.
3. *Evaluative ethnography*. The adjective refers to the use of ethnography for evaluative purposes in regard to the introduction of new technologies. The theme of the evaluation of technology is a particularly delicate one, not only because of the complexity and numerousness of the criteria, but also because the traditional evaluation methods, which operate on formal and pre-established criteria, are increasingly criticized and deemed inadequate or unsatisfactory.
4. *Re-examination of previous studies*. The ethnographic study of contexts already examined in the past is of particular interest because, from the theoretical point of view more than the practical one, it recognizes the principle of temporality and the fact that work contexts change over time because of new technologies. This principle is also important for the practical purposes of design, because it entails flexibility in the artefact, so that users and artefact can co-evolve in function of time and their interrelationships (Hughes et al., 1994, p. 432).

What is important in this scenario is not so much the 'purity' or otherwise of ethnographic methods as the change in the logic behind the analysis of work and the gradual abandonment of the analytical-prescriptive method (which breaks work down into individual tasks and actions) for an interpretative and descriptive method intended to reveal the overall meaning of the work, be it visible or 'invisible' (that is, embedded in the relationships that constitute the situational setting in which the work practice takes place).

In order to illustrate with examples from field research how practice-based design is developed, and how ethnography has proved to be the methodology best able to bring to light both the invisible work (Star and Strauss, 1999) of users and their practical knowledge, I shall refer to three communities of study that share similar approaches but also have different research traditions. I shall present examples drawn from particular areas of research which relate to Computer-supported Cooperative Work (CSCW), Participatory Design (PD) and Workplace Studies (WS) in order to illustrate how they have relaunched ethnography as a methodology with which to describe and understand work-in-situation, and by so doing, have contributed to developing the sociological analysis of working practices.

8.1 THE CSCW TRADITION

The term CSCW dates to 1984 when Irene Greif and Paul Cashman used it as the title of an interdisciplinary seminar which they organized to discuss how to support human work with computers (Greif, 1988). In the years that followed, the definition of CSCW was progressively refined. It was initially a generic 'umbrella term' used to group together researchers working in different disciplines so that they could meet to discuss issues concerning both the design of information systems and their use. Subsequently, the term denoted a field of inquiry centred on the role of the computer in group work. Thereafter, it referred to the endeavour of researchers to understand the nature and characteristics of cooperative work, the purpose being to design computer systems to support the latter. The focus on cooperative work, as a specific form of work, allowed the pioneers of this research field to define CSCW not as a research technique but on the contrary as a research *problem*.

The definition at present most widely used has been produced by Schmidt and Bannon (1992, p. 7, original emphasis): 'the professed objective of CSCW is to *support via computers* a specific category of work – cooperative work'.

This area of inquiry is highly heterogeneous because of the disciplinary origins of the researchers and the types of questions that it addresses: for example, what is the advantage of cooperative compared with individual work? How can ICTs solve the problems of the coordination required by . cooperative work more rapidly, more reliably and more flexibly? How is it possible to satisfy the requirements of cooperative work through the architecture of computer systems?

As will be seen from these questions, the CSCW area of research seeks both to understand and to support work. It therefore by definition requires an interdisciplinary competence, both in the social sciences (to analyse work in its 'natural' settings) and in the computer sciences to design ICT systems.

This interdisciplinarity raises a series of problems due both to the difficulty of conversing at the borders among communities consisting of very different 'professional visions', and to the difficulty of forming specific expertise. At present, the CSCW area of research is mainly concerned with design, but it collaborates with other areas able to deepen the analysis and interpretation of technologies-in-use and of the ways in which their users transform them.

The use made by CSCW studies of the ethnography of work stems from the crisis of the methodologies traditionally used to determine the requirements of the final users of information systems, and from dissatisfaction with their heuristic capacity to yield understanding of the work settings in which technologies are to be used. The traditional methods are based on task analysis of how duties are prescribed and how they should be performed. What evades this type of analysis is the discrepancy between prescribed work and work in practice, between the performance of a series of tasks in a routine context and the numerous unforeseen events that arise in an emerging context and which situated work absorbs. Another weakness of task analysis is that it is based on the analysis of individual work and therefore underestimates both spontaneous cooperation and articulation work.

According to Anderson (1994; 1997), the cause of this dissatisfaction was the realization that the practical working knowledge typical of those who work in a particular context is just as important as the knowledge possessed by the system designers, and it contributes to an equal extent to the success or failure of a new technology. This realization prompted innovative forms of intervention and design (Ehn, 1991; Mackay, 1990; Mumford, 1992; Norman and Drapper, 1986). Moreover, it was in this area of research and critical reflection that there developed the idea of the 'co-construction' of technologies, a neologism used to express the idea that innovations are produced at the point of encounter between designers and users, and that they are joint outcomes of the knowledge possessed by the former and the latter.

I now present (see Box 8.1) a classic study on office automation at a legal firm conducted by Blomberg et al. (1996; 1997). The purpose is to give an idea of how the analysis of the work, the design of the technology and its development in the work context considered, proceeded in parallel amid constant interaction between developers and users.

BOX 8.1   THE DEVELOPMENT OF AN ELECTRONIC DOCUMENT-PROCESS SYSTEM

The setting is a large law firm, to which the authors (researchers at a large company designing, producing and developing ICT technologies) have proposed a joint project whose purpose is to understand how the cooperative design of an electronic document-process system can be developed. This field has been selected both because of the central importance of paper-based documents in everyday legal work, and because of the willingness of the managers to collaborate on a project to determine what specific technologies were necessary to support legal work.

During negotiation of access to the field, the researchers and the managers set up a task force consisting of the director of technology in the law firm and a group of lawyers (who wanted to follow the new system's development). The initial agreement was that the researchers would spend some time in the firm in order to familiarize themselves with the environment and to identify the places and work phases in which image-processing technologies could be applied.

The researchers thus began to conduct a series of open-ended interviews with the lawyers who dealt with lawsuits, asking them to describe the litigation work process, their role in it, and their relations with the other lawyers and/or other people who assisted them in their work. These descriptions included an account of the 'document production' process. A large number of documents in the clients' files had to be located and then selected in relation to the case in question and their importance, as well as to prepare witness depositions and develop the legal arguments concerning the case. The firm had created a database for the cataloguing of documents, rather than digitizing the documents themselves. This process was described to the researchers as an illogical form of objective coding in which some self-evident elements of the documents (such as the author, content and date) were extracted and encoded in the database.

The researchers thus identified a central node in the work process, and they were interested in exploring how some applications (based on images or interfaces between users and documents) could support the working practices connected with litigation. Then, at this point of the research, they asked whether they could interact with the head of the litigation section. This manager was initially reluctant to collaborate with the researchers because of the little time at her disposal, and the researchers had to negotiate partial access to her section.

The researchers soon realized that a large amount of knowledge was necessary to support litigation, and they equally soon realized that the litigation section as a whole was under strong pressure from the firm's management to increase the efficiency of its services. This pressure was partly due to the management's simplistic view of the work necessary to maintain the database. This point became clearer to the researchers when a lawyer gave them a practical example showing very clearly the costs of the litigation support service. The lawyer told the researchers that he had just explained to a client the options available to him: if the service was provided by a local firm to which they often subcontracted, it would cost 190 (thousand dollars); the same service provided by an external firm headquartered in the Philippines would cost 110 (thousand dollars), and if provided by their firm, 350 (thousand dollars).

The manager of the litigation section also pointed out that the documents outsourced for cataloguing usually contained more errors, or that a document could be lost altogether. Moreover, the firm's lawyers did not consider the hidden costs for the firm of outsourcing the service, such as the hours spent converting data files produced externally within the firm's in-house search system.

There were few opportunities for the litigation support staff to dispute the lawyers' conception of the work of document coding (and the costs associated with it) because they were too distant from the lawyers' everyday work to be able to influence it. The litigation support staff had drawn up a list of the most frequent queries and devised a system for rapid consultation of the database. They had also prepared a description of the services furnished by their section so as to inform new lawyers about the type of support that they could provide. The litigation section constantly sought to introduce small innovations to improve the service, as well as alternative classification methods, in the belief that was it simpler to streamline the service than try and change the attitude of the lawyers.

Before the conclusion of the project, the litigation section had adopted an online coding system, something that would have been unthinkable only a year earlier. The change had been motivated by a simple desire to cut costs. Previously, there was one person who manually classified the documents using a paper support and a second person who inputted the data. The manager informed the researchers that this change had speeded up the system, which had previously required around an hour for 20–25 pages but with the online coding could process around 60 pages an hour. Moreover, because classifying a document often required a telephone call for clarification, and this required the workers to stop and think, the manager had tried to make the services as routinized as possible, thus moving it closer to the lawyers' conception of it. A budget had been fixed for each case, and it was the manager's task to ensure that it was not exceeded. Hence the workers had to mediate between the needs of accuracy and cost efficiency.

The design and research work therefore took place in a context in which there were considerable pressures for greater efficiency. Given the researchers' interest in developing a technological application based on image-processing, they started by proposing this solution. They initially encountered the scepticism of the litigation support staff, which did not think that another technology would make any difference. Subsequently, however, they saw the researchers as potential allies in changing the lawyers' view of codifying the work. In the end, the researchers developed an application that was of interest for their company and at the same time was also of interest to the workers in the litigation support section because it relieved the boredom of their more routine tasks and gave them more time to check the quality of what they produced. In their turn, the lawyers judged the technology in terms of what they imagined the classification work should be. They preferred the idea of automating the process to that of outsourcing it.

In this regard, the researchers had an opportunity to explain to the lawyers what the coding work consisted of and could show them that it required a margin of discretion and evaluation, thereby highlighting both the technical limits and the desirability of the service's complete automation.

When the researchers reflected on and wrote about their experience, they drew important conclusions on how new technologies engender changes in the international division of labour. In fact, despite the management's hopes of replacing human labour with information technology clashed with the empirical evidence on the limitations of automation, such hopes die hard precisely because it is new communication, data transfer and digital processing technologies that make alternative (and more economical) ways to do work possible. This example shows how the limits of current technological means for transforming paper documents into digital ones are off-set by the availability of cheap human labour which, although located at great geographical distances, is easily accessible to companies in the United States. Consequently, work is exported to the Philippines, to Singapore and to India. The authors of the study cite the claim by the promoters of this service that those who do the work need not have specific language skills. They only have to know how to locate the characters and numbers on the keyboard. Data entry work therefore only requires speed and accuracy. Of course, the authors of this study are not alone in denouncing the effects of globalization on workers in the industrialized countries. But their contribution is noteworthy because it evidences the contradictions inherent in new technologies, and the limits to their development and the capacity for technological innovation when alternative possibilities exist.

Source: Blomberg et al. (1996, pp. 250–264; 1997, pp. 278–85).

This example is instructive in regard to the interdependence among the priorities of management, the working practices of a group of professionals, and the knowledge needs of those who develop technological solutions to support human work. Researchers on technological innovation have realized over the years that knowledge about the work that should be supported by new technologies, and about the context in which these should be introduced, resides with those who do the work, even when they have a fragmentary, tacit knowledge which is difficult to access. Consequently, researchers on technological innovation have realized that the locus of product innovation and development is the interaction between users and developers (Von Hippel, 1976; 1988), but the main obstacles against greater involvement of the users originate from the organizational structures themselves, which take a short-term perspective and privilege prepackaged technologies over the search for solutions *in situ*.

8.2 PD TRADITION

To contextualize the historical and cultural significance of the Scandinavian experience of PD, one must go back to the 1960s and 1970s, when the industrial democracy movement was born in the Scandinavian countries and created both structures and cultures which promoted the participation of workers in the management of workplaces. This cultural heritage has given rise to numerous schemes whose common feature is cooperation on the development of new technologies among workers, future users and the trade unions. The declared objective is to design better jobs and to collaborate with the workforce to obtain closer control over technology and the organizational changes that it produces (Bjerknes et al., 1987; Greenbaum and Kyng, 1991).

The PD movement arose in open polemic with the growing intensification of work and with the rhetoric and practice of investing in technology so as to replace labour. The managerial rhetoric on labour-saving technology contained a contradiction: on the one hand, the introduction of new technology was justified on the grounds that the same work can be performed by a smaller number of workers; and on the other hand, the introduction of technology was cited as evidence of the upskilling of labour. The perverse effect of technological solutions imposed 'from above' and 'from outside' is the intensification of work, both because a smaller number of workers perform the same work previously performed by a larger group, and because new technologies often add work rather than eliminating it. Hence the ethos of PD research is connoted by a social commitment to the quality of work, the development of technologies to support human labour and ethnographic research (Blomberg et al., 1993).

I now illustrate a research study on PD that is considered paradigmatic of the methodology, and which also offers interesting considerations on the difficulties and the limits that such methodology encounters.

The example (see Box 8.2) concerns the AT project (Bødker, 1996) conducted jointly by the University of Aarhus, in Denmark, and the local branch of the Danish National Labour Inspection Service (NLIS), an institution which inspects and advises on workplace health and safety. When the project began, there were around 40–50 people working at the NLIS, ranging from secretaries, administrative workers, machinists, engineers, lawyers and therapists. Documents were mainly paper-based and were kept in large archives. The project therefore concerned office automation based on a centralized computer system (VIRK) which stored records of workplace inspections and correspondence with firms. Since the AT project, the terminal can also be accessed from personal computers. Today the project may seem very simple from a technological point of view, but

BOX 8.2   THE AT PROJECT

At the beginning of the project, the inspectors worked rather individually: each of them concentrated on a certain number of firms, and their work was assisted by the secretarial staff, who typed documents and managed the archive. During the project, the work was organized by groups according to the inspections that had to be carried out. The administrative work, that had previously been centralized, was distributed among the groups, and so were the secretaries. The groups were therefore multifunctional, and they had considerable autonomy, although control of the work became increasingly centralized (both at the local office and within the organization in general), and work was increasingly accounted according to quantitative standards. As regards managerial work, before the beginning of the project there was a general manager and two deputy managers (one responsible for inspections and one for administration). During the project, a new general manager arrived from headquarters, and the two deputy manager positions disappeared. This entailed further reorganization of the work and a managerial style completely different from the previous one.

At the end of the project, the work was again reorganized. The groups were changed because, with the advent of personal computers, the secretaries no longer had to write for the inspectors, so that the work of the inspectors now also included correspondence and large part of the work of retrieving data from the archive.

The shift of the boundaries among some occupational categories and others is a potential source of conflict which is not solely dyadic – between workers and management – but traverses numerous professional communities, whose working practices and competences are modified by technology. For instance, where the secretaries and the inspectors requested computer support and regarded technology as a 'tool' for their work, the managers wanted the technology to perform the 'control' function. Moreover, these two views clashed on what should be considered the purpose of inspections. Was it to make as many claims against firms as possible, or was it to establish long-term cooperative relations in order to improve working conditions? The contest between these two interpretations reflected the conflict between the efficiency of inspections (the management's concern) and the quality of inspections (the main concern of the inspectors).

In similar way, another conflict emerged between the secretarial staff and the inspectors. The introduction of computers had made 'life without secretaries possible' because the inspectors could write letters on their own. But what constituted a problem for the inspectors was the filing of material; an activity which had previously been meticulously performed by the secretarial staff. The inspectors were loathed to do this work. They did it less often and less conscientiously, thereby putting at risk the possibility of retrieving material previously saved.

Source: Bødker (1996, pp. 217–30).

it should not be forgotten that office automation is still the purpose of a good number of projects, and that 'simple' cases may teach a great deal precisely because of the ease of access to the underlying issues.

These tensions show that the concept of 'user participation' is problematic. A unique type of user does not exist, and the latter does not follow a unique a type of logic. Hence, the concept of participation should put into practice through the co-presence of different points of view, expectations and interests. What this experience of PD highlights is that the activity itself of technology design creates new conflicts and new 'threats' to existing situations and practices. This conflictual situation is reflected in, and generated by, the technology itself. The merits of PD are that it considers the latter as a resource for the development of alternative solutions and brings the contradictions among (or within) different occupations to light.

It is opportune to resume Susanne Bødker's (1996) reflections to conclude the discussion on how PD projects are accomplished *despite* the numerous problems that they encounter, such as:

- So-called 'collective participation' in reality concerns only the people directly involved in the project and only for its duration. Continuity in the experience, both among the workers and between one project and the next, is often lacking.
- Issues concerning power and resources are often not considered, and the 'users' are selected for participation without the support of their peer group. They do not have access to autonomous forms of inquiry; nor do they have the authority to convene meetings with colleagues during working hours. If the managers have the power to decide what to do and what not to do, the users are trapped: they are committed to supporting the system but they do not have the support of those whom they represent.

- The participants often have to devote time and energy to the development of systems without any form of compensation with respect to their normal workload or pay.
- Projects often do not have resources for the training of users.
- Finally, while the first PD projects in Scandinavia were supported by the trade unions and continued a commitment to the democratization of the workplace and technology, the position of the trade unions on these topics and their strength in the world of work have progressively weakened, even in the Scandinavian social democracies.

These initiatives have been important (and their analysis still continues) because they have highlighted the importance of developing theory on situated work and practical knowledge. Simultaneously, they have demonstrated the usefulness of the practical application of this knowledge for the development of technologies to support human labour.

8.3   WS TRADITION

WS share many themes and many authors with CSCW and PD. Nevertheless, they have developed a distinctive character of their own in how they study the ways in which people use technologies in relation to everyday working practices. They have developed a research programme aimed at respecifying technology according to working practices and their social organization.

According to Luff et al. (2000, p. 13), research which falls under the heading of WS has the following features:

1. An interest in the situated character of collaborative activities and the way in which tools, technologies, objects and artefacts manifest themselves in action and interaction in workplaces;
2. A naturalistic, ethnographic and descriptive methodology for the study of work;
3. A questioning of the categories currently used to understand technology.

To provide an idea of the type of research belonging within this tradition, I shall refer to an ethnographic study by Richard Harper (2000) on the International Monetary Fund (IMF), whose purpose was to understand whether (and how) to develop a technological network for information sharing. I cite this example of research to show how the analysis of working practices is useful for understanding when these *cannot/must not* be technologically supported.

The IMF can be conceived as a 'club' whose members are almost all the industrialized countries in the world. These countries contribute resources to be used in the form of short-period loans when a member-country must implement policies to deal with a problem in its balance of payments.[1] The IMF has a staff of around 3000 people, of whom 900 are economists who analyse economic and development policies. They are therefore interested in studying the circumstances associated with the emergence of financial imbalances, the policies with which to deal with them, and the corrective policy criteria for the issue of loans. This requires the economists to go on missions to the countries analysed. The assessments made in regard to the granting or otherwise of a loan are contained in the reports and documents used by the executive board when it makes its decisions.

To analyse the work of the economists, Harper (2000) (see Box 8.3) decided to study the 'life cycle' of a mission as follows:

- Following a hypothetical report in its trajectory through the organization, and interviewing all the parties that would be involved in its life cycle: the officers who wrote the reports, the chiefs who signed the reports, and the administrators and the research assistants. Moreover, further staff worked on the translating, printing and filing of the reports. To reconstruct the life cycle of a report in its entirety, Harper interviewed 138 people.
- Observing a mission and the associated practices of document production. This required participant observation of the preparatory meetings of the mission team, the meetings between the team and local authorities during the mission and the meetings held on conclusion of the mission. All the accompanying documents were also analysed.
- After the fieldwork, analytical descriptions of the work were produced and circulated. The comments on them were discussed with a number of informants, ranging from senior managers to junior economists.

This research work therefore led to the non-introduction of an information system because the managers believed that the system, although technically feasible, would not have been useful. The theoretical significance that Harper attributes to his study is that it shows the importance of analysing the inner logic of working practices (and how it is shared among the practitioners) as a prerequisite for technological design.

Finally, before concluding this chapter, I shall briefly expand the topic of information systems design to include the pervasive presence of

BOX 8.3   THE CASE OF THE IMF

The first thing that Harper (2000) did was seek to understand the logic of the desk officers' work and to appropriate their professional vision. In the words of one of them: 'I see my responsibilities as being as informed as possible about the current developments and I think most importantly, to have a basically coherent, albeit explicit analytic framework of understanding'.

Therefore, the work of the desk officers rotated around the construction of an 'analytical framework'. This, however, was important, not for its accuracy or completeness, but for communication with the local authorities of the member country. The officials, in fact, explained to the ethnographer that the importance of the framework was functional to the meeting with the local authorities (to have a common ground for discussion) and that it was during this phase of the work that the framework was modified and acquired clearer definition. Put very simply, for the officials it was enough to know what economic sectors produced wealth and what sectors consumed it.

How did the officials build an 'analytical framework? The core of this work, which the officials described as a sort of 'bricolage', consisted of assembling the important information and, especially, knowing how to select among an overabundance of information from diverse sources, such as similar ministerial or official sources, articles in specialized or non-specialized newspapers, specific databases and any other source that might be appropriate. The officials also had a more or less systematic method to create data time series or to file data which might prove useful in the future, but this work was anything but orderly or systematic. It became such only when there was an *ad hoc* need, but for the rest the officials complained about a lack of time or cited similar reasons for not doing something systematically for a variety of practical reasons.

Once Harper was able to understand the logic of the officials' work, after a dozen initial interviews, he continued his fieldwork by directly introducing the topic of networking technology which, together with accessory applications, would have allowed access to all the information that the officials collected and filed. In fact, Harper's intention was not to collect the opinions of the officials, but rather to understand how the technological network would have affected relations between the officials and the rest of the organization. The information system that Harper had in mind was rather simple and would have enabled access to all the information collected and stored in the organization. But he discovered that this system would have been inappropriate for current working practices. The reason was not the incomplete, chaotic or unsystematic nature of the information constituting the raw material of the work. It instead had to do with what could be shared and what could not/must not be shared: 'You could make sure that all the data we keep on the workstation was up to date and properly annotated [but] even if we were required to do that no one would use it. The only person who wants to use the information is the desk officer himself' (Harper, 2000, pp. 179–80).

This surprised Harper because, when information is being discussed, it is almost commonplace to say that one of the outputs of bureaucratic life is a collection of anonymous documents that are transformed in objective and voiceless bureaucratic documents. On the contrary desk officers' documents were 'authored'. To understand this paradox, Harper had to determine how a team of officials on a mission (usually four economists) worked together and what their collective work consisted of. Harper found that, during the mission, the initially rough data gradually became more complete; that the initial data served mainly to test the interpretations of one official against those of his/her colleagues; and, therefore, that the final report took shape through an interpretative and collective process. In the initial phase of a mission, the data the official possessed were still too rough to be shared and, although comprehensible to the other members, they would not have been relevant to them. Towards the end of the mission, the data became understandable and shareable because they had been processed and validated. The adequacy of the data was visible and comprehensible only to the members of the mission, because it was only they who knew what stage of completion the data have reached, while the officials who did not belong to that mission would find the data opaque and unusable.

Harper also realized that the work of officials was substantially different when they were in their offices in Washington and when they were on a mission, even if they were apparently still constructing their 'bricolage' of data. It thus also became clear why the officials regarded the computer system as useless for sharing their data. These, in fact, were important for the members of a mission only in preparation of it, and it was the same officials who, on signing the report, assumed responsibility for its content – that is, they guaranteed the process by which it had been generated.

Source: Harper (2000, pp. 172–82).

information and communication technologies within knowledge work, and how they form an environment of constant connectivity.

8.4   CONSTANT CONNECTIVITY

From the methodological point of view, a sociomaterial approach that reveals how contemporary knowledge work is itself a complex entanglement of social practices with the materiality of technological artefacts has been employed by Wajcman and Rose (2011) to rethink interruptions at work, and reframe what have been commonly understood as interruptions or multi-activity, in terms of 'constant connectivity'.

The proliferation of communication technologies reshapes work practices in the sense that people are now connected in multiple ways by devices and applications that make demands on workers' attention. This ubiquitous connectivity is inevitably giving rise to the fragmentation and constant interruption of working days, with the connected danger of stress, cognitive overload and human errors. CSCW has considered this issue in order to design improved technological interfaces which assist workers and minimize interruptions. Nevertheless, Wajcman and Rose's (2011) study is particularly significant in that it challenges the basic assumption that such 'interruptions' divert employee's attention away from their 'real work'.

On studying a major Australian telecommunications company, and shadowing a certain number of employees in their interactions with a range of technologies, Wajcman and Rose (2011) describe their everyday work practices as an ecology of constant connectivity. In the environment studied, the predominant mode of communication during the workday was technology mediated rather than face-to-face. Measurement and observation of interruptions indicated that such technologies seldom resulted in a change of work activity, whilst most of the face-to-face interruptions did so. In order to understand the role of mediated interactions and the role of employees' control over their technological work ecologies, the study considered how the knowledge workers' experience of and response to these mediated communications depended on the material properties of the particular device or application through which a message was transmitted. In fact, different communication media were equipped with alert devices, each reflecting a distinct power of appeal to the worker's attention:

> A hierarchy had emerged whereby communication via a mobile device, be it by voice communication or text message, signified that a matter was particularly urgent. Communication via a landline telephone indicated slightly less urgency, while email was generally interpreted as non-urgent. Participants took on board these meanings, which then influenced how they decided to interact with the various modes present in their work environment. (Wajcman and Rose, 2011, p. 957)

The study shows how the workers negotiated this obstinate presence of information about the potentially multiple-mediated communication that called for their attention by organizing the flow of work via communication technologies. This prioritizing process was based on a local knowledge of the organizational culture, norms and different job roles.

The study is of interest for the analysis of working practices for two reasons. The first is the fact that the proliferation of communication technologies is reshaping work practices and imposing competing demands on workers in coordination and control over their work flow (Datchary and Licoppe, 2007). The second reason concerns a methodological aspect relative to research on practices. The shadowing technique with people (or objects) as they do their work is variously used in qualitative sociology (Bruni, 2003), and it has proved particularly suited to understanding the temporality of events. For instance, in Wajcman and Rose's (2011) study, the use of shadowing rather than self-reporting made it possible to focus on interruptions not as isolated events, and therefore to see, instead of interruptions, an environment of constant connectivity in the interplay among the calls for attention from the various technologies.

8.5 TO SUM UP

When considering the application in organizations of methodologies deriving from practice-based studies, one should bear in mind that research on work as a situated activity has received particular impetus from issues that other disciplines – generally interested in the design and construction of technologies and ICT – have addressed in order to understand how human work can be supported by the work of non-humans.

The sociology of work has thus rediscovered its long tradition of ethnomethodology, ethnography and qualitative field studies applied to the solution of work problems or the design of working contexts. It increasingly collaborates in a multidisciplinary manner on applicative studies which start from the assumption that workplaces are sociotechnical contexts – that is, ecologies in which humans and non-humans are inextricably bound up with each other. Within information systems a critical perspective was born in opposition to its positivist tradition (Richardson et al., 2006) and critical research generally draws on the following themes: emancipation, critique of tradition, non-performative intent, critique of technological determinism and reflexivity (Howcroft and Trauth, 2005).

I then illustrated how the problem of applying knowledge about technological practices has been addressed by three contemporary strands of research: CSCW, PD and WS. I described three classical studies: the preparation of documents in a law firm; office automation at a labour inspectorate; and the work of economists at the IMF. All three cases therefore are based on ethnographic studies of practices and concerned the automation of paper-document processing work, but also the decision not to automate it. These three strands of research have numerous interconnections and exchanges, but also differences in the principal focus of their theoretical and methodological choices: CSCW centres on systems design, and therefore on analysis of the cooperative work functional to it; PD is distinguished by the active involvement of workers in the design of technologies and its emancipatory function; and, WS privilege the understanding of the social organization of work, and they subordinate technological design to the existing working practices. Finally, in order to complement the three traditions of research on the design of information systems I introduced the concept of constant connectivity to stress the main effect that ICT produces within working practices.

Practice-based studies have contributed to the demise of analytical methods for the description and interpretation of work (task analysis) based on tasks and their concatenation into working flows. They instead explore forms of interpretative analysis of working practices in which it is necessary to understand and reconstruct the logic internal to an occupation and the systems of categorization and construction that it uses to represent what people do when they work. What thus acquires importance for the researcher it is not so much what is done in terms of execution as how it is done, what sense it has and what relations it establishes. It is this strand of analysis, therefore, which forms the basis of my proposal to consider work not just as interaction but also as knowledge in action, as a practical knowing-how which links the elements of practices within a texture. The social dimension that underpins working practices is the collective dimension that stabilizes and institutionalizes a knowing-how which constitutes the stock of a community that continually debates the normative and aesthetic criteria that make a practice a good practice.

NOTE

1. Not discussed here are the conditions imposed by the IMF for the granting of loans, which have been frequently criticized, particularly because they have imposed on all member countries a standardized formula which has increased the economic difficulties of the most disadvantaged countries rather than alleviating them. See on this, Stiglitz (2002).

9. Towards a practice theory of organizing

In this book I have taken stock of an approach which first arose in the social sciences, and in particular within organizational learning and the sociology of practice. To this end, I have developed a methodological framework for analysing situated working practices with the focus on knowing as a practice phenomenon. In these conclusions I shall recall the implicit assumptions of the previous chapters in order to clarify my argumentative structure. I shall therefore present the theoretical and methodological framework of a practice-based approach to the study of situated work, and I shall conclude with brief discussion of the opportunities offered by this approach, but also its risks.

9.1 PRACTICE-BASED STUDIES: AN UMBRELLA CONCEPT

While the concept of practice has a long tradition both in philosophy and in sociology, its rediscovery within social sciences in general and within organization studies in particular dates to the end of the 1990s and beginning of the 2000s. Practice was indicated as a promising approach in anthropology (Ortner, 1984), in science and technology studies (Pickering, 1992), in education studies (Chaicklin and Lave, 1993), in organizational learning and knowledge management (Brown and Duguid, 2001) and in studies of technological design (Orlikowski, 2000).

At around the same time, the title of a very successful book edited by Schatzki et al. (2001) institutionalized the term 'practice-turn'. Later, in 2010, the scientific community working in the 'practice field' stressed that it was witnessing a 're-turn' to practice, and the editors of a special issue of *Organization Studies* (Miettinen et al., 2009, p. 1311) explained that this 're-turn' meant that although the concept of practice has a long tradition in philosophy and social sciences, that the 're-turn' was an invitation to start afresh with the re-examination of the concept and the development of new theories.

As an umbrella concept, practice has been used to assemble a plurality of conversations mostly interested in exploring the similarities, and not the differences, among several streams of research. In particular, within the organizational learning literature, the concept of practice was rediscovered as a third way between Scylla and Charybdis (Gherardi, 2000). In everyday language, reference to Scylla and Charybdis denotes a dilemma in which both options are equally undesirable. In the relationship between knowledge and organizations, Scylla and Charybdis can be represented, respectively, by a mentalistic vision of knowledge in organizations and by a commodification of knowledge. The desire to avoid the two dangers is shared – around the concept of practice – by intellectual inquiries which spring from different traditions. Practice was used as a prism through which to look at the phenomenon of situated knowing within organizations. At the same time the prism enables the researchers to see while distorting their vision. Every view is distorted because it is mediated by the viewing instrument, just as all knowledge is mediated by the means with which it is gathered: whence derives awareness of the irremediably reflexive character of the social sciences (Giddens, 1990). Practice can therefore be considered as a figure of the discourse on knowing and organizing.

When Roland Barthes (1977) introduced the concept of the figure in *Fragments d'un Discours Amoureux*, he wrote that the word should not be understood in its rhetorical sense, but rather in a much livelier way as the body's gesture caught in action. The figure is delineated in outline (as a sign) and is memorable (like an image or a tale). A figure is established if someone can say: 'That's so true! I recognize this scene of language' (Barthes, 1977, p. 4). The figure is a *topos* (a place) half coded and half projective: 'It is a modest supplement offered to the reader to be made free with, to be added to, subtracted from, and passed on to others' (Barthes, 1977, p. 5).

One of the figures of the discourse on knowledge in organizations states that knowledge resides in the heads of persons, and that it is appropriated, transmitted and stored by means of mentalistic processes. This figure works through the dichotomies of mind/body, thought/action, individual/organization. A second figure of discourse has been constructed by conversations in the economics of knowledge and in knowledge management. The starting point has been identification of knowledge as a production factor distinct from the traditional ones of capital, labour and land. This distinction has led to the definition of knowledge as 'strategic' and its location in the head of the organization (the management) and its work, and as a determinant of corporate performance. Practice as the third figure in the discourse of knowing in organizations articulates the image that knowledge does not reside in the heads of people, nor is it a commodity; rather, it is a collective, situated activity. Thinking of learning through participation in a practice enables us to focus on the fact that, in everyday practices, learning takes place in the flow of experience, with or without our awareness of it. In everyday organizational life, working, learning, innovating, communication, negotiation, conflict over goals, their interpretation, and history, are co-present in practice. Practice is both our production of the world and the result of this process. It is always the product of specific historical conditions resulting from previous practice and transformed into present practice.

The contribution made by practice-based theorizing is its methodological insight that, within a practice, knowing is not separate from doing. The following strands of research contribute to this ongoing conversation:

- *A cultural-aesthetic approach*, which views knowing as embedded in social interaction mediated by language. Aesthetic understanding is the form of knowledge that persons acquire by activating the specific capacities of their perceptive-sensorial faculties while they are engaged in the task at hand;
- *Situated learning theory*, which values learning as competent participation in a practice, and stresses that learning constitutes social systems and social identities;
- *Activity theory*, which focuses on objects of activity as partly given and partly emergent and maintains that knowing and acting are always and necessary embodied in particular, historical and culturally constituted settings;
- *Actor Network Theory (ANT)*, which illustrates how knowing is enacted in sociomaterial networks of human and non-human actants;
- *Workplace studies*, which are interested in the 'naturalistic' study of work settings, paying close attention to interactions and 'technology as a social practice', or technology-in-use.

These lines of inquiry have common roots in philosophical and sociological traditions dating back to the beginning of the century, mainly to Schütz (1962), Mead (1934) and Vygotsky (1934 [1987]). Dewey's pragmatism (1938) belongs to the same cultural milieu that influenced the theory of action developed by Joas (1997) and a pragmatist orientation within organizational learning (Elkjaer, 2003; Elkjaer and Simpson, 2011). A graphic representation of the roots of practice-based studies is provided in Figure 9.1. It illustrates more the 'modern' legacy of practice-based studies – to use Miettinen et al.'s (2009) terminology – than the more recent elaborations on practice as epistemology.

When we leave aside the commonplace use of the word 'practice' to denote what people do, it becomes evident that practice-based studies

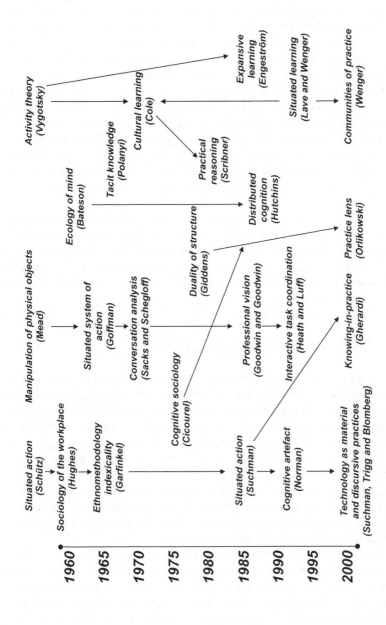

Figure 9.1   *The streams of practice-based studies*

converge on a common interest in understanding the production/con-sumption of knowledge and its circuit of reproduction. Practice, therefore, may be assumed as an empirical unit of analysis in order to study how, within a practice, people reach a practical agreement starting from het-erogeneous understandings and modes of cooperation with the material world. At the same time, the influence of practice theorists has been seen as more important as an epistemology for the study of working practices, and the kind of practical and 'hidden' knowledge that supports them. Usually, epistemology concerns itself with the validity conditions of knowledge (logic of verification) or, like pragmatism, with the conditions for the pro-duction of knowledge (logic of discovery). What is still beyond its reach is the study of the epistemological conditions of the circulation of knowl-edge, which means *how knowledge transforms itself through its use* – what we could term a 'logic of transformation'.

In this book I have used both perspectives, proposing a reading of practices as empirical phenomena, and using practice as an epistemologi-cal approach. In the conclusion I shall outline the conceptual framework that I propose in order to conceptualize practice, and the methodological framework that may be used in research on practices as empirical phenom-ena in organizations.

9.2   A CONCEPTUAL FRAMEWORK

A working practice is a collective activity undertaken in a particular place and at a particular time. It therefore assumes all the variability connected with the context that encloses it and makes it possible. It thus expresses a contextual rationality: that is, a form of action and practical reasoning applied to the work at hand, interactions with others, the setting and all the resources present in it. The jobs of a nurse, a lawyer, or a motorcycle courier consist of a set of working practices which are constantly repeated and adapted to the mutable circumstances in which they are performed. It is this set of working practices which make an occupation or a profession. Although these practices are constitutive of work and organizing, how they are executed depends on the specific situation.

Working practices can therefore be viewed as units of analysis of work. Partially already given and partially emergent, they are ways to order the work flow, to segment it into subsets of coherent and interdepend-ent activities, and to codify it in recognizable, recognized and socially sustained patterns. For instance, handovers from one shift to the next, fulfilling the quota or preparing a patient for anaesthesia are practices which, in the respective work settings, communicate 'what one is doing' to co-workers, and also have meaning for those who do not belong to the community of nurses, production workers or doctors. As *modes of ordering*, work practices create encoded situations comprising programmes of action (in situation X, do Y, Z . . .), but they are not binding on how that action is to be performed. Handovers from one shift to the next take place in diverse locations and situations and with varying contents, yet they are always recognized as 'handover practice'.

Distinctive of work practices, therefore, is not their internal variability, but rather their repetition. A practice is such precisely because it is practised, habitual, taught and learned as an activity that constitutes the job and requires expertise. It differs from an emergency, that is, a situation in which the usual operational parameters are altered (for instance, a sudden shortage of personnel or an unexpected inflow of patients) or from an unforeseen event (a flood in an operating theatre). Practices contain elements of habit, but they are not habits; they contain elements of action, but they are not actions. If the building in which we are working catches fire, its evacuation is an action for us, but a practice for the fire brigade.

The repetition (or recursiveness) distinctive of working practices is connected on the one hand with the development of skills and, on the other hand, with change as a re-specification for the practice's adaptation to contingencies or refinement. The two aspects are linked insofar as the constant reproduction of an activity generates within the community of its practitioners dynamics for the constant improvement (or disuse), adaptation or change in a practice as a response to altered conditions. Knowing-how is refined by being practised, just as excellence in knowing-how is a symbolic element which motivates, rewards, and celebrates the doing and the community of practitioners.

The third distinctive feature of practices (besides their nature as modes of ordering and their recursiveness) is that they reproduce society. Francis Bacon wrote in the seventeenth century that the persistence of society is just as problematic as its change. Four hundred years later, social scientists are still more interested in change than in persistence, in production more than reproduction. Yet a focus on practices entails the problem of society's competent reproduction. Tied to the recursiveness of practices is their stabilization by repetition, and therefore the iteration of the relations among the elements that make up the practice. But what motivates the reproduction of the same relations? According to an evolutionist explanation, only the more efficient practices, those that work better than others, survive. But this explanation fails to consider all the elements tied to tradition or to the emotional and symbolic dimension. A neoinstitutional explanation does not deny that technical superiority is a reason for the diffusion and reproduction of the practices, but it emphasizes the normative dimension and the process by which the community's work practices and how they are practised become institutionalized. In the communities of nurses, production workers, doctors or express delivery couriers, certain practices are considered 'the correct way to do things' because they are sustained by a set of values and by a constant debate on the ethical and aesthetic dimension of the occupation or profession. The effects of this debate are apparent in the negotiated order, rules, deontological code and the legislation. Agreement on practices does not necessarily mean their endorsement: indeed, almost all communities have conflicting schools of thought or visions of the world on what practice is more correct, more elegant or more efficacious. This internal debate augments the dynamism of the practice amid its recursiveness. It is the endogenous dynamic of change in the practice while it is being practised.

Having described the three salient features of work practices, I want to stress how practices, as the unit of analysis of working, knowing and organizing, can be studied as:

- *Containers* of activities and competences, situational domains in which collective abilities are created, transmitted, preserved or changed. The focus in this case is the activities that take place in the context of a practice, and how a common orientation is maintained among the participants during the performance of such activities.
- *Processes* which, as they unfold over time, follow a trajectory of becoming, mobilize resources and are pragmatically oriented. Emergent practices and cooperation in action are consequently the focus of the study.
- *Results* of stabilization through anchorage in the material world and institutionalization as the infusion of values and their upholding by limitation (norms, laws, codes and so on). Studied in this case are the normative system and the prescriptive relay as the outcome of, and precondition for, constant repetition of the practice 'for another first time'.

We have seen in the previous chapters how practices are simultaneously containers, processes and results because they reflexively create the context of their production. We have left in the background the relation among knowledge, competence and practice – a notion which we now introduce with a quotation from Lyotard (1984, p. 18):

Knowledge, then, is a question of competence that goes beyond the simple determination and application of the criterion of truth, extending to the determination and application of criteria of efficiency (technical qualification), of justice and/or happiness (ethical wisdom), of the beauty of a sound or color (auditory and visual sensibility), and so on Understood in this way, knowledge is what makes someone capable of forming 'good' denotative utterances, but also 'good' prescriptive and 'good' evaluative utterances.

According to Lyotard (1984), competence cannot be reduced to science, nor to knowledge. Knowledge is a set of statements which denote or describe objects, while science is a subcategory of knowledge constituted by a set of denotative statements to which certain acceptability conditions are applied. Knowledge does not consist solely of a set of denotative statements. It also comprises knowing how to do, knowing how to live and knowing how to listen. We can likewise emphasize the distinction between knowing a practice and knowing-in-practice, what we have called 'practical knowledge'. A researcher, like anyone else, may want to know a certain practice, but this does not mean that he/she is able to practise it. Knowing a practice in order to be a practitioner or a professional is different. In this case, the person is said to know that practice when he/she is able to reproduce it and knows how to do so autonomously, having acquired the necessary competence.

There are three types of relation between practices and practical knowledge:

- A *containment* relation, in the sense that practical knowledge is exercised within situated practices. On this definition, practices are objective entities (in that they have been objectified) of which their practitioners already have knowledge (that is, they re-know them as practices) and which contain items of knowledge anchored in the material world and in the normative and aesthetic system that has culturally processed them.
- A *reciprocal constitution* relation, in the sense that knowing and practising are not two distinct and detached phenomena; on the contrary, they interact with each other and produce each other.
- An *equivalence* relation: practising is knowing-in-practice, whether or not the subject is aware of it. Acting as a competent practitioner is synonymous with knowing how to connect successfully with the field of practices thus activated. The equivalence between knowing and practising is established when priority is denied to the knowledge which pre-exists its application, so that something already existing is not performed; rather, the action creates and expresses the knowledge formed in and through that same action.

We adhere to the third position because it enables us to propose a more sophisticated theory of practices seen from the point of view of the community that practises and therefore engenders them, and of knowledge as created and recreated competence. We are thus able to specify this book's underlying methodological framework more clearly.

9.3   A METHODOLOGICAL FRAMEWORK

To work, therefore, is not to know a series of practices; rather, it is to know-in-practice how a job or a profession is done. How can practical knowledge be studied empirically? We start by delimiting the phenomenon that we want to describe: knowledge as a practical activity. We have cited numerous examples of empirical research to illustrate a methodological apparatus able to analyse work practices as knowing-in-practice. We have assumed that all activities, both individual and collective, comprise elements that give them a collective, that is, social, character. By means of the metaphor of rock climbing, in which the handholds for action are constituted as such only through interaction, we have introduced the idea that the context of a practice furnishes the resources with which to identify 'what comes next'. That is to say, the practical accomplishment of a practice unfolds by discovering and relying on the resources available for its ongoing production.

As dynamic and indefinite practices emerge from activities, they progress by drawing on sensible knowledge, the materiality of the body, language and objects anchored in the social dimension, eliciting other people's activities and responding to them. In short, they are material-discursive practices. On the other hand, activities inscribe themselves concretely in the social organization through communities which structure them by defining roles (the division of labour), vocabulary and rules.

Work, therefore, is a knowing-how in situation, a knowing-how 'to work together' which weaves relations among people, objects, languages, technologies, institutions and rules. All these 'handholds' are found in the field of action. They are partly given, partly to be found and partly lacking, and they must be assembled into a meaningful network which holds them together and directs them towards a pragmatic goal. This is an image which recalls the activity of bricolage more than that of rational planning. We have in fact used concepts like articulation work, relational work, arbitrage, knotworking and alignment to convey the idea that the resources for action (material, interactive, communicative or normative) must be activated and interrelated in order to maintain a shared orientation. Before illustrating what these handholds and resources are, we introduce a metaphor for the relation between resources and practices by quoting a conversation between Marco Polo and Kublai Khan contained in Italo Calvino's book, *Invisible Cities* (1993, p. 83):

Marco Polo describes a bridge, stone by stone.
'But which is the stone that supports the bridge?' Kublai Khan asks.
'The bridge is not supported by one stone or another,' Marco answers, 'but by the line of the arch that they form.'
Kublai Khan remains silent, reflecting. Then he adds: 'Why do you speak to me of the stones? It is the arch that matters to me.'
Polo answers: 'Without stones there is no arch.'

Having talked about the arch, we may now consider the stones. In our case, the stones represent the handholds discovered as the practice unfolds and is skilfully activated to become a resource for accomplishment of an activity. The various chapters of this book have focused on specific handholds: the body – and with it sensible knowledge – technology, discursive practices, rules and institutions.

The body has received particular attention precisely because it has been taken for granted – if not systematically erased – by the classic sociology of work and organizations, which refers to a generic labour force without corporality or gender. The feminist critique has fiercely attacked this position. It claims that the labour force consists of men and women who bring their differences to work; it denounces the normative model of work as constructed on the male worker and as sustaining a normative model of masculinity; but above all it maintains that knowledge cannot be produced without starting from the body, and that different bodies have different experiences (and therefore constructions) of the world. We know through our bodies, and what lies outside us is first mediated by the body and its sensations. Sensible (aesthetic) knowledge is what is learned through the five senses and the aesthetic judgement passed on it. It is largely tacit, but social, knowledge. In many workplaces, it is the senses and the collective refinement of the sensory abilities that measure performance, just as they symbolize the competence expressed as 'having an eye, nose or ear' for something or having a light touch. Contrary to the Cartesian separation between mind and body, the study of practices valorizes the intimate connection between mind and body and the knowledge incorporated in bodily schemes, physical abilities and the collective development of a 'professional vision' made of experience and its codification.

Experience is not individual and unique; rather, it is a process which is both individual and collective. This conception of experience has been put forward by Teresa de Lauretis (1984, p. 159) as:

The process by which subjectivity is constructed. Through that process one places oneself or is placed in social reality, and so perceives and comprehends as subjective those relations – material, economic, and interpersonal – which are in fact social and historical. The process is continuous and daily renewed. For each person, therefore, subjectivity is ongoing construction, not a fixed point of departure or arrival from which one then interacts with the world. On the contrary, it is the effect of that interaction – which I call experience; and thus is produced not by external ideas, values, or material causes, but by one's personal, subjective, engagement in the practices, discourses and institutions that lend value, meaning, value, and affect to the events of the world.

This process is also collective. It is identity work and the sharing of experience in practices. It is the doing-in-situation which produces a collective identity and consolidates the practical knowledge transmitted to the novice (through co-piloting and scaffolding), through stories that 'do community', and through the rules that incorporate an experience and make it available after the event. When consideration is made of learning from experience, one should bear in mind that experiences leave traces of knowledge which become embedded and available beyond the individual occurrence. Objects embody past experiences. Script is the simplest technology with which to fix the past and update it to the present. The memory does not rely solely on the mental abilities; rather, humans utilize objects to remind them of things.

One of the most important contributions of the practice-based approach is that it directs attention to the sociomaterial domain. The material world lives with us, around us and through us. It is neither inert nor passive. When we say that the material world interpellates us, we refer to our interactions with objects: a notice tells us what we must or must not do; a machine alarm tells us that we must not touch it; a flashing light tells us that something is wrong and that the machine needs fixing; and so on. Tools anchor activities because they enable us to do things that we otherwise would not be able to do; technologies are extensions (prostheses) of our bodily abilities, and they increasingly incorporate knowledge and intelligence. Technologically dense work settings demonstrate that knowing-how is distributed between humans and non-humans, and that the knowledge specific to humans consists primarily in the ability to align and stabilize the sociotechnical system within an ecology of constant connectivity.

Working practices are then anchored in language in the form of technical vocabulary, classification systems and language-in-use. When we say that talking is working we imply that discursive practices are means of communication and interaction but also specific technologies. Institutional conversations, for example, perform a 'transformation' through speech. Service work is accomplished through talk-in-situation. Practical knowledge therefore also consists in communicative competence: that is, knowing how to use language appropriately in specific contexts of interaction.

Finally, the analysis of working practices as knowing-how in situation requires consideration of two further handholds: rules and institutions, which concern normation. These are resources with which to produce the negotiated order and learn how to move in the interstitial space of ordinary prescription, exploiting the incompleteness of rules and therefore opportunities between prescription and negotiation.

Hence, empirical study of organizing as knowing-in-practice requires analysis of how, in working practices, resources are collectively activated and aligned with competence. This activity is not extemporaneous; on the contrary, what makes practices 'plastic' – that is, relatively stable and mutable – is the activity that stabilizes the conditions for them. This book has amply described how the activation of resources accompanies their anchoring in the material world, in language, and in the institutional, normative and aesthetic dimensions.

Knowing-in-practice can therefore be analysed as it is manifest in the linguistic and cultural systems, and the technological and normative infrastructure, located in time and space, and as it is socially constructed and constantly developed.

9.4 TO STUDY PRACTICES IN ORDER TO CHANGE THEM

Just as the last century was characterized by the endeavour to increase the productivity of manual work, so this century has been distinguished by the endeavour to increase the productivity of knowledge work. This concerns two domains – technological and social – and therefore, on the one hand, the design of new ICT technologies, and on the other hand, the social contexts that work with them. But the true challenge in this regard is studying sociotechnical systems with the focus on situated work. As Heath et al. (2000, p. 316) put it:

> By turning attention to the details of work, and in particular the tacit, 'seen but unnoticed', social and interactional resources on which the participants relay in the practical accomplishement of organizational activities, we can begin to (re) consider how particular tools and technologies might support, enhance even transform what people do and the ways in which they do.

This quotation highlights one of the principal applicative interests of practice-based studies: technological practices and the construction of artefacts to support practices. Vice versa, little attention is paid to the more general context within which this interest is framed: that of the deliberate change made to practices by their practitioners. Knowledge about practices is obscure to their practitioners, and an important applicative field is that of the action research (broadly defined) which employs the representation of practices as a means to empower practitioners. This field raises numerous methodological problems for the study of practices, however, and it has generated interesting and innovative methodological experiments.

In this regard, there has been a revival of micro-social studies on work within the sociology of work and organizations, and increasing interest in interdisciplinary cooperation among people who work with information systems. Numerous schools of research and application have arisen in this field. A chapter of this book has been devoted to them, so that we will not return to the topic here. What we wish to emphasize in the conclusions is the openness of this strand of analysis. Indeed, it is necessary to consider in what directions it can develop, and the reasons for the 'renaissance' of the concept of practice.

Will the next few years see a new 'scientific work organization' movement? The aspects of work that were overlooked when it was studied as a task, now emerge when work is studied as a practical knowledge activity. Will they be incorporated into the management of work and workplaces as in Taylorism-Fordism when it was the model of organization?

The question is open, and it must remain so because it represents and defends a space for critical questioning. If knowledge is a new means of production, conflict over its control will shift in that direction, but, unlike land or labour, knowledge has a specific nature, with the consequence that the conflict will assume different forms.

Bibliography

Ackerman, M.S. and Halverson, C.A. (2000), 'Re-examining Organizational Memory', *Communication of the ACM*, **43** (1), 58–64.

Akrich, M., Callon, M. and Latour, B. (2006), *Sociologie de la Traduction. Textes Fondateurs*, Paris: Presses des Mines de Paris.

Anderson, R.J. (1994), 'Representations and Requirements: The Value of Ethnography in System Design', *Human-computer Interaction*, **9**, 151–82.

Anderson, R. (1997), 'Work, Ethnography, and System Design', *Encyclopedia of Microcomputing*, **20**, 159–83.

Antaki, C. (1985), 'Ordinary Explanation in Conversation: Causal Structures and Their Defence', *European Journal of Social Psychology*, **15**, 213–30.

Appadurai, A. (1986), *The Social Life of Things: Commodities in Cultural Perspective*, Cambridge: Cambridge University Press.

Atkinson, J.M. (1992), 'Displaying Neutrality: Formal Aspects of Informal Court Proceedings', in P. Drew and J. Heritage (eds), *Talk at Work*, Cambridge: Cambridge University Press, pp. 199–211.

Austin, J.L. (1962), *How to Do Things with Words*, Oxford: Clarendon Press.

Barad, K. (2003), 'Posthumanist Performativity: Toward an Understanding of How Matter Comes to Matter', *Signs*, **28** (3), 801–31.

Barad, K. (2007), *Meeeting the University Halfway: Quantum Physics and the Entanglement of Matter and Meaning*, Durham: Duke University Press.

Barley, S. and Kunda, G. (2001), 'Bringing Work Back In', *Organization Science*, **1**, 76–95.

Barthes, R. (1977), *Fragments d'un Discours Amoureux*, Paris: Editions du Seuil.

Bateson, G. (1972), *Steps to an Ecology of Mind: A Revolutionary Approach to Man's Understanding of Himself*, New York: Ballantine Books.

Beach, K. (1988), 'The Role of External Mnemonic Symbols in Acquiring an Occupation', in M.M. Grunberg, P.E. Morris and R.N. Sykes (eds), *Practical Aspects of Memory*, Vol. 1, Chichester: John Wiley and Sons.

Becker, H.S. (1982), *Art Worlds*, Berkeley: University of California Press.

Berg, M. (1997), *Rationalizing Medical Work*, Cambridge, MA: MIT Press.

Bergman, J.R. (1992), 'Veiled Morality: Notes on Discretion in Psychiatry', in P. Drew and J. Heritage (eds), *Talk at Work*, Cambridge: Cambridge University Press, pp. 137–62.

Bernstein, N. (1996), *Dexterity and its Developments*, Hillsdale, NJ: Lawrence Erlbaum Associates.

Bijker, W. (1995), *On Bikes, Bakelites and Bulbs: Towards a Theory of Socio-technical Change*, Cambridge, MA: MIT Press.

Bjerknes, G., Ehn, P. and Kyng, M. (eds) (1987), *Computers and Democracy – A Scandinavian Challenge*, Aldershot: Avebury.

Bjørkeng, K., Clegg, S. and Pitsis, T. (2009), 'Becoming (a) Practice', *Management Learning*, **40** (2), 145–60.

Blackler, F. (1995), 'Knowledge, Knowledge Work and Organizations: An Overview and Interpretation', *Organization Studies*, **6**, 1021–46.

Blackler, F. and Regan, S. (2009), 'Intentionality, Agency, Change: Practice Theory and Management', *Management Learning*, **40** (2), 161–76.

Blomberg, J., Suchman, L. and Trigg, R. (1996), 'Reflections on a Work-oriented Design Project', *Human-computer Interaction*, **3**, 237–65.

Blomberg, J., Suchman, L. and Trigg, R. (1997), 'Back to Work: Renewing Old Agendas for Cooperative Design', in M. Kyng and L. Mathiassen (eds), *Computers and Design in Context*, Cambridge: MIT Press, pp. 268–87.

Blomberg, J., Giacomi, J., Mosher, A. and Swenthon-Hall, P. (1993), 'Ethnographic Field-methods and Their Relation to Design', in D. Schuler and A. Namioka (eds), *Participatory Design: Principles and Practices*, Hillsdale, NJ: Lawrence Erlbaum Associates, pp. 123–55.

Bødker, S. (1996), 'Creating Conditions for Participation: Conflicts and Resources in Systems Development', *Human-computer Interaction*, **11**, 215–36.

Boje, D. (1991), 'The Storytelling Organization: A Study of Story Performance in an Office-supply Firm', *Administrative Science Quarterly*, **36**, 106–26.

Boje, D. (2001), *Narrative Methods for Organizational and Communication Research*, London: Sage.

Borzeix, A. (1994), 'Avant-propos', *Sociologie du Travail*, **4**, 413–17.

Borzeix, A. (2003), 'Language and Agency in Organizations', in A. Müller and A. Kieser (eds), *Communication in Organizations*, Frankfurt am Main: Peter Lang, pp. 65–79.

Borzeix, A. and Fraenkel, B. (2001), *Langage et Travail. Communication, Cognition, Action*, Paris: Editions du CNRS.

Borzeix, A., Fisher, S., Fornel, M. and Lacoste, M. (1995), 'La Lettre de Réclamation', in C. Quin (ed.), *L'Administration de l'Equipement et ses Usagers*, Paris: La Documentation Française, pp. 71–107.

Bourdieu, P. (1972), *Esquisse d'une Théorie de la Pratique Précédé de trois Études de Ethnologie Kabyle*, Switzerland: Librairie Droz S.A.

Bourdieu, P. (1990), *Le Sens Pratique*, Paris: Les Éditions de Minuit (trans. English, *The Logic of Practice*, Cambridge: Polity Press).

Boutang, Y.M. (ed.) (2002), *L'età del Capitalismo Cognitivo. Innovazione, Proprietà e Cooperazione delle Moltitudini*, Verona: Ombre Corte.

Boutet, J. and Gardin, B. (2001), 'Une Linguistique du Travail', in A. Borzeix and B. Fraenkel (eds), *Langage et Travail. Communication, Cognition, Action*, Paris: Editions du CNRS, pp. 89–112.

Boutet, J. and Maingueneau, D. (2005), 'Sociolinguistique et Analyse de Discours: Façon de Dire, Façon de Faire', *Langage et Société*, **114**, 15–47.

Bowker, G. and Star, S.L. (1999), *Sorting Things Out: Classification and Its Consequences*, Cambridge, MA: MIT Press.

Branthwaite, A. and Lunn, T. (1985), 'Projective Techniques in Social and Market Research', in R. Walker (ed.), *Applied Qualitative Research*, Aldershot: Gower, pp. 101–29.

Brogan, W. (1989), 'Plato's Pharmacon: between Two Repetitions', in H. Silverman (ed.), *Derrida and Decostruction*, London: Routledge, pp. 7–23.

Brown, J. and Duguid, P. (1991), 'Organizational Learning and Communities of Practice: Toward a Unified View of Working, Learning and Bureaucratization', *Organization Science*, **2**, 40–57.

Brown, J. and Duguid, P. (1996), 'Stolen Knowledge', in H. McLellan (ed.), *Situated Learning Perspectives*, Englewood Cliffs, NY: Educational Technology Publication.

Brown, J.S. and Duguid, P. (2001), 'Knowledge and Organization: A Social-practice Perspective', *Organization Science*, **12** (2), 198–213.

Brugère, F. (2000), *Le Goût. Art, Passions et Société*, Paris: Presse Universitaires de France.

Bruner, J. (1986), *Actual Minds, Possible Worlds*, Cambridge, MA: Harvard University Press.

Bruni, A. (2003), *Lo Studio Etnografico delle Organizzazioni*, Rome: Carocci.

Bruni, A. (2005), 'Shadowing Software and Clinical Records: On the Ethnography of Non-humans', *Organization*, **12** (3), 357–78.

Bruni, A. and Gherardi, S. (2001), 'Omega's Story: The Heterogeneous

Engineering of a Gendered Professional Self', in M. Dent and S. Whitehead (eds), *Knowledge, Identity and the New Professional*, London: Routledge, pp. 174–98.

Bruni, A. and Gherardi, S. (2007), *Studiare le Pratiche Lavorative*, Bologna: Il Mulino.

Bruni, A., Gherardi, S. and Parolin, L. (2007), 'Knowing in a System of Fragmented Knowledge', *Mind, Culture and Activity*, **14**, (1–2), 83–102.

Burawoy, M. (1979), *Manufacturing Consent: Changes in the Labour Process under Monopoly Capitalism*, Chicago: University of Chicago Press.

Butler, J. (1990), *Gender Troubles: Feminism and the Subversion of Identity*, London: Routledge.

Butler, J. (1993), *Bodies that Matter*, New York: Routledge.

Button, G. (1992), 'Answers as Interactional Products', in P. Drew and J. Heritage (eds), *Talk at Work*, Cambridge: Cambridge University Press, pp. 212–34.

Cacciatori, E. (2008), 'Memory Objects in Project Environment: Storing, Retriving and Adapting Learning in Project-based Firms', *Research Policy*, **37**, 1591–601.

Calvino, I. (1993), *Le Città Invisibili [Invisible Cities]*, Milan: Mondadori.

Carlile, P.R. (2002), 'A Pragmatic View of Knowledge and Boundaries: Boundary Objects in New Product Development', *Organization Science*, **13**, 442–55.

Carlsen, A. (2006), 'Organizational Becoming as Dialogic Imagination of Practice. The Case of the Indomitable Gauls', *Organization Science*, **17** (1), 132–49

Carr, A. and Hancock, P. (eds) (2003), *Art and Aesthetics at Work*, Basingstoke: Palgrave Macmillan.

Castells, M. (1996), *The Rise of the Network Society*, Oxford: Blackwell.

Chaicklin, S. and Lave, J. (eds) (1993), *Understanding Practice: Perspectives on Activity and Context*, Cambridge: Cambridge University Press.

Charreire-Petit, S. and Huault, I. (2008), 'From Practice-based Knowledge to the Practice of Research: Revisiting Constructivist Research Works on Knowledge', *Management Learning*, **39** (1), 73–91.

Chia, R. (2003), 'Ontology: Organization as "World Making"', in R. Westwood and S. Clegg (eds), *Debating Organization: Point–Counterpoint in Organization Studies*, Oxford: Blackwell Publishing, pp. 98–113.

Chia, R. and Holt, R. (2006), 'Strategy as Coping: A Heideggerian Perspective, *Organization Studies*, **27** (5), 635–55.

Chia, R. and Holt, R. (2008), 'On Managerial Knowledge', *Management Learning*, **39** (2), 141–58.

Cicourel, A.V. (1982), 'Interviews Surveys and the Problem of Ecological Validity', *American Sociologist*, **17**, 11–20.

Cicourel, A. (1986), 'La Connaissance Distribuée dans le Diagnostic Médical', *Sociologie du Travail*, **36**, 427–49.

Clegg, S., Kornberger, M. and Rhodes, C. (2005), 'Learning/Becoming/Organizing', *Organization*, **12** (2), 147–67.

Clot, Y. (1999), *La Fonction Psychologique du Travail*, Paris: Presses Universitaires de France.

Clot, Y. (2002), 'Clinique de l'Activité et Repetition', *Cliniques Méditeranéenne*, **66**, 31–53.

Clot, Y. (2005), 'Le Développement du Collectif: Entre l'Individu e l'Organisation du Travail', in Régine Teulier and Philippe Lorino (eds), *Entre Connaissance et Organisation: L'Activite Collective*, Paris: La Découverte, pp. 187–99.

Clot, Y., Faïta, D., Fernandez, G. and Scheller, L. (2001), 'Les Entretiens en Autoconfrontation Croisée: une Méthode en Clinique de l'Activité', *Éducation Permanente*, **146**, 17–27.

Cohen, I.J. (1996), 'Theories of Action and Praxis', in B.S. Turner (ed.), *The Blackwell Companion to Social Theory*, Cambridge: Blackwell Publishers, pp. 111–42.

Cole, M. (1998), *Cultural Psychology: A Once and Future Discipline*, Cambridge: Harvard University Press.

Conein, B. and Jacopin, E. (1994), 'Action Située et Cognition: le Savoir en Place', *Sociologie du Travail*, **94**, 475–500.

Cook, S. and Yanow, D. (1993), 'Culture and Organizational Learning', *Journal of Management Inquiry*, **2** (4), 373–90.

Cooper, R. and Fox, S. (1990), 'The Texture of Organizing', *Journal of Management Studies*, **27** (6), 575–82.

Cooper, R. and Law, J. (1995), 'Distal and Proximal Visions of Organization', in S. Bacharach, P. Gagliardi and B. Mundell (eds), *Studies of Organizations in the European Tradition*, Greenwich: Jai Press, pp. 237–74.

Corbin, J. and Strauss, A. (1993), 'The Articulation of Work Through Interaction', *Sociological Quarterly*, **1**, 71–83.

Corradi, G., Gherardi, S. and Verzelloni, L. (2010), 'Through the Practice Lens: Where Is the Bandwagon of Practice-based Studies Heading?', *Management Learning*, **41** (3), 265–83.

Crozier, M. (1963), *Le Phénomène Bureaucratique*, Paris: Editions de Seuil.

Czarniawska, B. (1997), *Narrating the Organization: Dramas of Institutional Identity*, Chicago: The University of Chicago Press.

Czarniawska, B. (2004), 'On Time, Space and Action Nets', *Organization*, **11** (6), 773–91.

Czarniawska, B. (2007), *Shadowing: And Other Techniques for Doing Fieldwork in Modern Societies*, Copenhagen: Liber.

Czarniawska, B. (2008), *A Theory of Organizing*, Cheltenham, UK and Northampton, MA, USA: Edward Elgar.

Datchary, C. and Licoppe, C. (2007), 'La Multi-activité et ses Appuis. L'exemple de la Présence "Obstinée" des Messages dans l'Environnement de Travail', *Activité*, **4** (1), 1–29.

Dean, J.W., Ramirez, R. and Ottensmeyer, E. (1997), 'An Aesthetic Perspective on Organizations', in C. Cooper and S. Jackson (eds), *Creating Tomorrow's Organizations: A Handbook for Future Research in Organizational Behavior*, Chichester: Wiley, pp. 419–37.

De Lauretis, T. (1984), *Alice Doesn't: Feminism, Semiotics, Cinema*, London: Macmillan.

Denis, J. (2007), 'La Prescription Ordinaire. Circulation et Énonciation des Règles au Travail', *Sociologie du Travail*, **49**, 496–513.

Dewey, J. (1938), *Logic: The Theory of Enquiry*, New York: Henry Holt.

Drew, P. and Heritage, J. (1992), 'Analyzing Talk at Work: An Introduction', in P. Drew and J. Heritage (eds), *Talk at Work*, Cambridge: Cambridge University Press, pp. 3–65.

Duboscq, J. and Clot, Y. (2010), 'L'Autoconfrontation Croisée comme Instrument d'Action au Travers du Dialogue: Objets, Adresses et Gestes Renouvelés', *Revue d'Anthropologie des Connaissances*, **2**, 255– 83.

Durkheim, Emile (1912), *Les Formes Elementaires de la Vie Religieuse: le Systeme Totemique en Austalie*, Paris: Alcun.

Ehn, P. (1991), 'Scandinavian Design: On Participation and Skill', in P. Adler and T. Winograd (eds), *Usability: Turning Technologies into Tools*, Oxford: Oxford University Press, pp. 96–132.

Eikeland, O. (2008), *The Ways of Aristotle. Aristotelian Phrónêsis, Aristotelian Philosophy of Dialogue, and Action Research*, Bern: Peter Lang.

Eikeland, O. (2009), '*Habitus*-validity in Organisational Theory and Research – Social Research and Work Life Transformed', in B. Brøgger and Olav Eikeland (eds), *Turning to Practice with Action Research*, Frankfurt am Main: Peter Lang, pp. 33–66.

Eikeland, O. and Nicolini, D. (2011), 'Turning Practically: Broadening the Horizon', *Journal of Organizational Change Management*, **24**, 164–74.

Elkjaer, B. (2003), 'Organizational Learning with a Pragmatic Slant', *International Journal of Life-long Education*, **22** (5), 481–94.

Elkjaer, B. and Simpson, B. (2011), 'Pragmatism: a Lived and Living Philosophy. What Can it Offer to Contemporary Organization Theory?', *Research in the Sociology of Organizations*, **32**, 55–84.

Elsbach, K., Barr, P. and Hargadon, A. (2005), 'Identifying Situated Cognition in Organizations', *Organization Science*, **16**, 422–33.

Emery, F. and Trist, E.L. (1965), 'The Causal Texture of Organizational Environments', *Human Relations*, **18**, 21–32.

Emirbayer, M. (1997), 'Manifesto for a Relational Sociology', *American Journal of Sociology*, **103**, 281–317.

Engeström, Y. (1987), *Learning by Expanding: An Activity Theoretical Approach to Developmental Research*, Helsinki: Orienta Konsultit.

Engeström, Y. (1999a), 'Expansive Visibilization of Work: an Activity Theoretical Perspective', *Computer-supported Cooperative Work*, **8**, 63–93.

Engeström, Y. (1999b), 'Activity Theory and Individual and Social Transformation', in Y. Engeström, R. Miettinen and R.L. Punamäki (eds), *Perspectives on Activity Theory*, Cambridge: Cambridge University Press, pp. 19–38.

Engeström, Y. and Blackler, F. (2005), 'On the Life of the Object', *Organization*, Special Issue, **12**, 307–30.

Engeström, Y., Engeström, R. and Vahaaho, T. (1999), 'When the Center does not Hold: The Importance of Knotworking', in S. Chaiklin, M. Hedegaard and U.J. Jensen (eds), *Activity Theory and Social Practice: Cultural-historical Approaches*, Aarhus: Aarhus University Press, pp. 345–74.

Engeström, Y., Brown, K., Engeström, R. and Koistinen, K. (1990), 'Organizational Forgetting: An Activity Theoretical Perspective', in D. Middleton and D. Edwards (eds), *Collective Remembering*, London: Sage, pp. 139–68.

Evered, R. and Louis, M.R. (1981), 'Alternative Perspectives in the Organizational Sciences. "Inquiry from the Inside" and "Inquiry from the Outside"', *Academy of Management Review*, **6**, 385–95.

Fabre, D. (1997), *Par Ecrit: Etnologie des Écritures Quotidiennes*, Paris: Edition de la MSH.

Feldman, M. (2000), 'Organizational Routines as a Source of Continuous Change', *Organization Science*, **11** (6), 611–29.

Feldman, M. and Orlikowski, W. (2011), 'Theorizing Practice and Practicing Theory', *Organization Science*, **22** (5), 1240–1253.

Feldman, M. and Pentland, B.T. (2003), 'Re-conceptualizing Organizational Routines as a Source of Flexibility and Change', *Administrative Science Quarterly*, **48**, 94–118.

Fele, G. (2008), 'The Collaborative Production of Responses and Dispatching on the Radio: Video Analysis in a Medical Emergency Call Centre', *Forum: Qualitative Social Research*, **9** (3), 1–44.

Foucault, M. (1975), *Surveiller et Punir. Naissance de la Prison*, Paris: Editions Gallimard.

Foucault, M. (1982), 'The Subject and Power', *Critical Inquiry*, **8**, 777–95.

Fox, S. (1997), 'Situated Learning Theory versus Traditional Cognitive Learning Theory: Why Management Education should not Ignore Management Learning', *Systems Practice*, **10**, 727–47.

Fraenkel, B. (1993), 'Pratique d'Écriture en Milieu Hospitalier: le Partage de l'Énonciation dans les Écrit de Travail', *Cahiers Langage et Travail*, **5**, Les Écrits au Travail.

Friedberg, E. (1993), *Le Pouvoir et la Régle*, Paris: Edition du Seuil.

Gabriel, Y. (2000), *Storytelling in Organizations. Facts, Fictions and Fantasies*, Oxford: Oxford University Press.

Gagliardi, P. (1996), 'Exploring the Aesthetic Side of Organizational Life', in S. Clegg, C. Hardy and W.R. Nord (eds), *Handbook of Organization Studies*, London: Sage, pp. 565–80.

Gagliardi, P. (2007), 'The Collective Repression of "Pathos" Organization Studies', *Organization*, **14** (3), 331–8.

Galegher, J. and Kraut, R.E. (1990), 'Technology for Intellectual Teamwork: Perspectives on Research and Design', in J. Galegher, R.E. Kraut and C. Egido, *Intellectual Teamwork: The Social and Technological Bases of Cooperative Work*, Hillsdale, NJ: Lawrence Erlbaum Associates, pp. 1–20.

Garfinkel, H. (1967), *Studies in Ethnomethodology*, Englewood Cliffs, NJ: Prentice Hall.

Garfinkel, H. (1996) 'Ethnomethodology's Program', *Social Psychology Quarterly*, **59** (1), 5–21.

Garfinkel, H. and Sacks, H. (1970), 'On Formal Structures of Practical Actions', in J. McKinney and E.A. Tiryakian (eds), *Theoretical Sociology*, New York: Appleton-Century-Crofts, pp. 337–66.

Garfinkel, H. and Wieder, D. (1992), 'Two Incommensurable, Asymmetrically alternate Technologies of Social Analysis', in G. Watson and R.M. Seiler (eds), *Text in Context: Studies in Ethnomethodology*, Newbury Park: Sage, pp. 175–206.

Geertz, C. (1983), *Local Knowledge*, New York: Basic Books.

Geiger, D. (2009), 'Revisiting the Concept of Practice: Toward an Argumentative Understanding of Practising', *Management Learning*, **40** (2), 129–44.

Gherardi, S. (1990), *Le Micro-decisioni nelle Organizzazioni*, Bologna: Il Mulino.

Gherardi, S. (1995a), *Gender, Symbolism and Organizational Culture*, London: Sage.

Gherardi, S. (1995b), 'When Will He Say: "Today the Plates Are Soft"? The Management of Ambiguity and Situated Decision-making', *Studies in Cultures, Organizations and Societies*, **1** (1), 9–27.

Gherardi, S. (2000), 'Practice-based Theorizing on Learning and Knowing in Organizations: An Introduction', *Organization*, Special Issue, **7**, 211–23.

Gherardi, S. (2001), 'From Organizational Learning to Practice-based Knowing', *Human Relations*, **54** (1), 131–9.

Gherardi, S. (2004), 'Translating Knowledge While Mending Organizational Safety Culture', *Risk Management: An International Journal*, **6** (2), 61–80.

Gherardi, S. (2006), *Organizational Knowledge: The Texture of Workplace Learning*, Oxford: Blackwell.

Gherardi, S. (2008), 'Situated Knowledge and Situated Action: What Do Practice-based Studies Promise?, in D. Barrry and H. Hansen (eds), *The SAGE Handbook of New Approaches in Management and Organization*, London: Sage, pp. 516–27.

Gherardi, S. (2009a), 'Community of Practice or Practices of a Community?', in S. Armstrong and C. Fukami (eds), *The Sage Handbook of Management Learning, Education, and Development*, London: Sage, pp. 514–30.

Gherardi, S. (2009b), 'Practice? It's a Matter of Taste!', *Management Learning*, **40** (5), 535–50.

Gherardi, S. (2009c), 'Spiral Case-study', in A. Mills, G. Durepos and E. Wiebe (eds), *Encyclopaedia of Case Studies Research*, London: Sage.

Gherardi, S. (2010), 'Telemedicine: A Practice-based Approach to Technology', *Human Relations*, **63** (4), 501–24.

Gherardi, S. (2011), 'Organizational Learning: The Sociology of Practice', In M. Easterby-Smith and M. Lyles (eds), *The Blackwell Handbook of Organizational Learning and Knowledge Management*, Malden, Oxford, Melbourne, Berlin: Blackwell, pp. 43–65

Gherardi, S. (2012), '*Docta Ignorantia*: Professional Knowing at the Core and at the Margins of a Practice', *Journal of Education and Work*, **25** (1), 38.

Gherardi, S. and Nicolini, D. (2000), 'The Organizational Learning of Safety in Communities of Practice', *Journal of Management Inquiry*, **9** (1), 7–18.

Gherardi, S. and Nicolini, D. (2002a), 'Learning in a Costellation of Interconnected Practices: Canon or Dissonance?', *Journal of Management Studies*, **39** (4), 419–36.

Gherardi, S. and Nicolini, D. (2002b), 'Learning the Trade. A Culture of Safety in Practice', *Organization*, **9** (2), 191–223.

Gherardi, S. and Perrotta, M. (2011), 'Egg Dates Sperm: A Tale of Practice Change and its Institutionalization', *Organization*, **18** (5), 595–614.

Gherardi, S. and Strati, A. (1990), 'The "Texture" of Organizing in an

Italian University Department', *Journal of Management Studies*, **27** (6), 605–18.

Gherardi, S., Nicolini, D. and Odella, F. (1998a), 'Toward a Social Understanding of How People Learn in Organizations: The Notion of Situated Curriculum', *Management Learning*, **29** (3), 273–98.

Gherardi, S., Nicolini, D. and Odella, F. (1998b), 'What Do You Mean by Safety? Conflicting Perspectives on Accident Causation and Safety Management Inside a Construction Firm', *Journal of Contingencies and Crisis Management*, **7** (4), 202–13.

Gherardi, S., Nicolini, D. and Strati, A. (2007), 'The Passion for Knowing', *Organization*, **14** (3), 309–23.

Gibson, J.G. (1979), *The Ecological Approach to Visual Perception*, Boston, MA: Houghton Mifflin.

Giddens, A. (1990), *The Consequences of Modernity*, Cambridge: Polity Press.

Goffman, E. (1956), *Encounters*, New York: Macmillan.

Goffman, E. (1959), *The Presentation of Self in Everyday Life*, Garden City, NY: Doubleday.

Goffman, E. (1971), *Relations in Public: Microstudies of the Public Order*, New York: Harper and Row.

Goffman, E. (1981), *Forms of Talk*, Oxford: Basil Blackwell.

Gomart, E. and Hennion, A. (1999), 'A Sociology of Attachment: Music, Amateurs, Drug Users', in J. Law and J. Hassard (eds), *Actor Network and After*, Oxford: Blackwell, 220–247.

Gomez, M.L. and Bouty, I. (2011), 'The Emergence of an Influential Practice: Food for Thought', *Organization Studies*, **32** (7), 921–40.

Goodwin, C. (1994), 'Professional Vision', *American Anthropologist*, **3**, 606–33.

Goodwin, C. (1997), 'The Blackness of Black', in L. Resnik, C. Saljo, C. Pontecorvo and B. Burge (eds), *Discourse, Tools and Reasoning. Essays on Situated Cognition*, Berlin: Springer, pp. 111–40.

Goodwin, C. and Goodwin, M.H. (1996), 'Seeing as Situated Activity: Formulating Planes', in Y. Engeström and D. Middleton (eds), *Cognition and Communication at Work*, Cambridge: Cambridge University Press, pp. 61–95.

Goodwin, M. (1995), 'Assembling a Response: Setting and Collaboratively Constructed Work Talk', in P. Ten Have and G. Psathas (eds), *Situated Order: Studies in the Social Organization of Talk and Embodied Activities*, Washington: University Press of America, pp. 173–86.

Goody, J. (1993), *Entre l'Oralité et l'Écriture*, Paris: PUF.

Greenbaum, J. and Kyng, M. (eds) (1991), *Design at Work: Cooperative*

Design of Computer Systems, Hillsdale, NJ: Lawrence Erlbaum Associates.

Greif, I. (ed.) (1988), *Computer Supported Cooperative Work: A Book of Readings*, San Matteo, CA: Morgan Kaufmann.

Grosjean, M. (2004), 'From Multi-participant Talk to Genuine Polylogue: Shift-change Briefing Sessions at the Hospital', *Journal of Pragmatics*, **36**, 25–52.

Grosjean, M. and Lacoste, M. (1999), *Communication et Intelligence Collective. Le Travail à l'Hopital*, Paris: PUF.

Grosjean, S. and Bonneville, L. (2009), 'Saisir le Processus de Remémoration Organisationnelles des Actants Humain et Non Humain au Cœur du Processus', *Revue d'Anthropologie des Connaissance*, **3** (2), 317–47.

Guillet de Monthoux, P. (2004), *The Art Firm: Aesthetic Management and Metaphysical Marketing from Wagner to Wilson*, Stanford: Stanford Business Books.

Gumperz, J.J. (1989), *Engager la Conversation. Introduction à la Sociolinguistique Interactionnelle*, Paris: Minuit.

Gumperz, J.J. (1992), 'Interviewing in Intercultural Situations', in P. Drew and J. Heritage (eds), *Talk at Work*, Cambridge: Cambridge University Press, pp. 302–27.

Habermas, J. (1979), *Communication and the Evolution of Society*, Boston, MA: Beacon Press.

Habermas, J. (1984), *The Theory of Communicative Action, Vol. 1 Reason and the Rationalization of Society*, Boston, MA: Beacon Press.

Habermas, J. (1989), *The Theory of Communicative Action, Vol. 2 Lifeworld and System: A Critique of Functionalist Reason*, Boston, MA: Beacon Press.

Habermas, J. (2003), *Truth and Justification*, London: Polity Press.

Hancock, P. and Tyler, M. (2000), '"The Look of Love": Gender and the Organization of Aesthetics', in J. Hassard, R. Holliday and H. Willmott (eds), *Body and Organization*, London: Sage.

Haraway, D. (1991), 'Situated Knowledges: The Science Question in Feminism and the Privilege of Partial Perspectives', in D. Haraway, *Simians, Cyborgs and Women: The Reinvention of Nature*, London: Free Association Books, pp. 183–202.

Haraway, D. (1997), *Modest_Witness@Second_Millenium.FemaleMan_ Meets_Oncomouse: Feminism and Technoscience*, New York: Routledge.

Harper, R. (2000), 'Analysing Work Practice and the Potential Role of New Technology at the International Monetary Fund: Some Remarks on the Role of Ethnomethodology', in P. Luff, J. Hindmarsh and C. Heath (eds), *Workplace Studies. Recovering Work Practice and*

Informing System Design, Cambridge: Cambridge University Press, pp. 169–86.

Heath, C. and Button, G. (2002), 'Special Issue on Workplace Studies: Editorial Introduction', *British Journal of Sociology*, **53** (2), 157–61.

Heath, C. and Luff, P. (1992), 'Collaboration and Control. Crisis Management and Multimedia Technology in London Underground Line Control Rooms', *Computer-supported Cooperative Work*, **1**, 69–94.

Heath, C. and Luff, P. (eds) (2000), *Technology in Action*, Cambridge: Cambridge University Press.

Heath, C., Knoblauch, H. and Luff, P. (2000), 'Technology and Social Interaction: The Emergence of "Workplace Studies"', *British Journal of Sociology*, **51** (2), 299–320.

Hennion, A. (2007), 'Those Things that Holds us Together: Taste and Sociology', *Cultural Sociology*, **1** (1), 97–114.

Hindmarsh, J. and Heath, C. (2000), 'Sharing the Tools of the Trade: The Interactional Constitution of Workplace Objects', *Journal of Contemporary Ethnography*, **29** (5), 523–62.

Hindmarsh, J. and Heath, C. (2007), 'Video-based Studies of Work Practice', *Sociology Compass*, **1**, 1–18.

Hindmarsh, J. and Pilnick, A. (2002), 'The Tacit Order of Teamwork: Collaboration and Embodied Conduct in Anesthesia', *The Sociological Quarterly*, **43**, 139–64.

Hindmarsh, J., Reynolds, P. and Dunne, S. (2011), 'Exhibiting Understanding: The Body in Apprenticeship', *Journal of Pragmatics*, **43**, 489–503.

Hochschild, A.R. (1983), *The Managed Heart: Commercialization of Human Feeling*, Berkley, CA: University of California Press.

Howcroft, D. and Trauth, E. (2005), 'Choosing Critical IS Research', in D. Howcroft and E. Trauth (eds), *Handbook of Critical Information Systems Research Theory and Application*, Cheltenham, UK and Northampton, MA, USA: Edward Elgar, pp. 1–15.

Hughes, E.C. (1958), *Men and their Work*, Glencoe: The Free Press.

Hughes, E.C. (1971), *The Sociological Eye*, Chicago: Aldine.

Hughes, J., King, V. and Rodden, T. (1994), 'Moving out of the Control Room: Ethnography in System Design', *Proceedings of CSCW 94*, Chapel Hill, NC: ACM Press, pp. 429–40.

Hutchins, E. (1990), 'The Technology of Team Navigation', in J. Galegher and R. Kraut (eds), *Intellectual Teamwork: Social and Technological Foundations of Cooperative Work'*, Hillsdale, NJ: Lawrence Erlbaum Associates, pp. 191–220.

Hutchins, E. (1995), *Cognition in the Wild*, Cambridge: MIT Press.

Hymes, D. (1974), *Foundations in Sociolinguistics. An Ethnographic Approach*, Philadelphia: University of Pennsylvania Press.

Iedema, R. (2007), 'On the Multi-modality, Materiality and Contingency of Organizational Discourse', *Organization Studies*, **28** (6), 931–46

Illich, I. (1982), *Gender*, New York: Pantheon Books.

Jedlowski, P. (2000), *Storie Comuni. La Narrazione nella vita Quotidiana*, Milan: Bruno Mondatori.

Joas, H. (1997), *Pragmatism and Social Theory*, Chicago: University of Chicago Press.

Jordan, B. (1992), *Technology and Social Interaction: Notes on the Achievement of Authoritative Knowledge in Complex Settings*, IRL Technical Report, Palo Alto: Institute for Research on Learning.

Jordan, S. (2010), 'Learning to Be Surprised: How to Foster Reflective Practice in a High-reliability Context', *Management Learning*, **41** (4), 391–413.

Joseph, I. (1994), 'Attention Distribuée et Attention Focalise. Les Protocoles de la Cooperation au PCC de la Ligne A du RER', *Sociologie du Travail*, **4**, 563–85.

Kirsh, D. (1995), 'The Intelligent Use of Space', *Artificial Intelligence*, **73** (1–2), 31–68.

Knorr Cetina, K. (1981), *The Manufacture of Knowledge. An Essay on the Constructivist and Contextual Nature of Science*, New York: Pergamon.

Knorr Cetina, K. (1997), 'Sociality with Objects: Social Relations in Postsocial Knowledge Societies', *Theory, Culture and Society*, **14**, 1–30.

Knorr Cetina, K. and Bruegger, U. (2002a), '"Traders" Engagement with Markets: A Postsocial Relationship', *Theory, Culture and Society*, **19**, 161–85.

Knorr Cetina, K. and Bruegger, U. (2002b), 'Global Microstructures: The Virtual Societies of Financial Markets', *American Journal of Sociology*, **107**, 905–50.

Knorr Cetina, K. and Preda, A. (eds) (2005), *The Sociology of Financial Markets*, Oxford: Oxford University Press.

Landri, P. (2007), 'The Pragmatics of Passion: A Sociology of Attachment to Mathematics', *Organization*, **14** (3), 407–29.

Latour, B. (1987), *Science in Action: How to follow Scientists and Engineers through Society*, Milton Keynes: Open University Press.

Latour, B. (1990), 'Drawing Things Together', in M. Lynch and S. Woolgar (eds), *Representation in Scientific Practice*, Cambridge, MA: MIT Press, pp. 19–68.

Latour, B. (1993), *We Have Never Been Modern*, London: Harvester Wheatsheaf.

Latour, B. (1999a), 'On Recalling ANT', in J. Law and J. Hassard, *Actor Network Theory and After*, Oxford: Blackwell, pp. 15–25.

Latour, B. (1999b), *Pandora's Hope: Essays on the Reality of Science Studies*, Cambridge, MA: Harvard University Press.

Latour, B. (2002), 'Morality and Technology. The End of the Means', *Theory, Culture and Society*, **19** (5/6), 247–60.

Latour, B. and Woolgar, S. (1979), *Laboratory Life: The Social Construction of Scientific Facts*, Beverly Hills: Sage.

Lave, J. (1988), *Cognition in Practice*, Cambridge: Cambridge University Press.

Lave, J. (1991), 'Socially Shared Cognition', in L. Resnick, J. Levine and S. Teasley (eds), *Perspectives on Socially Shared Cognition*, Washington DC: American Psychological Association.

Lave, J. and Wenger, E. (1991), *Situated Learning. Legitimate Peripheral Participation*, Cambridge, MA: Cambridge University Press.

Lave, J., Murtaugh, M. and de la Rocha, O. (1984), 'The Dialectic of Arithmetic in Grocery Shopping', in B. Rogoff and J. Lave (eds), *Everyday Cognition*, Cambridge: Harvard University Press, pp. 67–94.

Law, J. (1994), *Organizing Modernity*, Oxford: Blackwell.

Law, J. (2000), 'On the Subject of the Object: Narrative, Technology and Interpellation', *Configurations*, **8**, 1–29.

Léglise, I. (1998), 'Le Problème de l'Adresse en Situation d'Interaction Plurilocuteurs dans les Avions de la Patrouille Maritime', in K. Kostulski and A. Trognon (eds), *Communications Interactives dans les Groupe de Travail*, Nancy: PUN, pp. 183–205.

Licoppe, C. (2008), 'Dans le Carré de l'Activité: Perspectives Internationales sur le Travail et l'Activité', *Sociologie du Travail*, **50** (3), 287–302.

Linstead, S. and Höpfl, H. (eds) (2000), *The Aesthetics of Organization*, London: Sage.

Llewellyn, N. (2008), 'Organization in Actual Episodes of Work: Harvey Sacks and Organization Studies', *Organization Studies*, **29** (5), 763–91.

Llewellyn, N. and Hindmarsh, J. (eds) (2010), *Organization, Interaction and Practice: Studies in Ethnomethodology and Conversation Analysis*, Cambridge: Cambridge University Press.

Llewellyn, N. and Hindmarsh, J. (2011), 'Work and Organisation in Real Time: An Introduction', in N. Llewellyn and J. Hindmarsh (eds), *Organization, Interaction and Practice: Studies in Ethnomethodology and Conversation Analysis*, Cambridge: Cambridge University Press.

Luff, P., Hindmarsh, J. and Heath, C. (2000), *Workplace Studies. Recovering Work Practice and Informing System Design*, Cambridge: Cambridge University Press.

Lyotard, J. (1984), *The Postmodern Condition*, Manchester, UK: Manchester University Press.

MacIntyre, A. (1988), *Whose Justice? Which Rationality?*, Notre Dame: University of Notre Dame Press.

Mack, K. (2007), 'Senses of Seascapes: Aesthetics and the Passion for Knowledge', *Organization*, **14** (3), 367–84.

Mackay, W. (1990), 'Patterns of Sharing Customizable Software', *Proceedings of CSCW*, New York: ACM, pp. 209–21.

MacKenzie, D. and Millo, Y. (2003), 'Negotiating a Market, Performing Theory: The Historical Sociology of Financial Derivatives Exchange', *American Journal of Sociology*, **109**, 107–46.

March, J.G. (1988), *Decisions and Organizations*, New York: Basil Blackwell.

March, J. and Olsen, J.P. (1989), *Rediscovering Institutions. The Organizational Basis of Politics*, New York: Free Press.

Martin, P.Y. (2002), 'Sensations, Bodies and the "Spirit of a Place": Aesthetics in Residential Organizations for the Elderly', *Human Relations*, **7**, 861–85.

Martin, P.Y. (2003), '"Said & Done" Vs. "Saying & Doing". Gendered Practices/Practicing Gender at Work', *Gender and Society*, **17**, 342–66.

Matera, V. (2002), *Etnografia della Comunicazione: Teorie e Pratiche dell'Interazione sociale*, Rome: Carocci.

Mathieu, C.J. (2009), 'Practicing Gender in Organisations: the Critical Gap between Practical and Discursive Consciousness', *Management Learning*, **40** (2), 177–94.

Maynard, D. (1992), 'On Clinicians Co-implicating Recipients Perspective in the Delivery of Diagnostic News', in P. Drew and J. Heritage (eds), *Talk at Work*, Cambridge: Cambridge University Press, pp. 331–58.

Mazmanian, M., Orlikowski, W.J. and Yates, J. (2006), 'Ubiquitous Email: Individual Experiences and Organizational Consequences of BlackBerry Use', Best Paper Proceedings of the 65th Annual Meeting of the Academy of Management, Atlanta, GA, August.

McDermott, R. (1999), 'Why Information Technology Inspired but Cannot Deliver Knowledge Management', *California Management Review*, **41** (4), 103–17.

Mead, G.H. (1934), *Mind, Self and Society*, Chicago: University of Chicago Press.

Messner, M., Clegg, S. and Kornberger, M. (2008), 'Critical Practices in Organizations', *Journal of Management Inquiry*, **17** (2), 68–82.

Miettinen, R., Samra-Fredericks, D. and Yanow, D. (2009), 'Re-turn to Practice: An Introductory Essay', *Organization Studies*, **30** (12), 1309–27.

Mondada, L. (2002), 'Interactions et Pratiques Professionnelles: un Regard Issu des Studies of Work', *Studies in Communication Sciences*, **2**, 47–82.

Morgan, G. (1986), *Images of Organization*, Thousand Oaks, CA: Sage.

Mumford, E. (1992), 'The Participation of Users in Systems Design. An Account of the Origin, Evolution and Use of the ETHICS Method', in D. Schuler and A. Namioka (eds), *Participatory Design: Principles and Practices*, Hillsdale, NJ: Lawrence Erlbaum Associates, pp. 257–70.

Nicolini, D. (2006), 'The Work to Make Telemedicine Work: A Social and Articulative View', *Social Science and Medicine*, **62**, 2754–67.

Nicolini, D. (2007), 'Stretching out and Expanding Medical Practices. The Case of Telemedicine', *Human Relations*, **60** (6), 889–92.

Nicolini, D. (2009), 'Articulating and Writing Practice Through the Interview to the Double', *Management Learning*, **40** (2), 195–212.

Nicolini, D. (2010), 'Zooming In and Out. Studying Practice by Switching Lenses and Trailing Connections', *Organization Studies*, **30** (12), 1391–418.

Nicolini, D. (2011), 'Practice as the Site of Knowing. Insights from the Field of Telemedicine', *Organization Science*, **22**, 602–20.

Norman, D. (1993), 'Cognition in the Head and in the World: An Introduction to the Special Issue on Situated Action', *Cognitive Science*, Special Issue, **17**, 1–6.

Norman, D. (1998), *The Invisible Computer*, Boston: MIT Press.

Norman, D. and Draper, S. (1986), *User Centered System Design*, Hillsdale, NJ: Lawrence Erlbaum Associates.

Nyberg, D. (2009), 'Computers, Customer Service Operatives and Cyborgs: Intra-actions in Call Centers', *Organization Studies*, **30** (11), 1181–99.

Oddone, I., Re, A. and Briante, G. (1977), *Esperienza Operaia, Coscienza di Classe e Psicologia del Lavoro*, Torino: Einaudi.

Orlikowski, W.J. (2000), 'Using Technology and Constituting Structures: A Practice Lens for Studying Technology in Organizations', *Organization Science*, **11** (4), 404–28.

Orlikowski, W.J. (2006), 'Material Knowing: the Scaffolding of Human Knowledgeability', *European Journal of Information Systems*, **15**, 460–466.

Orlikowski, W.J. (2007), 'Sociomaterial Practices: Exploring Technology at Work', *Organization Studies*, **28** (9), 1435–48.

Orlikowski, W.J. (2009), 'The Sociomateriality of Organizational Life: Considering Technology in Management Research', *Cambridge Journal of Economics*, **34** (1), 125–41.

Orr, J. (1990), 'Sharing Knowledge, Celebrating Identity: War Stories and Community Memory in a Service Culture', in D.S. Middleton and D.

Edwards (eds), *Collective Remembering: Memory in Society*, Beverley Hills, CA: Sage, pp. 167–89.

Orr, J. (1996), *Talking About Machines: An Ethnography of a Modern Job*, Ithaka: Cornell University Press.

Ortner, S.B. (1984), 'Theory in Anthropology since the Sixties', *Comparative Studies in Society and History*, **26**, 126–66.

Østerlund, C. (2003), 'Documenting Practices: The Indexical Centring of Medical Records', *Outlines: Critical Social Studies*, **2**, 43–68.

Østerlund, C. (2004), 'Mapping Medical Work: Information Practices across Multiple Medical Settings', *Journal of the Centre for Information Studies*, **5**, 35–43.

Ottensmeyer, E. (1996), 'Too Strong to Stop, too Sweet to Lose: Aesthetics as a Way to Know Organizations', *Organization*, **3** (2), 189–94.

Pels, D., Hetherington, K. and Vandenberghe, F. (2002), 'The Status of the Object', *Theory, Culture and Society*, Special Issue, **19**, 1–21.

Pène, S., (1995), 'Traces des Mains sue les Écrit Gris', in J. Boutet (ed.), *Paroles au Travail*, Paris: L'Harmattan, pp. 103–22.

Pepper, S. (1942), *World Hypotheses*, Berkeley: University of California Press.

Perrotta, M. (2010), 'Situated Practices as the Locus of Technological Change', in S. Jordan and H. Mitterhofer (eds), *Beyond Knowledge Management: Sociomaterial and Sociocultural Perspectives within Management Research*, Innsbruck: Innsbruck University Press, pp. 147–69.

Pickering, A. (1992), *Science as Practice and Culture*, Chicago: University of Chicago Press.

Poggio, B. (2004), *Mi Racconti una Storia? Il Metodo Narrativo nelle Scienze Sociali*, Rome: Carocci.

Poggio, B. (2006), 'Editorial: Outline of a Theory of Gender Practices', *Gender, Work and Organization*, **13** (3), 225–33.

Polanyi, M. (1958), *Personal Knowledge. Towards a Post-critical Philosophy*, Chicago: University of Chicago Press.

Polanyi, M. (1966), 'The Logic of Tacit Inference', *Philosophy*, **41**, 1–18.

Rabardel, P. (1995), *Les Hommes et les Techniques, une Approche Cognitive des Instruments Contemporains*, Paris: Armand Colin.

Richardson, H., Tapia, A. and Kvasny, L. (2006), 'Introduction: Applying Critical Theory to the Study of ICT', *Social Science Computer Review*, **24** (3), 267–73.

Rogoff, B. (1995), 'Observing Sociocultural Activity on Three Planes: Participatory Appropiation, Guided Participation and Apprenticeship', in J.V. Wertsch, P. del Rio and A. Alvarez (eds), *Sociocultural Studies of Mind*, Cambridge: Cambridge University Press, pp. 139–64.

Rogoff, B. and Lave, J. (1984), *Everyday Cognition: Its Development in Social Context*, Cambridge, MA: Harvard University Press.

Roth, M.W. (2005), 'Textbooks on Qualitative Research and Method/ Methodology: Towards a Praxis of Method', *Forum: Qualitative Social Research*, online Journal, **7** (1) article 11, available at: www.qualitative-research.net/index/article.

Rouse, J. (2002), *How Scientific Practices Matter*, Chicago: University of Chicago Press.

Roy, D. (1952), 'Quota Restriction and Goldbricking in a Machine Shop', *America Journal of Sociology*, **57**, 427–42.

Roy, D. (1953), 'Work Satisfaction and Social Reward in Quota Achievement', *American Sociological Review*, **18**, 507–14.

Roy, D. (1959), 'Banana Time: Job Satisfaction and Informal Interaction', *Human Organization*, **18**, 158–68.

Roy, D. (1969), 'Making Out: A Counter-system of Worker Control of Work Situation and Relationships', in T. Burns (ed.), *Industrial Man*, Harmondsworth: Penguin, pp. 359–79.

Roy, D. (2006), 'Cooperation and Conflict in the Factory: Some Observations and Questions Regarding Conceptualization of Intergroup Relations within Bureaucratic Social Structures', *Qualitative Sociology*, **29**, 59–85.

Sacks, H. and Schegloff, E. (1974), 'Two Preferences in the Organization of Reference to Persons in Conversation and their Interaction', in N.H. Avison and R.J. Wilson (eds), *Ethnometodology: Labelling Theory and Deviant Behaviour*, London: Routledge and Kegan Paul.

Samra-Fredericks, D. (2003), 'Strategizing as Lived Experience and Strategists' Everyday Efforts to Shape Strategic Direction', *Journal of Management Studies*, **40** (1), 141–74.

Samra-Fredericks, D. (2005), 'Strategic Practice, "Discourse" and the *Everyday* Interactional Constitution of "Power Effects"', *Organization*, **12** (6), 803–41.

Sandberg, J. and Dall'Alba, G. (2009), 'Returning to Practice Anew: A Life-world Perspective', *Organisation Studies*, **30** (12), 1349–68.

Schatzki, T.R. (2001), 'Introduction. Practice theory', in T.R. Schatzki, K. Knorr Cetina and E. von Savigny (eds), *The Practice Turn in Contemporary Theory*, London and New York: Routledge, pp. 1–14.

Schatzki, T.R., Knorr Cetina, K. and von Savigny, E. (eds) (2001), *The Practice Turn in Contemporary Theory*, London and New York: Routledge.

Schmidt, K. and Bannon, L. (1992), 'Taking CSCW Seriously. Supporting Articulation Work', *Computer-supported Cooperative Work*, **1**, 7–40.

Schmidt, K. and Simone, C. (1996) 'Coordination Mechanisms: Towards a Conceptual Foundation of CSCW Systems Design', *Computer-supported Cooperative Work*, **5**, 155–200.

Schultze, U. (2000), 'A Confessional Account of an Ethnography about Knowledge Worker', *MIS Quarterly*, **24** (1), 3–41.

Schultze, U. and Boland, R. (2000), 'Knowledge Management Technology and the Reproduction of Knowledge Work Practices', *The Journal of Strategic Information Systems*, **9** (2–3), 193–212.

Schultze, U. and Orlikowski, W. (2004), 'A Practice Perspective on Technology-mediated Network Relations: The Use of Internet-based Self-serve Technologies', *Information System Research*, **15** (1), 87–106.

Schütz, A. (1962), *Collected Papers*, The Hague: Nijhoff.

Scribner, S. (1984), 'Studying Working Intelligence', in B. Rogoff and J. Lave, *Everyday Cognition*, Cambridge: Harvard University Press.

Searle, J. (1969), *Speech Acts*, Cambridge: Cambridge University Press.

Shapiro, D. (1994), 'The Limits of Ethnography', *Proceedings of CSCW 94*, Chapel Hill, NC: ACM Press.

Snook, S. (2001), *Friendly Fire*, Princeton: Princeton University Press.

Star, S.L. (1999), 'The Ethnography of the Infrastructure', *American Behavioural Scientist*, **43**, 377–91.

Star, S.L. (2002), 'Invisible Homes and Tiny Infrastructures', position paper for the workshop Managing as Designing, available at: http://design.case.edu/2002workshop.

Star S.L. (2010), 'Ceci n'est pas un Objet-frontière: Réflexions sur l'Origine d'un Concept [This is not a Boundary Object: Reflections on the Origin of a Concept]', *Revue d'Anthropologie des Connaissances*, **4** (1), 18–35.

Star, S.L. and Griesemer, J. (1989), 'Institutional Ecology, "Translations", and Boundary Objects: Amateurs and Professionals on Berkeley's Museum of Vertebrate Zoology', *Social Studies of Science*, **19** (3), 387–420.

Star, S.L. and Ruhleder, K. (1996), 'Steps Toward an Ecology of Infrastructure: Design and Access for Large Information Spaces', *Information Systems Research*, **7**, 111–34.

Star, S.L. and Strauss, A. (1999), 'Layers of Silence, Arenas of Voice: The Ecology of Visible and Invisible Work', *Computer-supported Cooperative Work: The Journal of Collaborative Computing*, **8**, 9–30.

Stein, W.E. (1995), 'Organizational Memory: Review of Concepts and Recommendations for Management', *International Journal of Information Management*, **15** (2), 17–32.

Stiglitz, J. (2002), *Globalisation and its Discontents*, New York: W.W. Norton and Company.

Strathern, M. (1991), *Partial Connections*, Savage: Rowan and Littlefield.

Strati, A. (1999), *Organization and Aesthetics*, London: Sage.

Strati, A. (2000), *Theory and Method in Organization Studies: Paradigms and Choices*, London: Sage.

Strati, A. (2003), 'Knowing in Practice: Aesthetic Understanding and Tacit Knowledge', in D. Nicolini, S. Gherardi and D. Yanow (eds), *Knowing in Organizations: A Practice-based Approach*, Armonk: M.E. Sharpe, pp. 53–75.

Strati, A. (2007), 'Sensible Knowledge and Practice-based Learning', *Management Learning*, **38** (1), 61–77.

Strati, A. (2008), 'Aesthetics in the Study of Organizational Life' in D. Barry and H. Hansen (eds), *The SAGE Handbook of New Approaches in Management and Organization*, London: Sage.

Strauss, A. (1978), *Negotiations*, San Francisco: Jossey-Bass.

Strauss, A. (1985), 'Work and the Division of Labor', *The Sociologcal Quarterly*, **26** (11985): 1–19.

Strauss, A. (1988), 'The Articulation of Project Work: an Organizational Process', *Sociological Quarterly*, **29** (2), 163–78.

Styhre, A. (2011), 'The Architect's Gaze: The Maintenance of Collective Professional Vision in the Work of the Architect', *Culture and Organization*, **17** (4), 253–69.

Suchman, L. (1987), *Plans and Situated Action: The Problem of Human-machine Communication*, Cambridge: Cambridge University Press.

Suchman, L. (1994), 'Working Relations of Technology Production and Use', *Computer-supported Cooperative Work*, **2**, 21–39.

Suchman, L. (1996), 'Constituting Shared Workspaces', in Y. Engeström and D. Middleton (eds), *Cognition and Communication at Work*, Cambridge: Cambridge University Press, pp. 35–60.

Suchman, L. (1997), 'Centers of Coordination: A Case and Some Themes', in L. Resnik, C. Saljo, C. Pontecorvo and B. Burge (eds), *Discourse, Tools and Reasoning. Essays on Situated Cognition*, Berlin: Springer, pp. 41–62.

Suchman, L. (2002), 'Practice-based Design of Information Systems: Notes from the Hyperdeveloped World', *The Information Society*, **18** (2), 139–44.

Suchman, L. (2005), 'Affiliative Objects', *Organization*, **12** (3), 379–99.

Suchman, L., Trigg, R. and Blomberg, J. (2002), 'Working Artefacts: Ethnomethods of the Prototype', *British Journal of Sociology*, **53** (2), 163–79.

Suchman, L., Blomberg, J., Orr, J.E. and Trigg, R. (1999), 'Reconstructing Technologies as Social Practice', *American Behavioural Scientist*, **43**, 392–408.

Svabo, C. (2009), 'Materiality in a Practice-based Approach', *The Learning Organization*, Special Issue on Knowing and Learning in Practice-based Studies, **16** (5), 360–370.

Swidler, A. (2001), 'What Anchors Cultural Practices', in T.R. Schatzki, K. Knorr Cetina, E. von Savigny (eds), *The Practice Turn in Contemporary Theory*, London and New York: Routledge, pp. 74–92.

Taylor, J.R. and Van Every, E.J. (2000), *The Emergent Organization: Communication as its Site and Surface*, Mahwah, NJ: Lawrence Erlbaum Associates.

Teil, G. (1998), 'Devenir Expert Aromaticien: Y a-t-il une Place pour le Goût dans le Goûts Alimentaires?', *Sociologie du Travail*, n. 4, 503–22.

Tiddi, A. (2002), *Precari, Percorsi di vita tra Lavoro e Non-lavoro*, Rome: Deriveapprodi.

Tolman, E. and Brunswick, E. (1935), 'The Organism and the Causal Texture of the Environment', *Psychological Review*, **42**, 43–77.

Townley, B. (1993), 'Performance Appraisal and the Emergence of Management', *Journal of Management Studies*, **30** (2), 221–38.

Tsoukas, H. (2006), 'Talking about Machines: Tenth Anniversary', *Organization Studies*, Special Issue, **27** (12), 1741–2.

Turner, B. (1971), *Exploring the Industrial Subculture*, London: Macmillan.

Vera, A. and Simon, H. (1993), 'Situated Action: a Symbolic Interpretation', *Cognitive Science*, Special Issue, **17**, 7–48.

Vermersch, P. (1994), *L'Entretien d'Explicitation*, Paris: ESF.

Von Hippel, E. (1976), 'The Dominant Role of Users in the Scientific Instrument Innovation Process', *Research Policy*, **5**, 212–39.

Von Hippel, E. (1988), *The Source of Innovation*, Oxford: Oxford University Press.

Von Hippel, E. (1994), '"Sticky Information" and the Locus of Problem-solving. Implications for Innovation', *Management Science*, no. 4, 429–39.

Vygotsky, L. (1934 [1987]), *Thinking and Speech*, New York: Plenum.

Wajcman, J. and Rose, E. (2011), 'Constant Connectivity: Rethinking Interruptions at Work', *Organization Studies*, **32** (7), 941–61.

Walsh, J.P. and Ungson, G.R. (1991), 'Organizational Memory', *Academy of Management Review*, **16** (1), 57–91.

Weber, M. (1922), *Wirtschaft und Gesellschaft*, Tubingen: Mohr.

Weick, K. (1979), *The Social Psychology of Organizing*, Reading, MA: Addison-Wesley.

Weick, K. (1995), *Sensemaking in Organizations*, Thousand Oaks, CA: Sage.

Weick, K. (1999), 'The Aesthetic of Imperfection in Orchestras and Organizations', in M.P. Cuhna and C.A. Marques (eds), *Readings in Organization Science*, Lisboa: Instituto Superior de Psicologia Aplicada.

Weick, K.E., Sutcliffe, K. and Obstfeld, D. (2005), 'Organizing and the Process of Sensemaking', *Organization Science*, **4**, 409–21.

Wenger, E. (1998), *Communities of Practice. Learning, Meaning and Identity*, New York: Cambridge University Press.

West, C. and Zimmerman, D. (1987), 'Doing Gender', *Gender and Society*, **1** (2), 125–51.

Whalen, J., Whalen, M. and Henderson, K. (2002), 'Improvisational Choreography in Teleservice Work', *British Journal of Sociology*, **53**, 239–58.

Winograd, T. and Flores, F. (1986), *Understanding Computers and Cognition: A New Foundation for Design*, Norwood: Ablex.

Woener, S.L., Orlikowski, W.J. and Yates, J.A. (2005), 'Scaffolding Conversations: Engaging Multiple Media in Organizational Communication', paper prepared for the 21st EGOS Colloquium Sub Theme 19 – Practice-based Studies of Knowledge, Work and Technology, Berlin, July.

Zucchermaglio, C. (1996), *Vygotskij in Azienda*, Rome: La Nuova Italia Scientifica.

Index

Computer-supported Cooperative
    Work (CSCW) 181–6
constant connectivity 194–5
Participatory Design (PD) 187–90
Workplace Studies (WS) 190–194
Excel workbook case and memory
    91–3
experience 144, 207–8
expertise, acquiring 57, 128
eyes 63–5

factories and production rules 135–40
feelings 58–9, 67, 121, 163
feet 51, 53, 54
Feldman, M. 133
figure concept 199–200
fluctuating configurations 110–111
Fox, S. 158–9
Fraenkel, B. 87, 111, 141
Friedberg, E. 141
front stage 114–16

Garfinkel, H. 6, 26, 27, 133–4, 155,
    159, 201
Geertz, Clifford 148
Geiger, D. 122–3
gender as a social practice 70–74
gender relations 6
Gherardi, Silvia 7, 11, 14, 15, 49, 55,
    57–9, 63–4, 65, 72–4, 109, 124–5,
    128, 129, 136–9, 147, 158, 159–62,
    164–5, 168–73, 175, 199, 201
Giddens, A. 27, 199, 201
glossing 159
Goffman, Erving 17, 37–8, 45, 98, 110,
    114, 116, 201
Gomez, M.L. 58
Goodwin, Charles 46, 62, 201
Goodwin, Marjorie 46, 62, 117, 201
Greif, Irene 181
Griesemer, J. 90, 93
Grosjean, Michèle 13, 32, 41, 88–9, 97,
    111, 112–13, 142–3, 144
group membership learning 96
Gumperz, J.J. 104, 105

Habermas, J. 120–123
handing over shifts 111–13, 130,
    202–3
hands 51–3, 74–5

Haraway, Donna 83, 179
Harper, Richard 190–194
Heath, Christian 7, 14, 15, 30–31, 32,
    35, 201, 209
Henderson, Kathryn 15, 98–101
Hennion, A. 20, 66
Heritage, J. 104–5, 106
hierarchical authority 145
highlighting 62–3, 75
Hindmarsh, J. 7, 32, 53, 115–16
historical-cultural anchoring 25, 45–6
hospital work 11–12
Hughes, E.C. 7, 35, 38
Hughes, John 15, 179–80
human activity 28, 42
human and non-human divide 83
Human–Computer Interaction (HCI)
    17
Hutchins, Edwin 15, 37, 38

identity
    collective 139, 208
    and gender 71, 73–4
Illich, I. 168
improvisational choreography 97–101,
    102
information and communication
    technology (ICT) 7–8, 123
    practice-based design of systems 82,
        178–97
information sharing case 190–194
informed, being 39
infrastructure, technological 24, 93–7
institutional conversation 104–6, 130,
    208
institutional interaction 106–10
instrumental discursive practice 106
instrumentality 97
interaction strategies 13
internalization 62
International Monetary Fund (IMF)
    190–194, 197
International Organization for
    Standardization (ISO) certification
    144
interruptions 194–5
interview with the double 162–5
invisibility
    of technologies 96
    in virtual encounters 125–7